AN INTRODUCTION TO ENGLISH LANGUAGE

Consultant Editors: Noël Burton-Roberts, *University of Newcastle* and Andrew Spencer, *University of Essex*

An Introduction to English Language

Sound, Word and Sentence

Koenraad Kuiper and W. Scott Allan

First published 1996 by
MACMILLAN PRESS LTD
Houndmills, Basingstoke, Hampshire RG21 6XS
and London
Companies and representatives
throughout the world

ISBN 0–333–62494–7 hardcover
ISBN 0–333–62495–5 paperback

A catalogue record for this book is available
from the British Library

10   9   8   7   6   5   4   3   2   1
05 04 03 02 01 00 99 98 97 96

Typeset in Great Britain by
Aarontype Ltd
Easton, Bristol

Printed in Great Britain by The Bath Press, Avon

To Alison, Gabrielle, Miranda and Sonya
Harriet, Imogen and Matthew

Contents

Preface

This book is written for students of English and their teachers. Its aim is to introduce you, our readers, to the English language: to its sounds, its words, and its sentences. We have supposed that you know little about these topics but are willing to learn. We also suppose that the best way to learn is through a combination of listening and doing. We have made our exposition relatively simple, trying always to present the essential nature of the phenomena rather than getting too caught up in the details. This book may therefore be seen (and hopefully used) both as a stand-alone introduction or as precursor to more advanced treatments of linguistic phenomena elsewhere.

In order to help beginners in the study of language we have included extensive glossaries at the end of each section (that is, at the end of the Introduction, and Parts I, II and III) where students can use them for reference and for revision. Professional linguists might take issue with some of our definitions of specialist terms. Our excuse is that we have tried to keep our definitions as simple as possible so that students may go on later to come to a deeper understanding of the theories that lie behind the terms.

At the end of each of the three parts of the book we also provide some additional reading and references dealing with the areas we covered in that particular part.

A large part of this book consists of exercises, which we hope you will do, rather than skim over. We have put stop signs in the form of a row of asterisks at the end of many exercises to suggest that you do not go on until you have actually tried the exercise.

The exercises are of three kinds. The first are expository exercises, which ask questions so as to set the scene for an expository section. These are indicated in the text by a shaded box. The answers to these exercises often follow directly in the text. The second are practice exercises, which should be done at the point where they appear in the book so that some skill in analytic technique is acquired at the appropriate time. The third type are applied exercises, which enable you to use some of the material you have learned to explore texts. There are more of both the latter at the end of chapters. Most exercises other than open-ended ones have answers provided at the end of the book. Readers should, of course, work through the questions for themselves before looking at our answers. A disagreement with our answer does not always mean that the student is wrong. Sometimes differences of opinion are the beginning of new understanding.

We wish also to justify creating a new textbook of this kind. It is our belief that a great many students of English around the world take introductory courses dealing with the English language. We have in mind a one-semester or full year course taken as a requirement or option for undergraduate students of English or trainee teachers. We believe that there are few purpose-built texts for such courses. Mostly students of English make do with books which are introductions to linguistics and which make use of data from languages other than English. Such books often include a variety of topics of interest to students of linguistics such as how children acquire languages and whether animals have languages. Although all these topics are of interest, we believe that such an approach is not the best one for students of English.

The courses for which this book is intended were in the past promoted as a way of learning to speak and write more effectively. It seems, however, that people learn to speak and write better not by studying the structure of the language they already speak, but by writing and speaking more and with appropriate audiences in mind and appropriate feedback.

This does not mean that there is no value in the study of a language by those who speak it or are learning to speak it. Students and teachers of English often need an informed way to talk about English. An agreed terminology and understanding of its use can be useful in pointing out particular problems in a student's writing, or in clarifying a complex passage. In addition, an ability to analyse language contributes significantly to the conscious appreciation of literary form and style. Since many students of English devote most of their studies to the reading and analysis of literature this seems a valuable ability to foster. Finally, and most importantly, an understanding of human language is essential to understanding what it means to be human. The acquisition of a human language is a major intellectual accomplishment, however effortlessly this acquisition comes about. So much else that we learn or accomplish throughout our lives depends on our ability to speak, write, read and understand a language.

We believe that this book aims clearly at these particular ends.

Both authors have developed the material in this book in the first-year courses in English which they teach at the Universities of Auckland and Canterbury. The students in these courses are usually correctly presumed to have little or no knowledge of the nature of the English language and its structure. The great majority of them take these courses as their only course in English language. We are grateful to them and their candid comments on our teaching material. This book is written therefore for students of English and their teachers in the hope that they find their language as interesting as we do.

It is impossible properly to acknowledge the help of all the very many people who have used and commented on this text and its precursors through their long and variable geneses, among them John Andreae, Mary Clark, Derek Davy and Doug Haggo. To all the many friends, colleagues and students who have used and commented on this material, our profound thanks.

We are grateful to Harriet Allan, Alison Kuiper, Francesca Hickey, Linda Whybrew and the Macmillan editors for many helpful suggestions during the drafting of the final versions. For those errors and infelicities that remain we take sole responsibility.

Both authors are grateful to their respective institutions for a period of study-leave during which this book went through its last revisions. The first author also gratefully acknowledges the assistance of the Research Institute for Language and Speech of Utrecht University and the Netherlands Scientific Organisation (NWO).

We would both value any comments and suggestions for the book's future improvement.

KOENRAAD KUIPER
Christchurch

W. SCOTT ALLAN
Auckland

Acknowledgements

Section 6 of Chapter 1 draws on D. Crystal and D. Davy, *Investigating English Style* (London: Longman, 1969).

The section dealing with phonological differences between dialects in Chapter 2 draws on J. D. O'Connor, *Phonetics* (Harmondsworth: Pelican, 1973), and I. C. Wells, *Accents of English* (Cambridge: Cambridge University Press, 1982).

The model of syllable structure in Chapter 2 is taken from that introduced in R. Lass, *Phonology: An Introduction to Basic Concepts* (Cambridge: Cambridge University Press, 1984). The discussion of stress placement is based on that found in P. Roach, *English Phonetics and Phonology: A Practical Course* (Cambridge: Cambridge University Press, 1983).

The terms *tone, tone group, tonic* relating to intonation are taken from D. Crystal, *The English Tone of Voice* (London: Edward Arnold, 1975), and M. A. K. Halliday, *A Course in Spoken English Intonation* (Oxford: Oxford University Press, 1970).

The authors and publishers wish to thank the following who have kindly given permission for the use of copyright material:

Curtis Brown (Aust.) Pty Ltd, on behalf of the author, for the extracts from 'Conversation' from *Inside us the Dead* (Longman Paul, 1976);

Faber and Faber Ltd, for the extract from W. H. Auden, 'Night Mail' in *Collected Poems*, edited by Edward Mendelson (1976);

the International Phonetic Association, for the International Phonetic Alphabet chart;

W. W. Norton & Company Ltd, for the extract from e.e. cummings, 'love is more thicker than forget' from *Complete Poems, 1904–1962*, edited by George J. Firmage; copyright © 1939, 1967, 1991 by the Trustees for the e. e. cummings Trust;

Oxford University Press, for the dictionary entries from the *Pocket Oxford Dictionary*, 8th edn (1992), the *Concise Oxford Dictionary*, 8th edn (1990), and the *Oxford English Dictionary*, 2nd edn (1989);

Laurence Pollinger Ltd, on behalf of the Estate of Frieda Lawrence Ravagli and Viking Penguin, a division of Penguin Books USA Inc., for the extracts from D. H. Lawrence, 'Gipsy' and 'A White Blossom' from *The Complete Poems of D. H. Lawrence*, edited by V. de Sola Pinto and F. W. Roberts (1964); copyright © 1964, 1971 by Angelo Ravagli and C. M. Weekly, executors of the Estate of Freida Lawrence Ravagli;

A. P. Watt Ltd, on behalf of Michael Yeats, for the extract from W. B. Yeats, 'The Moods' in *Collected Poems* (Macmillan, 1950);

Abbreviations and symbols

#	word boundary
*	indicates that the following is an ungrammatical form
/ /	slash brackets surrounding phonemic symbols
[ ]	brackets surrounding phonetic symbols or constituents of complex structures in morphology and syntax
A	adjective, adverb, numeral
ADJ	adjective
AP	adjective phrase, adverb phrase
AuxV	auxiliary verb
C	consonant
CD	compact disc
CD ROM	compact disc read-only memory
Co	coda
CONJ	conjunction
cons	consonantal
cont	continuant
cor	coronal
DEG	degree adverb
DET	determiner
IPA	International Phonetic Alphabet
LexV	lexical verb
N	noun
NP	noun phrase
Nu	nucleus
OED	*Oxford English Dictionary*

On	onset
P	preposition
POSS	possessive phrase
PP	prepositional phrase
PRON	pronoun
Rh	rhyme
S	clause or sentence
S′	embedded clause
Σ	syllable
strid	strident
V	vowel
V	verb
voi	voice
VP	verb phrase
|	tone unit boundary

CONSONANTS (PULMONIC)

	Bilabial	Labiodental	Dental	Alveolar	Postalveolar	Retroflex	Palatal	Velar	Uvular	Pharyngeal	Glottal
Plosive	p b			t d		ʈ ɖ	c ɟ	k g	q ɢ		ʔ
Nasal	m	ɱ		n		ɳ	ɲ	ŋ	N		
Trill	ʙ			r					R		
Tap or Flap				ɾ		ɽ					
Fricative	ɸ β	f v	θ ð	s z	ʃ ʒ	ʂ ʐ	ç ʝ	x ɣ	χ ʁ	ħ ʕ	h ɦ
Lateral fricative				ɬ ɮ							
Approximant		ʋ		ɹ		ɻ	j	ɰ			
Lateral approximant				l		ɭ	ʎ	ʟ			

Where symbols appear in pairs, the one to the right represents a voiced consonant. Shaded areas denote articulations judged impossible.

CONSONANTS (NON-PULMONIC)

Clicks	Voiced implosives	Ejectives
ʘ Bilabial	ɓ Bilabial	' as in:
ǀ Dental	ɗ Dental/alveolar	p' Bilabial
! (Post)alveolar	ʄ Palatal	t' Dental/alveolar
ǂ Palatoalveolar	ɠ Velar	k' Velar
ǁ Alveolar lateral	ʛ Uvular	s' Alveolar fricative

VOWELS

Front   Central   Back

Close: i y — ɨ ʉ — ɯ u
ɪ ʏ ʊ
Close-mid: e ø — ɘ ɵ — ɤ o
ə
Open-mid: ɛ œ — ɜ ɞ — ʌ ɔ
æ ɐ
Open: a ɶ — ɑ ɒ

Where symbols appear in pairs, the one to the right represents a rounded vowel.

OTHER SYMBOLS

ʍ Voiceless labial-velar fricative
w Voiced labial-velar approximant
ɥ Voiced labial-palatal approximant
ʜ Voiceless epiglottal fricative
ʢ Voiced epiglottal fricative
ʡ Epiglottal plosive

ɕ ʑ Alveolo-palatal fricatives
ɺ Alveolar lateral flap
ɧ Simultaneous ʃ and X

Affricates and double articulations can be represented by two symbols joined by a tie bar if necessary.

k͡p t͡s

SUPRASEGMENTALS

ˈ Primary stress
ˌ Secondary stress   ˌfoʊnəˈtɪʃən
ː Long   eː
ˑ Half-long   eˑ
̆ Extra-short   ĕ
. Syllable break   ɹi.ækt
| Minor (foot) group
‖ Major (intonation) group
‿ Linking (absence of a break)

TONES & WORD ACCENTS

LEVEL		CONTOUR	
e̋ or ˥	Extra high	ě or ˇ	Rising
é ˦	High	ê ˆ	Falling
ē ˧	Mid	e̗	High rising
è ˨	Low	e̖	Low rising
ȅ ˩	Extra low	e̍	Rising-falling etc.
↓ Downstep		↗ Global rise	
↑ Upstep		↘ Global fall	

DIACRITICS

Diacritics may be placed above a symbol with a descender, e.g. ŋ̊

̥ Voiceless	n̥ d̥	̤ Breathy voiced	b̤ a̤	̪ Dental	t̪ d̪
̬ Voiced	s̬ t̬	̰ Creaky voiced	b̰ a̰	̺ Apical	t̺ d̺
ʰ Aspirated	tʰ dʰ	̼ Linguolabial	t̼ d̼	̻ Laminal	t̻ d̻
̹ More rounded	ɔ̹	ʷ Labialized	tʷ dʷ	̃ Nasalized	ẽ
̜ Less rounded	ɔ̜	ʲ Palatalized	tʲ dʲ	ⁿ Nasal release	dⁿ
̟ Advanced	u̟	ˠ Velarized	tˠ dˠ	ˡ Lateral release	dˡ
̠ Retracted	i̠	ˤ Pharyngealized	tˤ dˤ	̚ No audible release	d̚
̈ Centralized	ë	̴ Velarized or pharyngealized	ɫ		
̽ Mid-centralized	ě̽	̝ Raised	e̝ (ɹ̝ = voiced alveolar fricative)		
̩ Syllabic	l̩	̞ Lowered	e̞ (β̞ = voiced bilabial approximant)		
̯ Non-syllabic	e̯	̘ Advanced Tongue Root	e̘		
˞ Rhoticity	ə˞	̙ Retracted Tongue Root	e̙		

The International Phonetic Alphabet
(revised 1993)

1 Introduction: what is a language?

1.1 Properties of human language

This book is written for students who are embarking on the study of the English language and so we will be looking at knowledge which people who speak English have already acquired. Since most of you who are looking at these words can read this book, you will already 'know' its content. You could not read English if you did not know English. This knowledge you have is unconscious and this book's aim is to bring it to your conscious awareness.

However, if you are studying English formally in a classroom the subject usually focuses on the use people make of the language. This can take the form of helping students to improve their reading, writing, speaking, and listening, or studying the use other people such as writers have made of the English language. In order to understand how writers and others have used language in particular ways and situations it is necessary first to know something about what language is; that is, what people know when they know it rather than what people do when they use it. So there is a practical point to knowing about the language you speak and write as well as an intellectual one.

So what do people know when they know a language? You would think that this is an easy question to answer since, as speakers of it, we all use our language frequently. The situation is rather like driving a car. Many people drive a car perfectly well without knowing how the car works. In the case of languages the situation is more difficult in that languages are not physical objects like cars. They exist only within the minds of speakers. There are many theories about how language works, but the more language is studied the more complex it seems to become.

When people know a language they must know how speech sounds relate to meanings. When speaking we produce sounds and our hearers hear sound. Speech sounds are the medium we use to represent what it is we are saying, that is, they represent content or meaning and both the speaker and hearer normally know the meanings which are conveyed by the sounds produced by a speaker (always provided that both the speaker and hearer speak the same language). But sounds convey meaning only indirectly. Speech sounds do not themselves have meaning.

Words (and some other units to be studied later) have meanings. Words when we use them come from our mouths as sounds. But not necessarily. In writing they take the form of marks on paper and in the case of some people who are deaf, words can take the form of signs made by the person's hands. However, for most speakers, a language is a complex relationship between speech sounds and the meanings they indirectly convey.

By way of contrast, whales and porpoises produce a large range of sounds: grunts, squeaks, whistles, among other things. If you were a marine biologist and following a school of whales, recording their sounds what would you be able to say about whale language on the basis of your observations of the whales' behaviour and the sounds they made? The answer must be 'very little'. You might be able to relate particular sounds to particular activities, such as feeding. However, this would not prove much since the sounds could indicate pleasure or the type of food being consumed or call signs that food was available and any number of other things. The problem is that as a marine biologist you cannot crack the code because you know nothing about how the code is organised or indeed if there is a code at all.

1.1.1 *Language is a code*

code
symbol

A language can be regarded as a code for conveying a great variety of information. The linguistic code uses symbols – signals which mean or convey something other than themselves. Think, for example, of traffic lights. What are the symbols in the traffic-light code, and what meaning does each convey? In the traffic-light code, each of a set of three, vertically arranged, coloured lights is associated with a particular instruction to the motorist. A red light conveys the instruction 'Stop'. A yellow light conveys the instruction 'Prepare to stop'. A green light conveys the instruction 'Proceed'. The relationship between a particular colour and the instruction it conveys is established by convention. It is quite easy to imagine a society which used different colours, or different signals, for the same instructions. There are relationships between what one light conveys and what the others convey. Unless the lights are not working, one of them is always on but they are never all on at once. The red light and the green light convey conflicting messages, and it would be contradictory to have them both on at the same time.

This simple example has some useful analogies with human languages. A language uses sounds as its basic medium rather than lights, but it too has a set of symbols. Each word of a language is a symbol, a sequence of sounds or letters which is related by convention to a particular meaning. As in the example of the lights, this relationship is arbitrary; the living creature which is represented in English by the sound sequence *horse* might just as easily be called *cheval*, *paard*, or *caballo* – as it is in other languages. Also there are relationships between symbols. For example, it is sometimes said that no two words of a language have exactly the same meaning. Stop for a moment and decide whether you think this is true.

1.1.2 *Linguistic symbols have function and form*

Not only does a language contain the set of symbols called words, but words are put together to make phrases and sentences. The phrases and sentences of a language (and, indeed, as we will see, the words themselves) have structure. What is a structure? Look, for examples, at a building, a flower, a scaffolding, a book. The structured things are organised according to some kind of principle or pattern. For instance, they may consist of sequences of similar items. Various bits may relate to each other in fixed ways. There may appear to be an overall plan to the thing.

phrase, sentence

structure

One of the most fundamental facts about language is that it has structure. To illustrate this, think of a simple sentence such as *Mary swims.* Say it out loud and listen to its sound. Just listening for sound, this sentence seems to be a totally unstructured sequence of noises, one merging into the next, like a whale melody. But as a sentence in a human language and one that we know, we can ask: what structure is there in this simple sentence, *Mary swims*?

The following features of the sentence appear to have structure:

1. Although the sound of the sentence *Mary swims* is continuous (we do not stop between letters) it is heard as a *sequence of sounds*. The first sound is a *m*, the second an *e*, as in *red* (or for some speakers as in *hairy*), and the third an *r* and so on. There are nine sounds altogether.

2. The nine sounds of this sentence are grouped into two words, the word *Mary* and the word *swims*. The word *Mary* is the name of a person or animal; *swims* designates an action. You may know that *Mary* is a noun and *swims* is a verb and that the *s* on the end of *swims* tells us that the swimming is not taking place in the past.

3. We may also perceive that during the saying of the sequence of individual sounds, emphasis is placed in some places more than others, and that there are, in fact, two main places where emphasis can be placed: either on the *a* of *Mary* or on the *i* of *swims*.

4. We might also perceive that the pitch of the speaker's voice rises and falls during the speaking. Normally it would fall at the end of *swims*.

In the structure of this sentence a sequence of units is built up from others. A sequence of nine sounds make up a sequence of two words. The first four sounds go to make up the first word and the rest go to make up the second word. We are simplifying here since it is not just sounds which make a word into a word. We suggested above that words also have meanings and grammatical properties such as being nouns.

constituent
linear
hierarchical

level
tree, box

The words in turn are the constituent parts (or constituents) of the sentence. Notwithstanding this we can see that the structure is linear, i.e. a particular set of units in a particular order, and it is hierarchical, i.e. one unit is made up of units lower down on the hierarchy. So the units are on different levels.

Such a hierarchy can be represented as a tree or box.

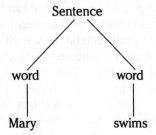

Figure 1.1 Tree Diagram

sentence	
word	word
Mary	swims

Figure 1.2 Box diagram

To gain an understanding of structures like this we can suppose sentences to be rather like some trains. Let us look at a train which consists of two engines at the front, a freight section, first- and second-class passenger cars, and a caboose or guard's van. Diagrams of such a train might look something like this:

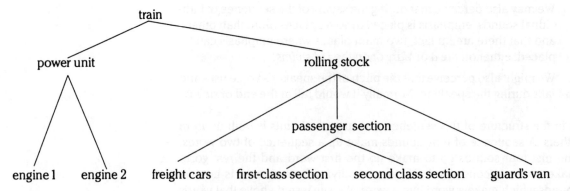

Figure 1.3 Tree diagram

train						
power unit		rolling stock				
			passenger cars			
engine 1	engine 2	freight cars	first class		second class	guard's van

Figure 1.4   Box diagram

Why choose a train as an analogy? Think for a moment of a train appearing out of a tunnel. You first see the engine and then various carriages until finally you see the guard's van or caboose. When a sentence comes from your mouth it is rather like the train emerging from the tunnel, first one word, then another and so on until the sentence reaches its end. We can only recognise words after they have started to appear from someone's mouth, just as we can only recognise carriages when they have at least partially appeared from the tunnel. Furthermore we do not know the structure of the sentence until the last word has been uttered, just as we do not know the train is completely out of the tunnel until the guard's van has appeared.

In describing the structure of a train or a sentence, each unit can be looked at in two ways. First, we can describe the function of the unit by **function** seeing what part it plays in the structure of the next highest unit. The power unit functions as the first unit of the train. Secondly, we can describe the form of the unit by examining its internal structure. The power unit of the train has the form of two engines coupled one behind **form** the other.

At the top level of the hierarchy units have no function because they do not play a role in higher structures. Trains as such are not parts of other units larger than trains. In the case of sentences it depends what one wishes to study. For people who study the grammatical structure of a language, the sentence can be regarded as the top level. It therefore has no function, not being part of a larger structure. But if one were studying people's writing, then sentences would function in larger units. In essays, sentences have a function in paragraphs, as topic sentences or as sentences that expand the topic in some way. Paragraphs have a function in the essay. There are introductory paragraphs, intermediate paragraphs, and concluding paragraphs, all of which have particular functions. However, because sentences have a special kind of structure that is different from that of an essay, grammatical analyses generally stop at the level of the sentence.

Classify the following units according to their form, i.e., their internal structure, and function, i.e. the role the unit plays in another: the caboose or guard's van in a train, a semicolon, the last couplet in a Shakespearian sonnet.

The caboose or guard's van *functions* as the last element in the structure of a train. As to its *form*, it is a rectangular car that may contain internal structure such as compartments where the train's crew sleep and eat.

A semi-colon *functions* as a mark of punctuation between two independent sections of a sentence. It has the form of a full stop over a comma.

The last couplet of a sonnet *functions* as a kind of concluding statement of the sonnet. It has the *form* of two lines of the same length with a rhyming pair of words at the end of each line.

1.1.3   *Linguistic units are constructed according to rules*

As we have seen, units of a language have a hierarchical organisation; that is, they are made up of a series of units, each of which may have an internal structure. Some linguistic units (for example, the words of a language) usually have to be learned one by one. However, larger units of the language are often put together in a systematic way by means of rules that combine or rearrange smaller units to form larger ones, and which assign a meaning to the result.

rule

Make a sentence out of each of the following sets of words. What does this tell you about word order in English sentences?

(a)   sleeps, a, baby, newborn
(b)   in, house, live, green, the, a, people
(c)   the, kicked, boy, ball, a

You will see that only a few word orders actually make English sentences. All other orders (including the original ones in the question) are contrary to the rules of English sentence construction.

What is the exact nature of the rules that determine how units in English may be combined? This is a difficult question but we can get some idea of the diversity of such rules by looking at how they operate in particular instances. Some rules determine which sequences of sound are permitted to be words in English. For example, of the words *blick* and *bnick*: only *blick* is a potential English word. Speakers of English can also locate which sequence is not permitted in the case of *bnick*, namely the *bn* sequence. In the first instance it might seem that the sequence is not allowed because it is more difficult to pronounce. However, that cannot be so because it occurs in places other than initially in a word, for instance in the word *hobnailed*, as in *hobnailed boots*, and when it does, speakers of English have no difficulty pronouncing it. This shows that this rule is a linguistic one and not a purely biological one. We shall have more to discover about such restrictions in Part I.

Other rules determine the sequencing possibilities of larger units within words. For example, whereas both the word *sanity* and the word *saneness* are possible, the word *bleakness* is possible but the word *bleakity* is not. The rules which determine these possibilities will be looked at in Part II.

Then there are rules which determine how words fit into sentences. For example, the sentence *Mary wheeled* is somehow unfinished because the word *wheel* (and not the word *Mary*) requires additional constituents to play a role in this sentence. We also know that there are, corresponding to the following statements: *John is eating his breakfast, John won't eat his breakfast, John should eat his breakfast, John ate his breakfast*, the related questions: *Is John eating his breakfast? Won't John eat his breakfast? Should John eat his breakfast?* and *Did John eat his breakfast?* Regardless of the particular form of the statement and regardless of whether you or any other speaker of English has ever come across the statement before, you will be able to form the related question. This suggests that there must be rules for relating statements to questions and there must be rules determining how sentences may be formed. They form the subject matter of Part III.

The important thing to realise at this point is that the knowledge you have just tapped into is knowledge of the rules by which smaller units of English must form larger ones. You were never taught these rules directly, either at school or by your parents. Somehow they have come to exist unconsciously in your mind. You use them almost without error whenever you speak, read, write, or listen to English. In a real way we have just tapped into your unconscious mind because that is where your language is.

Notice that we are using the word *rule* here in a different sense from that which it ordinarily carries. The rules we are concerned with here are not of the sort *Keep off the grass* or *Skirt hems must be no higher than two inches above the kneecap.* Our rules are descriptive, not prescriptive; **descriptive, prescriptive** this means they describe regularities in the structure of language, they do not tell you what to do.

We are now ready to return to our earlier questions: what is language? and what do we know when we know a language? Language is a code that allows us to represent thoughts and ideas by means of sounds (or letters). A special property of this code is that its symbols are complex; that is, they have internal structure. This means that the sounds do not directly convey meanings. Units have a structure which is rule-governed. As we have suggested, speakers of the language know these rules intuitively, although they are not able to say how. The rules are of many different kinds. Some of them are concerned with the combination of sounds, some with the formation of phrases and sentences, and some with the assignment of meaning. Some of these latter rules are extremely subtle. For example:

Whose dressing is under consideration in each of the following sentences?

(a)   Jill appealed to Mary to dress herself.
(b)   Jill appeared to Mary to dress herself.

In (a) it is Mary's dressing that is under consideration; in (b) it is Jill's. This switch in the identity of the person who is dressing is created by a change of just one letter in the written version of the sentence! Let us examine in more detail just what is going on in this example. The difference in the way these two sentences are understood by you, the speakers of English, rests not on the difference in the sounds 'l' and 'r' but in the words *appeal* and *appear*, which happen just to differ in form by this one sound. Furthermore the difference in meaning is not signalled by any difference in the order of the words in the two sentences. The order is exactly the same. It must therefore be that on the basis of important differences in the linguistic properties of *appear* and *appeal*, differences that are not apparent on the page, speakers of English understand the identical sequence of the other words in these two sentences quite differently. This suggests that the internalised rules we have been looking at are complex. It also shows that they are in the speaker's head and not on the page, since what is on the page is virtually identical. There is certainly nothing on the page which tells us who is getting dressed, Jill or Mary.

1.1.4   *Language is specifically human*

Imagine that you are an anthropologist entering a remote area of South America to study the language of a tribe of people whose existence has only recently been discovered. Assuming that the people are friendly and co-operative, how might you go about cracking the code that is their language?

However you proceed, the task is easier than your task with dolphins and whales because you know before even beginning that the language these people use will be organised in certain ways. That will be so because the people you are dealing with are human beings and you will rightly assume that their language and yours will have some common properties. (Of course if you are not trained in this task you might well be thoroughly mistaken about what those common properties are.) If, when you hold up a leaf and say 'leaf' in English, your new companions respond with the utterance *rogan*, you may suspect that this is the word for 'leaf' in their language. If you jump up and down or pretend to sleep, they may give you their words for 'jump' and 'sleep'. However wrong you may be in these guesses, throughout your investigation you can assume that the language you are studying uses *sound* to encode meaning, and that meaning is attached to something like the sound *sequences* that we call words. Furthermore, you can safely assume that the words you hear will belong to grammatical classes, such as *noun* and *verb*, and that these grammatical classes will be combinable into phrases and sentences. There will be ways of making statements, asking questions, giving commands, and making negative assertions. All these properties are true of every human language, a fact that will help you enormously in cracking the code of your new language.

1.1.5 *Language use is creative*

> Make up ten sentences you have never said before.
>
> (a)   Was it difficult?
> (b)   Did you feel creative?
> (c)   Were you, in fact, being creative?

Answers:

(a)   No.
(b)   Probably not.
(c)   Undoubtedly.

The reason you can perform this task so easily is that there are many words in English, and the rules of English permit these words to be combined in many different ways.

> How many times a day do you say the same sentence? How many times in a year/lifetime?

There are a few sentences that we repeat often. *How are you? Nice weather we're having* might be two of them. But by and large we do not repeat sentences. Most of the sentences we utter are put together on the spot.

> What is the longest English sentence?

There isn't one. You can keep adding to a sentence ad infinitum by using the little word *and*. Whenever you think you have reached the last sentence in the language, it is always possible to produce another by taking the last sentence, adding *and* to it and joining another sentence after the *and*. That way you get a new sentence. This means that there is no limit to the number of sentences which can be constructed in accordance with the rules of English.

The fact that we can create new sentences at will by adding on to old ones is by itself of little importance. What is more important is the fact that the rules of language allow us to put words together in *new ways* to create symbols for objects and ideas that have no pre-established symbols in the language. Lack of vocabulary is only a minor inconvenience. If you do not know the name of a student in your class, you can create one by specifying as many of their characteristics as are necessary to distinguish them from other students in the class. You can say 'that tall person with wavy blond hair and glasses and a long nose who sits in the second row near the window', continuing as long as is necessary to distinguish this one student from all others in the class. The same device is available for objects and concepts that have no conventional names. The four-year-old who says *I do it the way Mummy bakes a cake* has created a name for a way of doing things that has no name in English (or, presumably, any other language) – the way Mummy bakes a cake. Similarly, when the Bible was translated into African and American Indian languages that had no word for *snow*, the translators easily constructed phrases in each language that would convey the crucial properties of this substance.

We might reflect a moment at this point on just what we are, in fact, doing with language. We have seen that language is a code for linking speech sounds with meaning. If that code allows for the creation of new meanings because it allows for speakers to be creative, then just what are these meanings? In effect sentences are ways of representing not just the world outside us, but the worlds which we create in our minds. Look, for a moment, at what must happen when a pigmy from the African rain forest learns to read and reads about snow. In the process of coming to understand what snow is, such a reader is changing his or her mental representation of the world. It contains a new substance with a variety of properties. Yet the reader has never actually seen, felt or tasted it.

So language provides a key to open the door to possible worlds, worlds which differ from the one we currently live in in any way which we might imagine. By rearranging words into new sequences we can imagine the future, plan a space telescope or journeys to the moon, reconstruct the age of the dinosaurs, as well as write letters to friends.

1.1.6 *Language use is constrained*

While the rules of a language allow us a great deal of freedom to say whatever we like, external circumstances often place constraints on this freedom. While visiting grandparents, joining in a class discussion, or conversing with someone we think may not like us, we may find it necessary to exercise caution in our use of words.

List five situations you have been in where you were restricted as to what you could say or how you could say it? What was it that restricted you?

In all probability most of the situations you have listed are ones in which you were not at ease. You were the inferior party; you had not met the other person before; you were in a strange place. Notice that these factors have nothing to do with the English language; they have to do with the situation in which you *use* language.

Do a brief parody of a variety of English that you are familiar with: for example, a radio commentary, a TV weather report, a sermon, a political speech, a disc jockey's patter. What aspects of your language have you had to restrict, and how?

Each variety of a language restricts a speaker's choices in its own way. A minister or priest giving a sermon cannot use swear words. A person reading the news cannot address the viewers as 'Dearly beloved brethren'. Sounds, words, grammar and meaning are all potentially restricted.   **utterance**

Below are a number of utterances.
   What factors in the situation have influenced the choice of pronunciation, vocabulary, and grammar in each utterance? (You will have to use your imagination in describing the pronunciation.)

   (a)   My friends and fellow Americans, I speak to you tonight on one of the gravest issues facing our great nation, and at this time I want to make one thing perfectly clear...

   (b)   Canada is 3.8 million square miles in area. It is the second largest country in the world, covering more than half the North American continent.

   (c)   Johnson waits for the pitch. Here it comes...Swung at and missed! One down. That brings up Thomas.

   (d)   Tonight it appears that all the 247 passengers are dead. Search and rescue teams are making their way to the scene in order to start a full search at daybreak.

   (e)   The earth is the Lord's, and the fullness thereof; the world, and they that dwell therein: For he hath founded it upon the seas, and established it upon the floods.

   (f)   That's a good boy. Now you promise your grandpappy you won't do that again.

   (g)   My husband and I are pleased again to be visiting your beautiful country.

Answers:

   (a)   The speaker seems to be a politician. He or she is probably speaking on radio or TV. The audience therefore cannot reply; and the message sounds as though the speaker wants to persuade the audience about something.

   (b)   This is a piece of written language, probably from a geography book or tourist brochure. The author is anonymous, is not giving a personal view but merely trying to convey factual information.

   (c)   This is a commentary on a baseball or softball game. The speaker is a sports commentator. The purpose of the commentary is to tell the audience what is going on in the field and to hold their interest in the game.

(d)   Here a radio or TV news reader is reading a news item.

(e)   This sounds like a passage from the Bible. It also appears to have been written at an earlier period than our own.

(f)   The speaker appears to be talking to a child.

(g)   The speaker appears to be Queen Elizabeth II of England, using one of the introductions she often uses in a public speech, or someone imitating her.

Here are some general headings for the kinds of factors we have discovered:

1.   The speaker or writer is always a factor. Each speaker has his or her own identifying features. For example, in (a) the phrase 'I want to make one thing perfectly clear' is one that was frequently used by Richard M. Nixon, a former President of the USA. In (h) the phrase 'My husband and I' is particularly the 'property' of Queen Elizabeth II of England.

dialect

2.   Other aspects of a speaker's language reflect his or her dialect. In (f), for example, we have the word 'grandpappy', which is used particularly in certain regions of the USA. This is therefore a reflection of the place the person comes from. A person's social position can also be reflected in their language. For example, the sentence in (d) is being spoken in a middle-class social dialect. There are therefore at least two kinds of dialects, regional and social, reflecting a person's place of origin geographically and socially.

3.   The time at which the person is speaking or writing also influences their range of choices. This can be seen clearly in (e) with its old-fashioned words and expressions.

4.   The speaker's purpose can also have an effect. They can be trying to persuade, explain, inform, or entertain their audience. Each purpose involves choosing certain features of language over others.

mode

5.   The mode the speaker chooses to communicate in also influences their range of choice. If they are writing, as in (b) and (e), they can think about what they are doing and change it if necessary. If they are speaking, other options are available: the spoken rhetorical flourishes that would accompany (a), the slow, measured speed of (d), and so on.

media

6.   Speech or writing can be conveyed by different media. A medium can be thought of as a channel of communication. Writing can appear on a television screen, in a book, in lights on a building. Speech can come direct from speaker to hearer, over the radio, in a

film. Each medium places its own limitations on language. Only so much writing can fit on a TV screen; the screen then has to be wiped to display more writing. Speech on television, however, can come across in the normal way.

7. The audience also plays a part. It may be that they are passive, or absent altogether, in which case the speaker produces a monologue. Or it may be that they are present and actively involved in a dialogue.

8. The relationship of speaker and audience is conveyed linguistically. A US President speaking to the people can use an expression like 'My friends and fellow Americans' since Presidents are expected to speak in an elevated way and to have the interests of all Americans at heart. A street sweeper at the local shops could not seriously address shoppers this way. One important factor in such a relationship is the relative status of the two parties. Teachers talk differently to each other than they do to students. Status often influences style. This can, for example, involve differences in the choice of words and grammatical constructions. The more familiar the participants are, the more likely they are to use a colloquial, informal style. The less well they know each other, the more formal will be the style that they will tend to adopt.

9. Particular occupations and tasks also place restrictions on the language of the speaker. Doctors, news readers, politicians, when they are being doctors, news readers, or politicians, speak in the register **register** appropriate to their occupation. Of course, when the news reader gets home she does not tell her husband about her day's activities in the same way as she reads the news. Registers are restricted to particular uses and often to particular situations.

Language itself allows speakers to create new utterances whenever they choose. But this creativity is circumscribed by the social forces that surround the speaker. The rest of this book will largely be concerned with the linguistic resources that we have as speakers of English, and to a lesser extent with how our choice of them is influenced by the situations in which our language is used.

Glossary

Box diagram Box diagrams are a way to picture hierarchies by representing lower levels on a hierarchy as being enclosed within boxes which are then enclosed within boxes representing higher levels on the hierarchy. These can be paraphrased as 'what is in the outer box has as constituents what is in the inner boxes'.

Code   A code is a system of symbols that allows things to represent others for the purpose of communicating. Morse code, for example, uses sounds of only two different lengths to represent all the different letters of the alphabet.

Constituent   Any grammatically coherent component part of a sentence. *See* Chapters 7 and 8.

Descriptive rule   A descriptive rule is a statement of a regular pattern that actually exists; unlike a **prescriptive rule**, where someone attempts to prescribe that people should follow a rule which they actually do not follow (at least some of the time).

Dialect   Regional or social variety of a language.

Form   The form of a unit is what it looks like, particularly on the basis of its internal structure.

Function   The function of a unit is the role the unit plays in a larger unit.

Hierarchical   Having the form of a hierarchy. In the description of languages, the hierarchies that are used usually represent units which consist of sub-units. The sub-units are lower on the hierarchy.

Level   When linguists describe languages the description is usually subdivided into different levels. Each level of description deals with different kinds of units, all of which together go to make up the way the language works.

Linear   In the form of a line.

Medium   The channel through which an utterance is conveyed, e.g. telephone, television.

Mode   of an utterance. Whether the person producing the utterance is speaking or writing.

Phrase   Grammatically coherent constituent part of a sentence. *See* Chapter 7.

Register   Occupational variety of a language, e.g. the speech of market criers.

Rule   A rule is a statement of a regular pattern.

Sentence   A sequence of words having a structure which is grammatically independent of that of other sentences. *See* Chapters 7 and 8.

Structure   A structure consists of parts that are organised in some way. For example, a bridge is a structure that has many parts all of which are organised to make the whole.

Symbol   Symbols have two aspects: a form and a meaning. The two are arbitrarily linked. For example, the symbol of the Campaign for Nuclear Disarmament consists of a circle with a letter Y upside down with a line down the middle of it, inside the circle. There is nothing about the symbol that makes this graphic particularly apt for its purpose. It is a matter of convention.

Tree diagram   Tree diagrams are a way to picture hierarchies. Tree diagrams are so called because they look like trees turned upside down. Tree-diagram representations can be paraphrased as 'what is given higher up in the tree has as constituents what is connected to it lower in the tree'.

Utterance   What a speaker says or a writer writes at a particular point in time.

Further reading

Bolinger, D., *Aspects of Language*, 2nd edn (New York: Harcourt Brace Jovanovich, 1975).

Crystal, D. and Davy, D., *Investigating English Style* (London: Longman, 1969).

Falk, J. S., *Linguistics and Language: A Survey of Basic Concepts and Applications* (Lexington, Mass.: Xerox College Publishing, 1973).

Finegan, E., *Language: Its Structure and Use*, 2nd edn (New York: Harcourt Brace Jovanovich, 1994).

Fromkin, V. and Rodman, R., *An Introduction to Language*, 5th edn (New York: Harcourt Brace Jovanovich, 1993).

Miller, G. A., *Language and Speech* (San Francisco, Cal.: W. H. Freeman, 1981).

Traugott, E. C. and Pratt, M. L., *Linguistics for Students of Literature* (New York: Harcourt Brace Jovanovich, 1980).

PART I

Sounds

Introduction to Part I

Concepts

Part I deals with the sounds of the English language. We will look at the way speech sounds are produced and the way these sounds are organised in English into distinctively different segments of sound, and suprasegmental sound patterns. To deal with articulatory phonetics we will look at the organs of speech, speech production processes, and provide an introduction to the phonetic transcription of speech and the International Phonetic Alphabet. In dealing with segmental phonology we will introduce the basic concepts of segmental phonology. These include phonemes, allophones, distinctive features, contrastive, complementary, parallel and defective distribution, phonotactics and allophonic rules. We will also introduce a number of the more common allophones and allophonic processes in English. Then we will look at the syllable and how syllables are structured, stress patterning, rhythm, tone and intonation.

Skills

By the end of this part of the book you should be able to identify the organs of speech, describe speech production and any individual speech sound. You should be able to produce and read transcriptions of English in IPA. You should also be able to identify phonemes and their allophones, write allophonic rules and identify the more common allophonic processes in English. You should also be able to distinguish syllables of English and their structure, and the major stress and intonation patterns of English.

2 Speech sounds

We take our capacity to communicate through speech for granted. Each day we may utter tens of thousands of words without stopping to consider what we are doing or how we do it. Although communication through speech is our most common form of communication, the study of the production of speech is the farthest removed of all the branches of linguistics from our intuitions about language. We have intuitions about the grammaticality of sentences, and the meaning and structure of words, but we have few intuitions about how we produce speech sounds. For example, few speakers have any precise notion of what is physically involved in the production of the word *eye* (which consists of a single speech sound), or the production of the two sounds that constitute the word *me*. Furthermore, they would probably find it difficult to describe how these sounds are produced.

This lack of intuition where the production of speech sounds is concerned is all the more surprising when we consider that we often make social judgements about people from their speech. We may locate them geographically and socially from their pronunciation of a single sentence. Yet we often have no idea, in precise phonetic terms, why the speech of one speaker differs markedly from that of another. Furthermore, although some speakers are able to mimic successfully the speech of others, they may have no precise idea of how they achieve this.

The study of the production, perception, and analysis of speech sounds is called 'phonetics'. Phonetics is not a new or recent subject **phonetics** but is centuries old. The Sanskrit grammarian Panini, who lived in India in *c.* 500 BC, included material on the subject in his grammar of Sanskrit. In George Bernard Shaw's play *Pygmalion*, and the musical *My Fair Lady*, one of the main characters, Professor Henry Higgins, is a phonetician. He records in detail, using a special set of symbols, what a speaker says so that he can reproduce it exactly.

In this chapter we are going to look at the production of speech sounds (phonetics). But first we shall look at the relationship between sound and spelling, because letters on a page are usually considered to represent the speech sounds of a language.

2.1 Sounds and spelling

The spelling system of English aims to represent in writing the sounds used by speakers of English when they speak their language. It should be fairly easy to achieve this aim. All we have to do is identify the sounds of English, and then assign a unique symbol to each sound. However, what seems straightforward in theory turns out to be a little more complex in practice.

Your answers may be something like this:

Consider the following words. Say them out loud and write down how many sounds you make for each one.

(a)	fill	(b)	feel	(c)	tree	(d)	bitter
(e)	thesis	(f)	sing	(g)	drunk	(h)	single
(i)	marry	(j)	Mary	(k)	jungle	(l)	meander
(m)	theory	(n)	beer	(o)	furious	(p)	tune
(q)	chew	(r)	stew	(s)	cheer	(t)	phone

(a)	3	(b)	3	(c)	3	(d)	4 or 5
(e)	5	(f)	3	(g)	5	(h)	5 or 6
(i)	4	(j)	4	(k)	5	(l)	6 or 7
(m)	4 or 5	(n)	3	(o)	7	(p)	3 or 4
(q)	2	(r)	3 or 4	(s)	3	(t)	3

It would appear that the number of spelling symbols or letters in a word does not necessarily correspond to the number of sounds. Consequently, we cannot tell how many sounds there are in a particular word just by looking at its spelling.

The relationship, in English, between spelling and sounds is not one-to-one. Each spelling symbol does not necessarily correspond to a single sound. Some words have fewer sounds than letters, for example *fill*, *bitter*, *phone*, and *sing*. In these cases there is no sound associated with some of the spelling symbols. Other words have the same, for example *drunk*; while a third set has the same but the relationship is opaque, for example *cube*. *Cube* contains four spelling symbols and four sounds, but there is no spelling symbol associated with the second sound, and *e* doesn't represent any sound – it is 'silent'. Finally, there are cases where a word consists of more sounds than spelling symbols. For example, *Cuba*, which in some versions of English contains five sounds. There is no spelling symbol that corresponds to the second sound in this word. This frequent mismatch is not the only problem with the English spelling system.

> (a) How many different ways can you find to spell the sound represented by the *ee* of *keep*?
>
> (b) How many different pronunciations can you find for the spelling ... *ough*?

Answer:

(a) *e* as in *me*; *ey* as in *key*; *e* ... *e* as in *scene*; *ee* as in *keep*; *ea* as in *reap*; *ie* as in *belief*; *ie* ... *e* as in *believe*, *ei* as in *receipt*; *ei* ... *e* as in *receive*; *i* ... *e* as in *machine*; *oe* as in *amoeba*.

(b) *though, cough, through, bough, thought, rough.*

Clearly there is more than one way of spelling a single sound, and a particular spelling may represent more than a single sound. This takes us farther away from our seemingly achievable goal of one sound, one spelling symbol.

To make matters worse, the spelling of a word may contain 'silent' letters. These letters have no sound associated with them (although they may have been pronounced at some earlier time in the history of English). Furthermore, the pronunciation of a word may include a sound that is not represented in the spelling.

> (a) What silent letter can you find in the words *sword, knight, mortgage, doubt, align, would, psychology, honest, who*?
>
> (b) What 'extra' sound can you find in the pronunciation of the words *use, cute,* and *one*?
>
> (c) What mismatch do you find between the pronunciation and the spelling in the words *answer* and *salmon*?

Answer:

(a) s*w*ord, *k*night, mor*t*gage, dou*b*t, ali*g*n, wou*l*d, *p*sychology, *h*onest, *w*ho.

(b) A *y* sound before the *u* in *use* and *cute*, a *w* sound at the beginning of *one*.

(c) There is no *w* sound associated with the *w* in *answer*, and no *l* sound in *salmon*.

The following exercise is a listening one. The aim is to listen to words for sounds that are the same.

Can you find examples of the same sound as that italicised in the initial word, in the sentence that follows it?

For example: fea*t*   The old *t*ree in the garden

(a) *f*oot   Taking off his gloves, he coughed.

(b) *b*ook   The bomb went off.

(c) s*c*ene   You must clean the window.

(d) *ch*in   To which gin did you switch?

(e) *y*our   Pure acid is bad for the digestion.

(f) *z*oo   This is a bad business.

(g) l*u*ck   I have had enough trouble today.

(h) ba*th*   There's a draught out there.

(i) *w*atch   Which question was that?

(j) sa*y*   I saw the fish take the bait.

Having completed this exercise, what can you tell about the relationship between spelling and sound?

Answer:

(a) Taking *off* his gloves, he cou*gh*ed.

(b) The *b*omb went off.

(c) You must cl*ea*n the windows.

(d) To whi*ch* gin did you swit*ch*?

(e) P*u*re acid is bad for the diges*ti*on.   [*second one only for some pronunciations*]

(f) This is a bad bu*s*iness.

(g) I have had en*ou*gh tro*u*ble today.

(h) There's a dr*au*ght out there.

(i) Which question *w*as that?   [*first one only for some pronunciations*]

(j) I saw the fish t*a*ke the b*ai*t.

Some things are again obvious from this exercise:

1. The same written letter does not always represent the same sound.

2. The same sound is not always represented by the same letter.

3. Some letters are not pronounced at all.

4. We pronounce sounds in some places where there is no letter.

Find examples of each case in the above exercise.

Many people find spelling difficult. It takes years of practice to be a good speller, and one reason for this is that English spelling does not always directly reflect the sounds people make when they say a word.
From all the above exercises, it is clear that:

1. We interpret words as sequences of sound segments rather than as continuous streams of sound. This is important because we tend to think of words as written rather than spoken objects.

2. The number of letters in the written version of a word, and the number of sound segments in the spoken version, are not necessarily the same.

3. Sometimes the same word can be pronounced with different sequences of sound segments. For example, *single* can be pronounced with or without a second vowel, *single* or *singil*.

So our orthographic or spelling system, which is based on Roman orthography, does not enter into a one-to-one relationship with the sounds of our language. This problem is not unique to English. It occurs, for example, with French, Gaelic, and Irish. However, there are other languages, for example Dutch, German, Italian, and Maori, where the relationship between the sounds of the spoken language and the letters of the written language, which represent those sounds, is much more regular than that of English. Even in these languages it is not perfect. **orthography**

Given the problems associated with the English spelling system discussed above, it is clear that it is not an ideal means for recording the sounds of English. Furthermore, many languages possess sounds for which there is no symbol in the English spelling system. For example, one of the click sounds found in the Zulu language Xhosa is represented by the English spelling symbol !.

2.1.1   *The International Phonetic Alphabet*

To allow the sounds of English, and any other language, to be written down, a phonetic alphabet was developed – the International Phonetic Alphabet (or IPA). In this alphabet the relationship between symbol and sound is one-to-one. Although we shall be discussing it in relation to English, it should be kept in mind that the IPA is universal, that is it contains symbols for all the sounds in all known languages. The symbols required for English form a subset of the IPA. In this book we shall be interested only in the symbols that represent the sounds of English.

Table 2.1 *Consonantal sounds of English and their descriptive labels*

Stops

[p]	voiceless labial stop	put capable cup
[b]	voiced labial stop	but abandon cub
[t]	voiceless alveolar stop	tab butter put
[d]	voiced alveolar stop	done edit pad
[k]	voiceless velar stop	cat succulent break
[g]	voiced velar stop	get begging drug

Nasals

[m]	voiced labial nasal	mint examine drum
[n]	voiced alveolar nasal	nut money can
[ŋ]	voiced velar nasal	finger drink sing

Fricatives

[f]	voiceless labio-dental fricative	fly coffee calf
[v]	voiced labio-dental fricative	verb cave having
[θ]	voiceless dental fricative	thin moth
[ð]	voiced dental fricative	the wither bathe
[s]	voiceless alveolar fricative	sing blessing cats
[z]	voiced alveolar fricative	zinc breeze rose
[ʃ] or [š]	voiceless post-alveolar fricative	ship crush brushing
[ʒ] or [ž]	voiced post alveolar fricative	rouge measure seizure
[h]	voiceless glottal fricative	hope ahead

Affricates

[tʃ] or [č]	voiceless post-alveolar affricative	chalk catching clutch
[dʒ] or [ǰ]	voiced post-alveolar affricate	jump digest rage

Approximants

[w]	voiced labio-velar approximant	watch away
[l]	voiced alveolar lateral approximant	lie pulling pull
[r]	voiced alveolar approximant	roast pouring
[j]	voiced palatal approximant	yacht cube

The symbols in the left-hand column represent the consonant sounds of English. We may define each symbol in two ways. First, each is assigned a three-term label, which provides a phonetic definition of how the sound represented by a symbol is articulated. These labels are given in the centre column and the terms are explained in section 2.2.

Secondly, each phonetic symbol may be associated with a spelling symbol or symbols. Each phonetic symbol represents the sound associated with the underlined spelling symbols in the right-hand column.

Table 2.2   *The vowel sounds of English*

Monophthongs

[iː]	b<u>ea</u>d	[biːd]
[ɪ] or [ı]	b<u>i</u>d	[bɪd]
[e] or [ɛ]	b<u>e</u>d	[bed]
[æ]	b<u>a</u>d	[bæd]
[ɑː]	b<u>a</u>rd	[bɑːd]
[ɒ]	h<u>o</u>t	[hɒt]
[ɔː]	b<u>ou</u>ght	[bɔːt]
[ʊ]	b<u>oo</u>k	[bʊk]
[uː]	b<u>oo</u>ed	[buːd]
[ɜː]	b<u>ur</u>n	[bɜːn]
[ʌ]	b<u>u</u>d	[bʌd]
[ə]	<u>a</u>bout	[əbaut]

Diphthongs

[ei]	b<u>ay</u>	[bei]
[ai]	b<u>uy</u>	[bai]
[ɔi]	b<u>oy</u>	[bɔi]
[ou]	b<u>oa</u>t	[bout]
[au]	b<u>ou</u>gh	[bau]
[iə]	b<u>eer</u>	[biə]
[eə]	b<u>ear</u>	[beə]
[uə]	t<u>our</u>	[tuə]

The above vowel sounds are based on a non-rhotic dialect of English. In non-rhotic dialects *r* is pronounced only when it is followed by a vowel sound. Speakers of rhotic dialects always pronounce *r* no matter what follows. This difference leads to differences in some of the vowel sounds: **rhotic**

		Non-rhotic	*Rhotic*
[iə]	b<u>eer</u>	[biə]	[biːr]
[eə]	b<u>ear</u>	[beə]	[beir]
[uə]	t<u>our</u>	[tuə]	[tuːr]
[ɔː]	f<u>our</u>	[fɔː]	[four]
[ɜː]	b<u>ur</u>n	[bɜːn]	[bʌrn]

The symbols in the left-hand column of this table represent the vowel sounds associated with the underlined spelling symbols in the words that form the centre column. A transcribed version of each word is given in the right-hand column.

Exercise 2.1

Using the above tables convert the following piece of phonetic script into regular English spelling. Notice that in the phonetic script no use is made of either capital letters or punctuation. You will need to add these to the orthographic representation yourself.

[bʌt ðə riːl hɒrə ʌmʌŋst spaidz wəz mɔː laiklɪ tə biː eŋkauntəd ɪn ðə lævətrɪ ɪtself ðɪs wəz ðə red bæk ðə red bæk ɪz meinlɪ blæk wɪθ ə skaːlət straip weə ɪts spain wʊd biː ɪf ɪt wɜː ə vɜːtɪbreit]

(Clive James, *Unreliable Memoirs*)

* * * * * * * * * *

Exercise 2.2

Using the above tables transcribe the following text into phonetic script. Remember that you do not use either capital letters or punctuation in your transcribed version

One of the most interesting things about the six-headed Omni-Quarrgs of the planet Cygo-Swarreldong in the star system of Grudni-Vogar-Actinax, in the constellation of 'Go-and-upset-another-scrabble-board-Les-I-need-a-new-name', is that they have only one word to stand for all 400 million nouns, adjectives, prepositions, verbs and adverbs.

(from *The Faber Book of Parodies*, ed. Andrew Marshall and David Renwick)

* * * * * * * * * *

We can see from the above tables that the phonetic alphabet establishes a one-to-one correspondence between symbol and sound. Each sound is represented by one and only one symbol, while each symbol represents one and only one sound. Given any sound, we can represent it with a single symbol, and given a single symbol, we know exactly which sound it represents. This differs from regular English spelling (or orthography), where one symbol may represent a number of different symbols. As an illustration, first consider the orthographic letter *a*, which represents three different sounds. For example, *a* represents the vowel in the words: *bad*, *bard*, and *bade*. We transcribe these sounds as [æ], [ɑː], and [ei] respectively. Secondly, consider the sound [f], which may be represented in English orthography by *f* as in *fine*, *ph* as in *physics*, or *gh* as in *laugh*.

Furthermore, the symbols retain their value irrespective of which language is being described. For example, the symbol [t] (which represents the final sound in *put*) represents the same sound in all languages.

The above tables introduce various terms, for example stop, fricative, labial, velar, and monophthong, which are used by phoneticians to describe sounds. To understand these terms we need to consider how sounds are produced.

2.2 Articulatory phonetics

Articulatory phonetics is the name given to the study of how we produce sounds. To understand how we produce speech sounds, it is necessary to identify the organs involved in the articulation of these sounds.

2.2.1 *Organs of speech*

In identifying the organs of speech, we shall start at the lips and work our way down to the lungs.

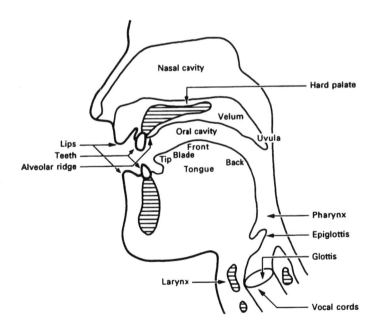

Figure 2.1

labial

1. Upper and lower lips
   These are used in the production of labial sounds, and certain vowels. When at rest, the lips usually remain in the closed position, forming an air-tight seal.

2. Upper and lower teeth

3. The roof of the mouth: if you run the tip of tongue backwards from your upper front teeth you should feel:

alveolar

(a) The alveolar ridge: a hump directly behind the teeth.

hard palate

(b) The hard palate: running your tongue tip back from the alveolar ridge you should feel a bony structure, which may rise up quite steeply before it levels out. This is the hard palate.

soft palate, velum, uvula

(c) The soft palate or velum, and uvula: as you continue to run your tongue tip back along the hard palate you should detect a change from the bony hard palate to the soft velum, which ends in the uvula. The velum is a muscle, which can be raised against the back wall of the pharynx to create an air-tight seal between the oral and nasal cavities. When the velum is closed, air from the lungs is directed out through the oral cavity. During normal breathing the velum is in the lowered position and, with the lips forming a seal, air is forced through the nasal cavity.

4. The tongue: this is a complex muscle, whose flexibility allows it to be moved into a number of different positions and shapes. Although there are no obvious divisions on the surface of tongue itself, for the description of sounds it may be divided into a number of sections.

(a) tip or point,
(b) blade – this lies below the alveolar ridge,
(c) front – this is the middle section which lies below the hard palate,

back

(d) back – this section lies opposite the velum and the uvula;

pharynx

(e) root – a relatively vertical section which faces backwards towards the back wall of the pharynx.

The tongue is larger than the portion we can see when we look in the mirror. When it is not being used, it does not lie on the floor of the mouth but is held mid-way between the roof and floor of the mouth, approximately in the position it would be if we were to make the vowel sound at the end of *sofa*.

5. The upper and lower jaws: these bones contain the teeth. The lower jaw is attached to the skull at a point just in front of the bottom of the ears. If you place your first fingers in this position and move your jaw up and down you will feel the hinge. Only the lower jaw may move. The upper jaw is part of the skull.

6. The larynx and the vocal cords – the larynx is positioned at the top of the trachea (windpipe). It is a box-like construction consisting of cartilage. The protuberance known as the Adam's apple is the top of the larynx. The vocal cords are located inside the larynx just below the level of the Adam's apple. If you place your thumb and first finger on your larynx and make the sound at the beginning of *mouse* you should feel the vocal cords vibrating.

larynx

We refer to the space bounded by the lips and the vocal cords as the vocal tract. It is usual to divide the vocal tract into two cavities:

(a) the pharynx – this begins behind the velum and ends at the larynx and
(b) the oral cavity (mouth) – this runs from the velum to the lips.

The pharynx and the oral cavity are two of the three resonating cavities of the head and neck. The third of these cavities is the nasal cavity, which is divided from the oral cavity by the hard palate. As we noted above, it may be either cut off from or connected to the vocal tract by the action of the velum.

2.2.2 *Speech production*

The production of speech involves three distinct processes. Although each process is independent of the other two, they may interact with each other. It is the interaction of these processes that allows for the great range of possible speech sounds. The three speech production processes are:

(a) initiation (b) phonation and (c) articulation.

initiation, phonation articulation

Let us consider each of these three processes in relation to the production of consonant sounds.

2.2.2.1 *Initiation*
The production of any speech sound requires the creation of an airstream in the vocal tract. The airstream may be created by either compressing or rarefying the air in the tract. In English the airstream is initiated by the lungs. When the lungs contract, they push air out, creating an out-flowing airstream. We call this airstream 'pulmonic egressive' – pulmonic because it is initiated by the lungs, and egressive because it is out-flowing. The advantages of this airstream can be easily

illustrated. Take a deep breath and as you breathe out count aloud. Note how high you managed to count before you ran out of breath. Now breathe out and as you breathe in try counting aloud again. Note how high you manage to count before it becomes impossible to count any further. You should find that you cannot count as high when you breathe in as you can when you breathe out. Speaking while breathing in requires considerably more effort than when breathing out. Imagine the difficulties that would arise if we used only an ingressive airstream.

Although all languages use a pulmonic egressive airstream, there are some languages that use alternative initiation types besides the pulmonic egressive one. Xhosa, a language spoken in South Africa, uses velaric suction to produce some of its sounds called 'clicks'. One click sound is similar to the 'tutting' sound we make when telling off someone. The click sounds do not require air to flow either in or out of the lungs, but air does flow into the oral cavity. Consequently, you can make clicks for as long as you like. Try making this sound slowly and see how you create the suction which allows the air to flow in past the tongue and teeth making the clicking, sucking sound.

2.2.2.2 *Phonation*

voice

The pulmonic egressive airstream, as it passes through the larynx, may be modified by the vocal cords, through the introduction of voice. Without voice speech would be reduced to an inaudible whisper. When the vocal cords are brought together, air passing out from the lungs causes them to vibrate, and voice is produced. Sounds produced with the vocal cords vibrating are called voiced. If the vocal cords are

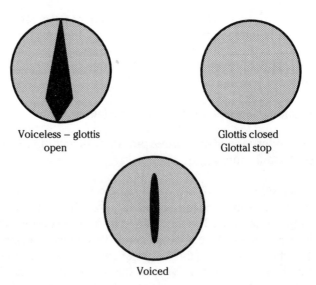

Voiceless – glottis
open

Glottis closed
Glottal stop

Voiced

Figure 2.2

pulled back, they cannot vibrate. Sounds produced without the vocal cords vibrating are called voiceless. When we breathe, the vocal cords are pulled back allowing the air to pass freely in and out of the lungs.

To identify voiced and voiceless sounds, place your thumb and first finger on either side at the top of your larynx. Now make the sound at the beginning of the word *zoo*. You should feel the vocal cords vibrating. Keep your fingers in position but this time make the sound at the beginning of the word *sue*. This time you should not feel your vocal cords vibrating. The first example is a voiced sound, and the second is a voiceless one.

Exercise 2.3

Below is a list of words. Say each one out loud, and decide if the sound associated with the italicised letter (or letters) is voiced or voiceless.

	Voiced	Voiceless		Voiced	Voiceless
ba*c*on			*ch*eese		
sa*l*ami			crea*m*		
ri*c*e			*sh*rimp		
ora*ng*e			*f*lour		
*w*alnut			gra*p*e		

* * * * * * * * * *

2.2.2.3 *Articulation*

As the airstream passes through the vocal tract, it may be modified by the movement of the articulators, that is by the lips and the tongue obstructing its passage through the vocal tract to varying degrees. This process is called articulation. The obstruction of the airstream may occur at any point in the vocal tract, and is the result of an active articulator moving towards a passive articulator. The active articulators are the lips and the tongue, and the passive articulators are locations on the roof of the mouth, for example the alveolar ridge, hard palate, etc.

We usually subdivide the articulatory process into two sections – place (where in the vocal tract obstruction of the air flow occurs) and manner (the degree to which the flow of air is obstructed). The second term of the three-term phonetic labels introduced in Table 2.1 (section 2.1.1) refers to a place of articulation, and the third to a manner of articulation. In the following sections we shall define and discuss these terms.

articulators

active articulator
passive articulator

2.2.2.3.1 *Place of articulation* The number of places of articulation may vary from one language to another. The following are those which are required for English and were introduced in section 2.1.1:

1. Labial: these are sounds formed by the articulation of the upper and lower lips, for example [p] as in *pit*.

2. Labio-dental: labio-dental sounds are produced by the lower lip and the upper incisors, for example [f] as in *fat*.

dental

3. Dental: make the sound at the beginning of *thick* and prolong it. You should find that the tip of your tongue makes contact with your incisors. It may either make contact with the back of your incisors or protrude slightly between them. The symbol for this sound is [θ].

alveolar

4. Alveolar: to produce an alveolar sound the blade (or tip and blade) of the tongue touches or comes close to the alveolar ridge. The sounds associated with the underlined segments in the following words are all alveolar: *tip* [t], *dip* [d], *sip* [s], *zip* [z], and *nip* [n].

5. Post alveolar (sometimes called alveopalatal or palato-alveolar): these sounds are produced by the blade of the tongue articulating with the junction of the alveolar ridge and the hard palate. In English the sound at the beginning of *church* [tʃ] is post-alveolar.

palatal

6. Palatal: make the sound at the beginning of *yacht* and prolong it. This is a palatal sound produced by the front of the tongue articulating with the hard palate. (Remember the front of the tongue is the middle section and not the tip.)

7. Velar: velar sounds are the result of the back of the tongue articulating with the soft palate or velum. [k] in *cat*, [g] in *golf*, and [ŋ] in *hang* are all velar.

The places of articulation described above are those necessary for the description of English. Although they are sufficient for some other languages, there are many languages whose speakers use speech sounds which require additional places of articulation. For some French speech sounds the back of the tongue articulates with the uvula. The Dravidian languages of southern India have a series of retroflex consonants for which the tongue is curled backwards so that the underside may make contact with the alveolar ridge.

2.2.2.3.2 *Manner of articulation* Just as the vocal tract may be obstructed at any point, it is also possible to vary the degree of obstruction, giving a range of manners of articulation. To describe the consonant sounds of English we require the following manners of articulation:

Nasal vs oral
                                                                                    nasal
As we saw in 2.2.1 above, the nasal cavity is one of the three cavities of the head and neck involved in speech production. The flow of air from the lungs into the nasal cavity is controlled by the velum, which may be either raised or lowered. If it is lowered then air is free to flow out through the nasal cavity. We call segments produced with air flowing through the nasal cavity 'nasals'. The addition of voice will result in nasal resonance. Any segment produced with the velum raised, closing off the nasal cavity, is oral.

If you make the sound at the beginning of *mad* you should find that although your lips form an air tight seal, air flows out through the nasal cavity. Now make the sound at the beginning of *bad*. You should find that no air flows out at all. Not only do the lips form an air-tight seal, as with the *m* of *mad*, but the velum is raised, sealing off the nasal cavity.

The position of the velum may be varied independently of the other speech production processes. Consequently, it is possible to nasalise any segment type, or to have voiceless nasals. For example, French has a set of nasalised vowels, and Hopi (a North American native language) has a set of voiceless nasals.

There are three nasal segments in English – labial [m], alveolar [n] and the velar [ŋ]. All other sounds are oral, that is the velum is raised and the airstream from the lungs is forced to flow out through the oral cavity.

Figure 2.3(a) Position of the articulators for a bilabial oral stop.

Note that the lips are shut and the velum is shutting off the nasal passage.

Figure 2.3(b)   Position of the articulators for a bilabial nasal stop.

Note that the lips are shut but the velum is away from the back wall of the pharynx opening the nasal passage.

stop

Stops

To make a stop the articulators form an air-tight seal somewhere in the vocal tract, and the air flow in the vocal tract is completely obstructed. [p b t d k g] are all stops.

The nasals [m n] and [ŋ] are also stops. Although air from the lungs is free to flow out through the nasal cavity, each of these sounds involves a complete obstruction at some point in the oral cavity. Consequently, we classify nasals as stops.

We can identify three stages in the production of a stop consonant. The first is the closing stage, where the active articulator approaches the passive one. In the hold stage, the active articulator forms the air-tight seal. As air continues to come out of the lungs, the air pressure behind the seal increases. The release stage occurs when the active articulator is pulled rapidly away from the passive one. This is accompanied by a small explosion as the air behind the seal is released. Occasionally stops may lack the closing or release stages, but they must always have a hold stage.

fricative

Fricatives

In the production of a fricative, the active articulator comes close enough to the passive one to restrict the flow of air but not to stop it completely.

Figure 2.4   Position of the articulators for an alveolar oral stop – [t] or [d]

Note the blade of the tongue is completely blocking the airflow at the alveolar ridge and the velum is shutting off the nasal passage.

As the air is squeezed through the narrow gap between the articulators, it becomes turbulent and an audible hiss is produced. [f v s z] are all fricatives.

Approximants

approximant

With approximants the vocal tract is narrowed by the movement of the active articulator towards the passive one. However, unlike fricatives the gap is not narrow enough to produce turbulence. Consequently no audible hiss is produced. The sound at the beginning of *yacht* – [j] is an approximant as is [r].

We can divide the set of approximants into two classes – liquids [l r], and semi-vowels or glides [j w]. The glides are phonetically like vowels. If you make the sound at the beginning of *yield*, that is [j], and prolong it, you should find quite quickly that you are actually making [iː] – the vowel sound in *bead*. The articulation of [j] is almost identical [iː], but is extremely short. The articulation of [w] is close to that of [uː]. As with [j], if you prolong the initial sound of *wood*, you will find that, just as a prolonged [j] quickly developed into [iː], a prolonged [w] will develop into [uː]. [j] is an extremely short [iː], and [w] is an extremely short [uː].

liquid
glide

Figure 2.5   Position of the articulators for an alveolar oral fricative –
[s] or [z].

Note that the velum is shutting off the nasal passage while a very small gap between the
alveolar ridge and the blade of the tongue exists.

consonant
consonantal

Despite being phonetically vowels, the glides behave like consonants,
and we shall still classify them as such. We can easily illustrate the consonantal behaviour of the glides. In English the indefinite article occurs
as *a* before a noun beginning with a consonant, for example, *a mouse, a
frog*, and *an* before a noun beginning with a vowel, for example, *an aardvark, an emu*. Before nouns beginning with either [j] or [w], we find the
pre-consonantal form *a*, for example, *a yacht, a wombat*. We shall return
to the glides in section 3.7.3.

affricate

Affricates
Like stops, affricates involve a complete obstruction of the air flow at
some point in the vocal tract. However, unlike stops, the obstruction is
released gradually. The gradual movement of the active articulator
away from the passive one allows the air, which has built up behind
the obstruction, to squeeze through the gap, creating turbulence. As
with fricatives, the turbulence creates audible friction. [tʃ], as in the
initial sound in *church*, and [dʒ], as in the initial sound in *judge*, are
both affricates.

Figure 2.6 Position of the articulators for an alveolar approximant − [r]

Note that the articulators are in almost the same position as for [s] and [z] but the blade of the tongue and the alveolar ridge are a little further apart.

Trills, taps and flaps

trills, taps, flaps

These three manners are less common than those discussed above but do occur in some dialects of English.

For trills the active articulator is held in such a position that the airstream flowing over it causes it to vibrate rapidly against the passive one. The vocal tract is alternately open and closed. In some dialects of Scottish English, the sound at the beginning of *rabbit* is a voiced alveolar trill.

In the articulation of taps and flaps, the active articulator makes a single fast contact with the passive one. In many US dialects of English the alveolar stops are articulated as taps when they occur between two vowels, for example the *t* in *phonetic* would be a voiced alveolar tap − [ɾ].

Central vs lateral

central, lateral

This distinction describes the route the airstream takes as it passes out through the oral cavity. In the production of all consonantal segments, except stops, the passage of the pulmonic airstream through the oral cavity may be either central or lateral.

Central. Make [ʃ] but instead of breathing out, breathe in. The centre of your tongue should feel cold as the air passes over it. [ʃ] is a central sound. For these sounds, the side rims of the tongue form an air-tight seal with the upper molars and gums. This forces the airstream out over the centre of the tongue.

Lateral.   Make [l] and, as above, breath in. This time the sides of your tongue should feel cold as the air passes over them. For lateral segments, a closure is formed somewhere in the centre of the vocal tract. Air passes round this obstruction and out over the sides of the tongue. In English only [l], for example *like*, is lateral. All other segments are central.

Exercise 2.4

From the list of English words below, put the underlined segments into classes according to manner of articulation:

   cabin, ships, thanks, yacht, gather, drop

                 * * * * * * * * * *

We can use the speech production processes to provide a descriptive framework for consonants. As we saw in section 2.1.1, it is possible to identify most English consonant segments by a three-term label.

   1.   The first term will always be either 'voiced' or 'voiceless'.
   2.   The second term will always refer to the place of articulation, for example 'labial', 'alveolar' or 'velar'.
   3.   The third term always refers to the manner of articulation, for example 'stop', 'fricative', 'affricate', 'approximant', or 'nasal'.

Consider, as an example, [k]:

   In the production of this segment the vocal cords do not vibrate, therefore, [k] is 'voiceless'.

   To produce [k] the back of the tongue articulates with the velum. The place of articulation is 'velar'.

   The airstream is completely blocked. Segments produced in this manner are 'stops'.

[k] is a 'voiceless velar stop'.

   [l] requires an extra label. It is usually described as a 'voiced alveolar lateral approximant'. The term 'lateral' is required to distinguish [l] from [r], which is a 'voiced alveolar approximant'. Note that as all segments in English, apart from [l], are central, we do not include central in our description of consonants.

Exercise 2.5

Provide three-term labels for the following segments:

[p]

[g]

[z]

[j]

* * * * * * * * * *

Exercise 2.6

In this exercise do not be misled by the orthography.

(a) Identify all the words in the following that contain an alveolar fricative between two vowel sounds:

craze, case, rose, busy, doze, electricity, ace, raising, pleasing

(b) Identify all the words in the following that begin with an approximant:

link, talk, quick, unit, sew, judge, youth, write, onion

(c) Identify all the words in the following that end with a voiceless fricative:

dogs, laugh, boxes, rags, cuts, through, bath, tough

(d) Identify all the words in the following that end with a vowel sound:

fly, put, stop, flow, lime, bit, name, through, rose, type

* * * * * * * * * *

2.2.3 *Vowels*   **vowel**

The description of consonants is based on a combination of the following: the degree of obstruction of the air flow, for example stop, fricative or approximant; place of obstruction, for example, dental, alveolar, or palatal; and voicing, that is all consonants are either voiced or voiceless. Since it is the combination of voice, place, and manner that defines the quality of each consonant, by using these three qualities we are able (as we saw above) to provide descriptive labels for all English consonants. Unlike consonants, the quality of a vowel is not the product of a combination of voice, and place and manner of articulation but is determined by the shape of the vocal tract.

We can alter the shape of the vocal tract by varying the position of the tongue and the lips: the height of the tongue, which part of the tongue is raised or lowered, and the shape of the lips. With the addition of voice we create a range of different vowel sounds.

In describing vowels we refer to the position of the tongue and lips, and not to the place or degree of obstruction. Tongue position may be specified in two ways: vertically (how high or low is the tongue) and horizontally (which section of the tongue is raised or lowered). The lips are either rounded or unrounded. It is these three parameters (vertical and horizontal tongue position, and lip rounding) that are used to describe the articulation of vowels.

2.2.3.1 *Tongue position*

In section 2.2.1 we claimed that, when at rest, the tongue does not lie on the floor of the mouth but is held mid-way between the roof and the floor of the mouth, approximately in the position for the final vowel sound in *sofa*. It we take the rest position as the starting point, we may plot tongue position in the articulation of vowels in terms of movement from this point.

To establish the rest position of the tongue, produce the final vowel in *sofa* – [ə]. Try to maintain this articulation and then make the vowel in *bead* – [i:]. Alternate between these two vowels until you feel confident about your perception of the movement of your tongue. Do you detect any movement and if so in which direction?

In producing [i:], you should detect a forward and upward movement of the front of your tongue from the rest position towards the hard palate. You may check this by making [i:] and then, while articulating this vowel, move your tongue up until it touches the roof of your mouth and forms a stop. The front of your tongue will most likely be in contact with your hard palate. Now try alternating [ə] with [æ], as in *bad*. As you articulate [æ], you should detect a downward movement of both the front of your tongue and your lower jaw (away from the rest position and hard palate).

high
low
Relative to [ə], the tongue moves forwards and up for [i:]. Consequently we refer to [i:] as a high vowel. For [æ] there is lowering of the tongue and jaw relative to [ə], and therefore we refer to [æ] as a low vowel.

mid
If you alternate [ə] with the vowel in *bed* – [e], your tongue will move forwards but will probably only move up or down very slightly if at all. Given this lack of vertical movement, we refer to this vowel as a mid vowel. This gives us a three-place scale for tongue movement in the vertical axis – high, mid, and low. Try articulating these three vowels in sequence. You should become aware of the progressive lowering of the tongue and opening of your mouth as your lower jaw moves down.

For some languages we may require a four-place scale, for example if we have [iː], [e], [ɛ] and [æ]. It is easy to accommodate this series into our three-place division by dividing the mid-point in two, giving high-mid – [e], and low-mid – [ɛ].

high-mid
low-mid

In the articulation of [iː], [e], and [æ] it was the front of the tongue that moved, either up (towards the hard palate) or down (away from the hard palate). Vowels that involve the movement of the front of the tongue in the region below the hard palate we shall label as front. This now gives us a two-term label for each of these vowels. [iː] is a 'high front vowel', [e] is a 'mid front vowel', and [æ] is a 'low front vowel'. The first term defines the position of the tongue in the vertical axis while the second identifies which horizontal section of the tongue is involved.

front

> If [iː], [e], and [æ] are all front vowels, then what horizontal section is involved in the articulation of the vowels in *bard, bought,* and *booed* – [ɑː], [ɔː], and [uː]? In attempting this exercise, contrast each of the vowels given above with [ə] as in the previous exercise. It may be useful to begin with [uː] and then [ɑː].

With [ɑː], [ɔː], and [uː] you should notice that it is the back of your tongue that moves from the rest position. In the articulation of [uː], the back of the tongue moves up and back from the rest position towards the soft palate or velum. You may check this by articulating [uː] and then moving the tongue slightly up until it makes contact with the soft palate. At this point you should have made a velar stop, either [k] or [g] depending on whether or not you retain the voicing of the vowel. [uː] is a 'high back' vowel. For [ɑː] your tongue (and perhaps your lower jaw) will move down. [ɑː] is a 'low back' vowel. In articulating [ɔː] your tongue may move only slightly up or down (if at all) but will move back. [ɔː] is a 'mid back' vowel.

back

It is not just the front and the back of the tongue that are involved in the articulation of vowels, the centre is also used. In English, [ə], [ʌ] and [ɜː] are all central vowels. The middle of the tongue is involved in the articulation of these vowels.

2.2.3.2 *Lip position*
The position of the lips, as well as the tongue, contributes to vowel quality. Alternate the vowels [iː] and [uː]. You should notice that, apart from sounding like a klaxon, you change the position of your lips as you move from one to the other. For [iː] the lips are unrounded, whereas for [uː] they are rounded. Lip position may be varied independently of the tongue position. Make the [iː] vowel again, round your lips but do not move your tongue. When you round your lips you should produce a close front rounded vowel. This vowel is identified by the symbol [y] and occurs in French *bureau*. While making a close front rounded vowel, move your tongue from the close position to the open position.

How open does the vowel become before it ceases to be round? You should be able to produce high, high-mid, and low-mid front rounded vowels. It is rather difficult to produce a low rounded vowel. The symbols [ø] and [œ] are used to represent the high-mid and low-mid front rounded vowels, respectively. Such vowels occur in many languages, for example French, German, Swedish, and Danish. Just as it is possible to find front rounded and unrounded vowels in languages, central rounded and back unrounded vowels also occur in languages, for example, Mandarin, Japanese, and Fe?Fe? (an African language) all have a high back unrounded vowel – [ɯ].

2.2.3.3 *Monophthong and diphthong*

monophthong

Monophthong – one sound. If the sound of a vowel remains relatively unchanged during its production, then we call it a monophthong. [e] and [ɑ:] are monophthongs.

diphthong

Diphthong – two sounds. If the sound of a vowel continually changes within a single syllable then we call it a diphthong. The change in sound quality may be achieved by a movement of the tongue and/or lips. The vowels in *toy*, *tie*, and *town* ([ɔi], [ai], and [au] respectively) are all diphthongs.

It is possible to represent graphically the position of the tongue in the articulation of vowels using a vowel quadrilateral. The quadrilateral represents the shape of the inside of the mouth. The vertical axis represents the vertical position of the tongue on the high–low scale, while the horizontal is used to identify which section of the tongue is involved in the vertical movement. Using these two axes, we may position vowels on the chart in relation to the position of the tongue in their articulation.

While monophthongs may be indicated by a single point on the chart, diphthongs require a starting point, direction of movement, and a finishing point.

Figure 2.7

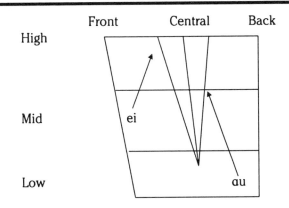

Figure 2.8

2.2.3.4 *Long and short vowels*

Vowels in English, and other languages, may be either long or short. This is referred to as 'length' or 'quantity'. (The difference between the vowel sounds is referred to as 'quality'.) All vowels are either long or short. [ɪ e æ ʌ ə ɒ] are all short in English. The remaining monophthongs and all diphthongs are long.

To conclude this section on speech production, we can compare the whole process, and the anatomy that makes it possible, with the bagpipes. Bagpipes consist of a bag, which is full of air, connected to pipes. Similarly, the lungs are a pair of bags connected to tubes. The pipes of the bagpipes have a double reed inside at their base. When the bag is compressed, the air is forced out and passes between the reeds causing them to vibrate just like the vocal folds are caused to vibrate when the lungs are compressed. The sound created by the vibration in both cases then travels along the rest of the tube and we hear a single note droned by the pipe. This is much the same as the nasal cavity, whose air volume cannot be changed. If the sound created at the vocal folds produces a single note that passes out through the nose, we will hear a single note being droned. One of the pipes on the bagpipes, called the chanter, has holes in it so that the volume of air may be more radically altered. As the player covers or uncovers the holes, the note changes appreciably. This is like the oral cavity, which can have the volume of air within it changed by the degree to which the jaw is open, and by the placement of the tongue and the position of the lips. As a result it can produce different harmonics of the note created at the vocal folds.

In essence then, the vocal mechanism looks rather like the diagram in Figure 2.9.

The differences between the vocal tract and the bagpipes are also of course important. The note created by the vocal folds can change in a way that the double reed's note in a bagpipe cannot. The vocal tract has a valve in the form of the velum, which allows the airway to the

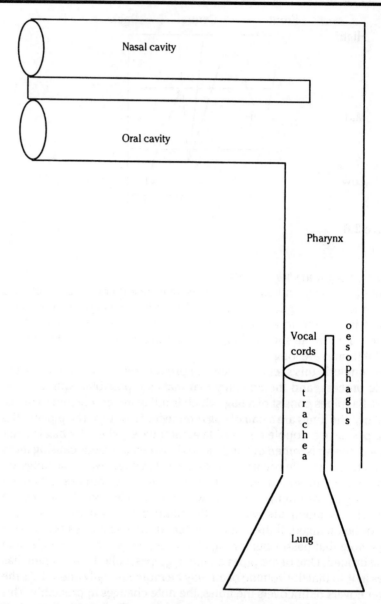

Figure 2.9   Schematic representation of the vocal tract

nasal passage to be cut off. Bagpipes have no tongue within the chanter and no moveable lips at its extremity. Notwithstanding all these differences, you can see from the diagram in Figure 2.9 that the oral tract is essentially a bent tube through which exhaled air passes. As it passes out it may be modified in a variety of ways, many of which create speech sounds.

Further exercises

Exercise 2.7

For each of the following phonetic labels provide the correct symbol and a word that begins with that sound.
For example: voiced labial stop   [b]   *bin*

(a) voiced palatal approximant

(b) high back vowel

(c) voiceless post-alveolar fricative

(d) voiced alveolar nasal

(e) voiced labio-dental fricative

(f) high front vowel

(g) voiced velar stop

(h) voiceless dental fricative

(i) low front vowel

(j) voiced alveolar lateral approximant

Exercise 2.8

Convert the following passages of phonetic script into regular English orthography. Notice that in the phonetic script no use is made of either capital letters or punctuation. You will need to add these to the orthographic representation yourself.

[ɪf ə red bæk bɪt ju: ɒn ðə bəhaind ju: wɜ: left wɪθ ðə prɒbləm əv weə tə put ðə tuənəkei ənd nɒt lɒŋ tə θɪŋk əbaut ɪt nɔ: kʊd ju: ɑ:sk eni:wʌn tə sʌk aut ðə pɔizən ʌnles ju: nju: ðəm verɪ wel ɪndi:d]

(Clive James, *Unreliable Memoirs*)

[hi: mʌst həv hɜ:d hau bɔ:rɪŋ ðei wɜ: sɪns i: nevə əpiəd bʌt ɪt wɒz nɒt fə wɒnt əv hævɪŋ ɪz neim ɪnvoukt ðə houl fækəltɪ sælɪveitəd ɒn mæs ət ðə miə menʃən əv ɪm]

(Clive James, *Unreliable Memoirs*)

Exercise 2.9

Study the following piece of transcription carefully and then answer the questions below

[ðə fɜːst vjuː əv ɑustreiljə wɒz ðə koust niə pɜːθ riːfs whɑit biːtʃəz ʃælow wɔːtə laik ðə juːs of emrəldz huːndrɪds əv swɪmɪŋ puːls ðə kʌlər əv pɔːl njuːmənz ɑiz ətestəd tʊ æfluːəns]

(Clive James, Flying Visits)

There are three errors in the transcription of vowels, and four errors in the transcription of consonants. Identify and list each of these errors, and provide a correct transcription of the words in which they occur. For example, [qwɪk] – [q] should be [k] giving [kwɪk].

Pick out one word that begins and ends with a voiceless stop, one that contains a diphthong between two alveolar approximants, and one that contains a cluster of three consonants.

Exercise 2.10

Convert the following passages into phonetic script.

> I caught this morning morning's minion, king-
>> dom of daylight's dauphin, dapple-dawn-drawn Falcon, in his
>>> riding
>> Of the rolling level underneath him steady air, and striding
> High there, how he rung upon the rein of a wimpling wing

(Gerard Manley Hopkins, The Windhover)

. . . so I made my way out, saying goodbye to Todd and Alison and Sue and all the other wonderful new friends, I'd made, and stole a cab. No, not literally. It's an old-established New York custom: when you see a luggage-laden traveller hailing a cab, you obstruct his passage while he's trying to haul his gear and jump into the cab ahead of him, laughing heartily as you do so.

(Stephen Brook, New York Days, New York Nights)

There was trouble over the oranges. The customs officers started asking questions and making difficulties. Perhaps the right man wasn't on duty or hadn't been paid enough. It seemed a lot of fuss over a crate of fruit. Were the oranges stuffed with drugs, or diamonds, or explosives? Fantastic explanations proposed themselves more readily than answers.

(Simon Loftus, A Pike in the Basement)

Exercise 2.11

For each of the following symbols provide the correct phonetic label and a word that begins with that sound.

For example: [s] voiceless aveolar fricative   *stop*

(a)   [d]

(b)   [m]

(c)   [ʌ]

(d)   [f]

(e)   [dʒ]

(f)   [ɒ]

(g)   [w]

(h)   [k]

(i)   [r]

(j)   [e]

3 The phonology of English

Introduction – sounds: same vs different

In section 2.2, we established a framework for the description of sounds. This framework is based on articulatory phonetics. Although we concentrated on English, with some additions to the framework it is possible to describe all sounds produced in the vocal tract. Furthermore, it is possible to describe any sound in detail.

Consider the following words:

    1. s*t*em   2. *t*ip   3. no*t* yet   4. a*t*las   5. no*t* now   6. eigh*t*h   7. ha*t*pin

Pronounce the first word with your hand held just in front of your mouth, and then pronounce the second word. Do you perceive any difference in your pronunciation of *t* between the two words?

aspirated

You should feel a burst of air as you make the *t* in the second word, but not in the first. The second *t* is usually described as aspirated, while the first is a voiceless alveolar stop. We do not introduce a completely new symbol to represent the second *t* sound but add a diacritic, an additional mark, to the original symbol. These diacritics have no sound value in themselves but give us more detail concerning the pronunciation of the symbol to which they are added. The diacritic that signals aspiration is a raised *h*, which occurs to the right of aspirated consonant. For *t* this gives [t^h].

Now pronounce 3–7 in the list above, paying attention to the position of your tongue in the articulation of *t*. Compare the position of your tongue in each case to its position for the *t* in *stem*. In 6 try closing your teeth together as you make the *t*.

You should find that your articulation of *t* varies for each word. For *not yet*, your tongue is probably further back towards the hard palate. In this example [t] is described as 'palatalised'. The diacritic for palatalisation is a raised *j* placed to the right of the symbol for the palatalised sound. This gives [t^j]. If you say these words quickly enough you will probably pronounce the sequence of [t] + [j] as [tʃ].

In *atlas* we have a sequence of two alveolar consonants – a voiceless stop and a lateral approximant. (We refer to sequences of consonants with the same place of articulation as homorganic sequences.) In releasing the stop you do not move the entire blade of the tongue but only the sides. The centre remains in contact with the alveolar ridge. We call this lateral release and transcribe the *t* in this instance with a superscript *l* – [t^l].   **homorganic**   **lateral release**

We have another homorganic sequence in *not now* – a voiceless stop and a nasal. As with the *t* in *atlas* you do not release the *t* by moving the tongue from the alveolar ridge. In fact the tongue does not move at all. In this case the stop is released through the nasal cavity. The velum is in the raised position for the oral stop but is lowered for the homorganic nasal. The compressed air trapped in the oral cavity can then escape through the nasal cavity. We call this nasal release and transcribe this *t* with a superscript *n* – [t^n].   **nasal release**

If you try to close your teeth for the *t* in *eighth*, you may have found your tongue in the way. In this case we have a dentalised version. For many speakers, their tongue protrudes between their incisors when they articulate dental or dentalised sounds. Speakers who do not put their tongue between their incisors for this sound will probably articulate this *t* by placing the tip of their tongue on the back of their incisors. Dentalisation is indicated by a diacritic, which resembles a small incisor, placed below the appropriate symbol: [t̪].

In the final example, your tongue may move towards the alveolar ridge, and it may even make contact, but it is more than likely that you do not release the stop. If you consider your pronunciation carefully, you will probably find that you make and release the labial stop at the beginning of *pin*, but you do not release the stop at the end of *hat*. In this example [t] is described as 'unreleased', and transcribed as [t˥], where ˥ is the diacritic for an unreleased stop.

This exercise demonstrates that there are, at least, seven types of *t* in English. It is possible, with an expanded phonetic framework, to describe these sounds in some detail. If there are seven types of *t* in English, then what use do speakers of the language make of these sounds? The answer is none. Until you were asked to consider carefully your pronunciation of the above words, you were probably unaware of these differences but simply thought of them all as *t*. Although they are all phonetically quite different you probably 'heard' them all as *t*. For speakers of English, whether a *t* is aspirated, dentalised, palatalised, or unreleased, is unimportant. None of these phonetic properties seems to be involved in the recognition of *t*. Speakers of English are unaware of these differences. In fact, they consider all seven *t*s to be 'the same'. This point may be simply illustrated. Aspirate the *t* in *stem*. Does the substitution of the unaspirated *t* by the aspirated version change the meaning of the word? No. Substitution of one *t* sound for another does not produce a different word. It simply results in a somewhat unusual pronunciation of that word. You can test this further by replacing all the *t* sounds by the dentalised version. In each case the result will be the same. The meaning of the word will not change but your pronunciation will be slightly odd (and in some cases difficult).

Consider again *tip*. Using the table of consonant sounds of English introduced in section 2.1.1, try replacing the initial sound (a voiceless alveolar stop) by another single consonant sound from the list, for example [d] (a voiced alveolar stop). Each time replacement results in a different word, record the consonant involved and its three- (or four-) term label.

You should have found that at least: [p] voiceless labial stop, [d] voiced alveolar stop, [n] voiced alveolar nasal, [s] voiceless alveolar fricative, [z] voiced alveolar fricative, [l] voiced alveolar lateral approximant, and [w] voiced labio-velar approximant, may be substituted for [t] and make another word. Whereas the phonetically different *t* sounds in the earlier exercise could be considered as the 'same' sound, speakers of English clearly consider each of the sounds in the above exercise to be different. These sounds are used to distinguish one English word from another.

Phonetic properties such as aspiration and palatalisation are not distinctive in English. Their use does not distinguish one word from another. However, properties such as voiced, voiceless, labial, alveolar, stop, fricative, approximant, and nasal are distinctive. They are used to distinguish one word from another. A change in one or more of these phonetic properties in a single sound may result in what a speaker considers to be a different sound, or if that sound is part of a word, then such a change may result in a different word.

In English, phonetic properties such as aspiration and palatalisation are automatic, that is, they are not within the speaker's control. Native speakers of English have to try hard not to aspirate the *t* sound in words like *ten* or *top*. However, phonetic properties like voiced and voiceless; labial, dental and velar; and stop, fricative and approximant, are within the control of the speaker. It is these properties that speakers of English use to distinguish one sound from another, and one word from another.

It would appear that we can identify two different sets of phonetic properties in English. First, there are those that distinguish one sound from another, and therefore one word from another. These properties are information-bearing. If we change the initial voiceless stop of *tip* to a voiced one, we know that a different word has been uttered. Secondly, there is the set of properties that provide a more detailed description of the pronunciation of a sound, but do not distinguish one sound (or word) (or word) from another. The members of this second set are not informa-tion-bearing. In distinguishing the initial sound of *tip* from that of *dip*, a property such as aspiration is unnecessary or redundant. The presence versus absence of aspiration is not necessary to distinguish [t] from [d], whereas voiceless versus voiced is.

The first set of (information bearing) properties we shall describe as distinctive, and the second as non-distinctive. This division of phonetic properties may be extended to the segments themselves. We have a set of distinctive segments that are defined solely by distinctive phonetic prop-erties and are used to distinguish one word from another. We shall call the members of this set phonemes, and indicate their status by placing **phoneme** them inside slanting brackets, for example /t/ and /d/. Sounds whose description includes one or more non-distinctive properties, and does not distinguish one word from another, we shall call allophones ('other **allophone** sounds') and place them inside square brackets, for example [tʰ] and [t⁻] in English. The identification and study of these distinctive sounds, and their relation to the non-distinctive sounds is called phonology. **phonology**

The set of properties that are distinctive is not constant throughout the world's languages. Consequently, the set of distinctive sound segments may differ from language to language. Although, for example, aspiration is non-distinctive in English, it is distinctive in languages such as Korean and Thai. Speakers of these languages will hear the difference between, for example [tʰ] and [t]. These two languages have phonemic voiceless aspirated stops /pʰ tʰ kʰ/, whereas in English such segments are allo-phones of the voiceless stops. A speaker of English does not 'hear' the difference between the aspirated and unaspirated voiceless stops, but a speaker of Korean or Thai listening to English will hear the difference. Furthermore, whereas the distinction between voiced and voiceless stops is distinctive in English, there are languages such as Maori and Tongan where it is not. In these languages phones such as [b d g] are not phonemes, but are allophones of /p t k/ respectively. Speakers of Tongan do not 'hear' the difference between /p/ and /b/ in English. For them these two sounds are the 'same'.

3.1   Identification of phonemes

We may test whether the difference between two sounds is phonologi-cally important by substituting one sound for another in a word. If this substitution produces a different word then we have identified a pho-neme. For example, earlier we replaced the [t] in *tip* with [d]. This gave us *dip*, which is different from *tip*. We can conclude that [t] and [d] are phonemes and as such we place them in slanted brackets rather than square ones to identify them as phonemes, that is /t/ and /d/, rather than [t] and [d].

minimal pair test
minimal pair

This method of testing for the phonological importance of a sound is called the minimal pair test. The two words, for example *tip* and *dip*, which differ in one and only one sound are called a minimal pair. Any two words that differ in one and only one sound are a minimal pair, for example *cheap* and *jeep* – [tʃiːp] vs [dʒiːp], *wing* and *sing* – [wɪŋ] vs [sɪŋ], and *fill* and *kill* – [fɪl] vs [kɪl]. Pairs of words that differ in more than a single sound are not minimal pairs, for example *kill* and *thrill* – [kɪl] vs [θrɪl], and *wing* and *fling* – [wɪŋ] vs [flɪŋ] are not minimal pairs. To establish the phonemic status of a sound, it is only necessary to identify one minimal pair. Always remember that we are considering sounds and not spelling symbols. *Hand* and *hang* differ in a single spelling symbol but in two sounds – [hænd] vs [hæŋ], and therefore are not a minimal pair.

Consider the word *pin* – /pɪn/. Substitute the other consonant sounds from Table 2.1 for /p/. Which ones, when substituted for /p/, give another English word?

You should have found that /b t d k f θ s ʃ tʃ dʒ w l/ (*bin, tin, din, kin, fin, thin, sin, shin, chin, gin, win*, and *Lynn*) can all be substituted for /p/ to give another English word.

In the above exercise, we established a phonetic frame – [__ɪn], and then substituted various sounds in the initial position of this frame. Each time the placing of a sound in this frame resulted in a different word, we identified a phoneme of English. All the sounds that can be substituted for /p/ to make another English word are phonemes of English.

This method of identification of phonemes (the minimal pair test) is based on the notion of 'minimal contrast'. Two or more sounds in a language contrast if they can appear in the same position in the same frame. All the sounds you identified above appear in the same position in the same frame, that is, before [ɪn]. These sounds are said to be in contrastive distribution. The minimal pair test relies on the notion of contrastive distribution.

contrastive distribution

Although we have applied the minimal pair test only to the consonant phonemes of English, it is possible to use this method to identify the vowel phonemes of English. For example, taking /pɪn/ as our frame, we can try substituting various vowel sounds for /ɪ/, and as for the consonants, each time we get a new word we have identified a vowel phoneme of English, for example *pen, pan, pain, pun,* and *pine* – /pen pæn pein pʌn pain/. We can also substitute other consonant sounds for /n/, for example *pip, pit, pill, pith, pitch, pick, pig,* and *ping.* – /pɪp pɪt pɪl pɪθ pɪtʃ pɪk pɪg pɪŋ/.

Exercise 3.1

How many minimal pairs can you find for (a) *pill*, (b) *hot*, and (c) *high*?

* * * * * * * * * *

3.1.1 *Complementary distribution*

In the introduction to this chapter we identified a number of different *t* sounds. All of these *t* sounds appear in different (or mutually exclusive) environments, for example the laterally released allophone occurs only before a lateral, the dental allophone only before a dental, and the palatalised allophone only before a palatal sound. We never find the palatalised allophone before a dental sound or the laterally released allophone before a palatal. For example, we never find [eitʲθ]. Sounds in a language that never occur in the same environment can never contrast or have the potential to contrast. Therefore, they cannot be in contrastive distribution. We say that sounds that only ever occur in different (or mutually exclusive) environments are in complementary distribution.   **complementary distribution**

Sounds that are in complementary distribution are allophones of phonemes. For allophones to be assigned to a particular phoneme, not only must they be in complementary distribution, but they must also be pho-   **phonetically similar**
netically similar. If we consider again the many different *t* sounds, not only are they in complementary distribution, but they are also phonetically similar. We would have no objections to assigning these sounds to the phoneme /t/. They are allophones of the phoneme /t/.

Phonetic similarity is not a formal notion, but rather intuitive. There are no rules or cut-off points that help us to decide to which phoneme a particular allophone should be assigned. However, it is easy for us to arrive at such decisions.

3.1.2 *Defective distribution*

Consider the sounds [h] and [ŋ] in English. What is the distribution of these sounds?

These two sounds would appear to be in complementary distribution. [h] never occurs in word-final position, or before another consonant. In fact, it appears only in syllable-initial position. [ŋ] never occurs in word-initial position, but does occur in word- and syllable-final position. Given that these two sounds are in complementary distribution, we could claim that they are allophones of the same phoneme. However, intuitively this seems wrong. In this example the notion that they are allophones of the same phoneme is rejected on grounds of lack of phonetic similarity. Furthermore, native speakers of English would never consider [h] and [ŋ] to be allophones of the same phoneme. Unlike the allophones of /t/, which native speakers perceive as the 'same', no native speaker perceives [h] and [ŋ] as the same. They are clearly different.

The fact that /h/ and /ŋ/ fail to appear in contrastive distribution, but appear in complementary distribution, is an extreme example of defec-   **defective distribution**
tive distribution. This term is used to describe any phoneme that appears in some environments but not in others.

3.1.3 *Parallel distribution*

The minimal pair test is a simple and effective means for identifying the phonemes of a language, and only a single minimal pair is required for the phonemic status of a sound to be established through contrastive distribution. However, it may not always be possible to find a minimal pair.

When we cannot find minimal pairs and we are certain that the sounds in question are not allophones of a single phoneme, we consider the distribution of the sounds in question. What this means is that we look at the range of positions in a word in which the specific sounds may appear. For example, we might consider word-initial or word-final position, or which consonants and vowels the sounds under consideration may precede or **parallel distribution**   follow. If the distribution of two sounds overlaps then they are in parallel distribution. Sounds that are in parallel distribution have the potential to contrast with each other and, therefore, are phonemes. They cannot be allophones, because allophones, as we discussed above, appear in mutually exclusive positions. To establish parallel distribution, we have to find only a single environment in which both sounds appear.

As an illustrative example, let us consider the distribution in English of /θ/ and /ʒ/. In word-final position, we find that the same vowels may precede /θ/ and /ʒ/:

Final /θ/	Final /ʒ/	Vowel
teeth	liege	iː
faith	beige	ei
bath	camouflage	ɑː
booth	rouge	uː

We now have four environments in which both sounds appear, that is, after /iː ei ɑː/ or /uː/. Given the above examples, we can establish parallel distribution. /θ/ and /ʒ/ have the potential to contrast, and therefore must be assigned phonemic status.

Parallel and contrastive distribution are related. All sounds in contrastive distribution are also in parallel distribution. Minimal pairs, for example *slip* vs *snip* – [slɪp] vs [snɪp], contrast in a single sound. These sounds, which contrast, must appear in the same environment – [s_ɪp]. Therefore, they are also in parallel distribution. However, the reverse is not necessarily true. Sounds in parallel distribution, as we have seen in the above exercise, do not always occur in contrastive distribution.

The notions of contrast and distribution are fundamental concepts in phonology. It is through these notions that we identify all the phonemes of a language (its phonemic system) and the allophones of those phonemes. For reference, these concepts are summarised below.

Contrastive distribution involves two or more sounds that occur in identical environments and for which at least one minimal pair can be found. A minimal pair is a pair of words that differ in one, and only one, sound.

Parallel distribution involves two or more sounds that occur in identical environments. It is not always possible to find minimal pairs for sounds in parallel distribution.

Complementary distribution involves two or more sounds that never occur in identical environments and for which no minimal pairs will ever be found.

Without a sound understanding of parallel, contrastive, and complementary distribution, we cannot proceed with our study of phonology. Before continuing you should attempt exercises 3.2 to 3.5. These are devised to reinforce the notions of contrastive, parallel, and complementary distribution. In attempting these exercises you will find it useful to set out a distribution table for the sounds whose distribution you have been asked to investigate. The use of such a table will make it easier for you to identify the distribution of the sounds in question.

Positions to consider in setting up your table might include: #__ (word-initial), __# (word-final), V__ (after a vowel), __V (before a vowel), V__V (between two vowels), C__ (after a consonant), __C (before a consonant), and C__C (between two consonants).

You should choose only those positions in which the sounds in question occur in the data you have been asked to consider. For example, if the sounds in question do not appear in either word-final or word-initial positions, do not include these in your table. If the sounds under investigation are consonants, and there are no consonant clusters in the data, then do not include C__, C__C, or C__. Similarly, if you are considering vowels and there are no clusters of monophthongs, then do not include V__, V__V, or __V in your table.

As an illustrative example, consider the distribution of [x] and [ç] in the following data based on German:

[dɑx]	roof	[mɑnç]	many
[deçɒʁ]	roofs	[çemi]	chemistry
[bu:x]	book	[taoxən]	dive
[by:çɒʁ]	books	[ho:x]	high
[lɒx]	hole	[miç]	me
[lœçɒʁ]	holes	[lɑxən]	laugh
[stɒʁç]	stork	[milç]	milk

Given the environments in which [x] and [ç] appear in the data, our distribution table for these data would be as shown in Table 3.1.

Table 3.1

	#___	___#	V___	___V	V___V	C___
x	—	√	√	√	√	—
ç	√	√	√	√	√	√

From this table it appears that [x] and [ç] are in partial parallel distribution, and therefore could be separate phonemes. However, notice that only [ç] appears in word-initial position, and although both appear in word-final position, only [ç] may be preceded by a consonant. Whenever [x] occurs in word-final position, it is always preceded by a vowel, and never a consonant. These observations suggest that we should take a closer look at the environments in which both [x] and [ç] occur.

If [x] and [ç] are in complementary distribution, then they must occur in different (mutually exclusive) environments. As we noted above, only [ç] occurs in word-initial position and word-final preceded by a consonant. In these positions it is in complementary distribution with [x]. Both appear before, after, and between vowels. Closer inspection of the vowels that occur next to [x] and [ç] may show that these consonants are in complementary distribution. Before we proceed, can we eliminate any of the three environments (_V, V_, and V_V) from consideration?

Above we noted that although both sounds occur in word-final position, only [ç] is preceded by a consonant. This suggests that the difference in environment is what precedes the sound and not what follows. If both sounds occur word-finally then they are in parallel distribution, but if only one can be preceded by other consonants then they are in complementary distribution. Let us look at the vowels that precede [x] and [ç], as shown in Table 3.2.

We can see that [x] and [ç] are in complementary distribution. [x] is always preceded by [ɑ ɒ oː uː], and [ç] is preceded by [e yː i œ]. The vowels that precede [x] are all back, while those that precede [ç] are all front. Based on these data, [x] and [ç] are allophones of a single phoneme.

In answering the following problems, set up distribution tables to help you analyse the distribution and arrive at the status of the sounds

Table 3.2

	ɑ	e	ɒ	oː	uː	yː	œ	i
x	√	—	√	√	√	—	—	—
ç	—	√	—	—	—	√	√	√

in question. As in the above example, you should begin with more general environments, for example word-final, word-initial, between vowels, etc., before proceeding to more specific ones, for example, before front vowels, before back vowels, etc.

Exercise 3.2

The following data are based on Italian:

[kɑpo]	[gɑmbɑ]	[tʃenɑ]	[dʒiɑrdino]
[kurɑ]	[gufo]	[tʃirkɑ]	[dʒentile]
[kolle]	[governo]	[tʃelebre]	[dʒenero]
[koɲato]	[grɑnde]	[kutʃinɑ]	[kudʒino]
[krude]	[gloriɑ]	[kontʃepire]	[intellidʒente]
[biskotto]	[lɑgo]	[innotʃente]	[voldʒeri]
[sikuro]	[orgɑno]		
[lokɑle]	[negotsio]		
[perikolo]	[lɑguno]		

Consider [k] and [tʃ], and [g] and [dʒ] in the above data. The members of each pair are in complemenatry distribution with each other. Provide a statement of the distribution of each member of the pair confirming that they are in complementary distribution.

* * * * * * * * *

Exercise 3.3

Consider the following data based on Castilian Spanish:

[tiβio]	*tibio*	'lukewarm'	
[balsa]	*balsa*	'raft'	[la βalsa]
[luθiðo]	*lucido*	'lucid'	
[demenθia]	*demencia*	'dementia'	[la ðemenθia]
[reɣaθo]	*regazo*	'backlog'	
[gola]	*gola*	'throat'	[la ɣola]

The voiced stops and the voiced fricatives are in complementary distribution. Provide a statement of the distribution of these sounds to support this claim.

* * * * * * * * *

Exercise 3.4

Consider the following data based on Italian:

[skudo]	*scudo*	'shield'	[zbadato]	*sbadato*	'careless'
[sabato]	*sabato*	'Saturday'	[zlitta]	*slitta*	'sleigh'
[seta]	*seta*	'silk'	[zmalto]	*smalto*	'glaze'
[sfida]	*sfida*	'dare'	[zgorbio]	*sgorbio*	'daub'
[sindakato]	*sindacato*	'union'	[zvestire]	*svestire*	'undress'
[solo]	*solo*	'alone'	[vazo]	*vaso*	'vase'
[sperone]	*sperone*	'spur'	[ezame]	*esame*	'survey'
[stampo]	*stampo*	'stamp'	[uzo]	*uso*	'use'
[sudore]	*sudore*	'sweat'	[vizo]	*viso*	'face'
[aspettare]	*aspettare*	'await'	[mizeria]	*miseria*	'misery'
[vista]	*vista*	'view	[tezoro]	*tesoro*	'treasure'

[s] and [z] are in complementary distribution. Provide a distribution table for each sound.

* * * * * * * * * *

Exercise 3.5

Consider the following data from British English:

[li:p]	*leap*	[bli:p]	*bleep*	[fi:ɫ]	*feel*	[heɫd]	*held*
[led]	*lead*	[glu:m]	*gloom*	[feɫ]	*fell*	[sɒɫt]	*salt*
[leik]	*lake*	[mɪljən]	*million*	[pu:ɫ]	*pool*	[ɒɫrɔ:it]	*alright*
[læp]	*lap*	[ɔilɪ]	*oily*	[ɔiɫ]	*oil*	[fɪɫm]	*film*
[lu:m]	*loom*	[səlekt]	*select*	[pouɫ]	*pole*	[brɫz]	*bills*
[lɒk]	*lock*	[jelou]	*yellow*	[peiɫ]	*pale*	[ʌɫsə]	*ulcer*

In British English [l] (clear *l* – voiced alveolar lateral, as described in section 2.2.2), and [ɫ] (dark *l* – voiced velarised alveolar lateral) are in complementary distribution. What is the distribution of these two sounds?

* * * * * * * * * *

3.1.4 *Free variation*

In the previous section we used the notions of parallel and contrastive distribution to identify phonemes.

Consider the following transcriptions:

[iːðə]   [aiðə]   [niːðə]   [naiðə]   [ekɒnɒmɪks]   [iːkɒnɒmɪks]

How many different words are there?

Although there are six different transcriptions, there are only three different words. We know that /iː/, /ai/, and /e/ are all phonemes in English (see section 2.1.1) but in the above examples substitution of, for example, /ai/ for /iː/ in [iːðə] does not result in a new word. In these examples, the phonemic contrast between these vowels would appear to have been suspended. We call this situation, where the contrastive nature of the phoneme is suspended in isolated words, free variation.

free variation

Although phonemic contrast is suspended in free variation, some sociolinguists have argued that free variants are often sociologically significant. The choice between variants is often conditioned by the social situation. For example, one variety might be associated with a particular social group or geographical area, or may be of higher prestige. These aspects will clearly influence the speaker's choice. Often this is a matter of degree. Speakers with higher social prestige may use one free variant more frequently than speakers with lower prestige so that people living in a wealthy suburb may more often say [ekɒnɒmɪks] while people in the same town but in a poor neighbourhood might more often say [iːkɒnɒmɪks]. Only a careful sociolinguistic study will establish social rules that determine the occurrence of the variants.

This approach may be applied to cases of free variation both with phonemes and also with allophones. Speakers may have a choice of two (or more) allophones in a particular environment. For example, after a stressed vowel speakers may choose either [t] or [ʔ] – a glottal stop – as allophones of /t/. The selection of one of these allophones may depend on such factors as the class, sex, age, and even religion of the speaker. For example, in a study of Scottish English, Macaulay and Trevelyan (1977) found that members of the professional and managerial class are less likely to use [ʔ] than members of the semi-skilled and unskilled class.

3.1.5 *Variation and dialects*

Free variation accounts for only a fraction of the variation in language. Most of the variation we encounter results from exposure to different

dialect

geographical dialects. In the introduction to Chapter 2, we noted that we may locate speakers geographically and socially from their pronunciation of the language. We usually say that a speaker has a particular

accent

accent, which we may describe geographically, for example Birmingham, Glasgow, New York, Australian or New Zealand, or more subjectively, for example posh, plummy, broad, rustic, northern, or soft.

Variation between different geographical and social dialects of English may be accounted for in four different ways:

systemic difference
phonemic system

Systemic differences

Dialects that differ systemically have different phonemic systems. For example, Scottish English has a voiceless velar fricative, /x/, which other English dialects lack. Whereas *lock* and *loch* are a minimal pair in Scottish English (/lɒk/ vs /lɒx/), in other dialects they are homophones, that is they sound identical. As a further example, many dialects of English lack /ʍ/, the voiceless counterpart of the voiced labio-velar approximant /w/. In fact many books which deal with the phonetics of English no longer include /ʍ/ as a phoneme of English. The opposition between the two sounds is still reflected in English orthography. *Wh* represents /ʍ/ and *w* represents /w/. Some words whose distinctiveness rested solely in this opposition are now, for many speakers, homophones (they sound identical), for example *whine* and *wine*, *which* and *witch*, and *whether* and *weather*.

distributional difference

Distributional differences

With distributional differences, the phonemic systems may be the same, but the distribution of certain phonemes may differ between the dialects in question. This is best illustrated by an example. All dialects of English possess a voiced alveolar central approximant – /r/. However, if we were to compare Ulster English with southern British English, we would find that the distribution of this phoneme differs in these two dialects. In southern British English /r/ is restricted to pre-vocalic position only, that is only before vowels. However, in Ulster English /r/ has a full distribution. It occurs before vowels, consonants, and pauses. We call dialects, such as southern British English, which have only pre-vocalic /r/, 'non-rhotic'. Those dialects in which /r/ has a full distribution are 'rhotic'. Scottish, Welsh, West Country, and General American are all rhotic. Most dialects of British English, and Australian and New Zealand English are non-rhotic.

realisational difference

Realisational differences

As with distributional differences, two dialects may possess the same number of phonemic oppositions but differ in the phonetic realisation of all instances of particular phonemes. For example, both southern British English and New Zealand English possess an opposition between the vowels in *bit* and *bet*. However, in New Zealand English the vowel in *bit* is more central than its counterpart in southern British English, while the vowel in *bet* is realised slightly higher. These realisational differences apply to all occurrences of the vowel phonemes in question.

Selectional differences

selectional difference

With selectional differences, two dialects have the same set of phonemic contrasts but particular words select different phonemes in each dialect. Again this is best illustrated with an example. The vowels /i:/ and /ɪ/ occur in both British and New Zealand English. However, for example, in *cloudy* speakers of New Zealand English select /i:/, while British English speakers select /ɪ/.

3.2 Phonemes and allophones revisited

From the discussion in this chapter as far as section 3.1.1, it would appear that a phoneme is the minimal unit of sound in a language capable of distinguishing one word from another. For example, if [t] in *tip* is replaced by [d] this gives *dip*, which differs in meaning from *tip*. Therefore /t/ and /d/ must be phonemes of English.

Allophones of a single phoneme are in complementary distribution (they never contrast), and are usually phonetically similar. Furthermore, allophones are the predictable realisations of phonemes, and the factors that condition the occurrence of allophones are usually found in the immediate environment of the word in which the allophone occurs. This means that for a given phoneme we can predict where each of its allophones will occur, and we can capture such predictable behaviour in a rule. In the *t* example above it is possible to write rules that will predict where each allophone will occur. For example /t/ will be realised as [t̪] when it occurs next to a dental consonant. Similarly, /t/ will be realised as [tʲ] when it occurs next to a palatal sound. Although it is possible to predict where the allophones of a phoneme will occur, it is impossible to predict where phonemes will occur. We cannot write a rule to account for the distribution of, for example, /t/ in English.

In the above discussion we claimed that allophones were the predictable realisations of phonemes. If allophones are phonetically real, then what exactly do they realise? What is the status of the phoneme?

In our discussion of the phoneme in the first section of this chapter, we identified two types of properties – distinctive and non-distinctive. Speakers do not 'hear' the non-distinctive properties but do 'hear' the distinctive ones. For example, because aspiration is non-distinctive in English, a speaker of English will 'hear' [kʰ] in, for example, *catch* as a voiceless velar stop, and not as an aspirated voiceless velar stop (which is what the speaker produced). Speakers listen for the distinctive properties of a sound – those on which contrasts are based – and not for the non-distinctive properties. Implicit in this is the claim that the phoneme is, in some sense, psychologically real. We may claim that the phoneme is an abstract psychological unit.

Speakers of English never realise, for example, /k/ exactly the same each time it is said. Yet neither speaker nor hearer is ever in any doubt over what was said. To allow for such variations, we can claim that both speaker and hearer must have a mental pattern of the sound. Speakers attempt to match their production to this mental pattern, and hearers match incoming sounds to their mental patterns. These mental patterns may also be defined in terms of the distinctive properties of the language. Allophones of a phoneme will be matched against these patterns and assigned to the closest one. For example [kʰ], which is voiceless, velar, aspirated and a stop, will be matched against /k/, which is (ideally) voiceless, velar, and a stop. As aspiration is non-distinctive, the hearer disregards it. In one sense the hearer does not 'perceive' it.

Further evidence for the psychological approach may be drawn from the behaviour of speakers when they encounter sounds that are not part of their own language. Speakers, in pronouncing non-native words, will match sounds that do not occur in their own language with the closest ones that do. For example, speakers of English often replace French nasalised vowels by vowel + nasal sequences, and realise the voiceless velar fricative of German as a voiceless velar stop. French, Dutch, and German have no dental fricatives, and speakers of these languages will often substitute dental stops or alveolar fricatives for these sounds when speaking English, for example, a German speaker might, when speaking English, say [sɪŋ] or [tɪŋ] but mean [θɪŋ].

If an individual phoneme is an abstract unit, then any phonemic representation of a word form must also be abstract. For example the phonemic representation of *pin* is /pɪn/. This consists of three phonemes − /p/, /ɪ/, and /n/. If each of these is an abstract entity then any unit that consists wholly of abstract entities must also be abstract. We often refer to phonemic representations of word forms as underlying representations. Underlying representations are also often referred to as lexical or dictionary representations, and are thought to be the form in which a speaker stores words in their mental lexicon or dictionary.

underlying representation

3.3   Phonemic analysis

phonotactics

There are three parts to a phonemic analysis of a language: the phonemic system, a statement of the phonotactics, and a set of allophonic rules, which link phonemes to their allophones. Let us look at all of these.

3.3.1   *The phonemic system*

This is a list of all the consonant and vowel phonemes of the language in question. The phonologist will identify the phonemes of a language through a careful analysis of phonetic data. Phonemic status will be assigned only to those units that occur in contrastive or parallel distribution. Units in complementary distribution are allophones of phonemes and will, on the basis of distribution and phonetic similarity, be assigned to the appropriate phoneme.

Here only the consonant phonemes of standard British English have been given. There are twenty-four consonant phonemes in the phonemic system of standard British English. These may be divided into:

seventeen obstruents (oral stops, fricatives and affricates)

/p t k b d g f v θ ð s z ʃ ʒ tʃ dʒ h/,

seven sonorants, consisting of

three nasals	/m n ŋ/
two glides or semi-vowels	/j w/
two liquids	/l r/

3.3.2 *Phonotactics*

Consider the following transcriptions:

[sprʌldʒ]   [strɔiʃt]   [θmɜːjŋ]   [fniːz]   [gruːltʃ]   [swɒŋk]

Which of the above words could be English and which could not?

Answer:

[sprʌldʒ], [gruːltʃ] and [swɒŋk] could all be words of English, whereas [strɔiʃt], [θmɜːjŋ], [fniːz] could not.

Although you are unlikely to have encountered any of the above words before, you should have had few, if any, problems in separating those words that could be English from those that could not. This is possible because, as part of your knowledge of English, you recognise which combinations of segments are possible, and which combinations do not occur, that is you know the phonotactics of English.

The phonotactics of a language are a list of restrictions on the distribution of segments, possible combinations of segments into clusters, and admissible syllable types. Although there are twenty-four consonant phonemes in English, and consonant clusters both before and after vowels are permitted, it is certainly not the case that consonants may combine at random up to the maximum permitted limit. Some clusters are simply too difficult to pronounce, and free combination would place quite a burden on the language learner.

What is the largest cluster of consonants that may occur at the beginning of an English word? How many different clusters of this size can you find?

Answer:

The largest initial consonant cluster in English contains three consonants. There are only ten such clusters in English. They are:

s + p + l, r, j

s + t + r, j

s + k + l, r, j, w

s + m + j

Each of these clusters begins with /s/, the second element is always a stop, and the third is one of the non-nasal sonorants. Apart from /smj/, that occurs only in *smew* (the name of a bird), the second consonant in all other clusters is always a voiceless stop. In general initial CCC clusters in English are of the form: /s/ + voiceless stop + approximant.

However, we have to add four exceptions to this rule. First, there is /smj/, which is not covered by our general statement. Secondly, there are three combinations of /s/ + /p t k/ + /l r j w/ that do not occur. There are no /spw/, /stl/ or /stw/ initial clusters in English. These three clusters are different from clusters such as /pdz/, /bfn/ or /gtb/, which are ruled out by the general phonotactic restrictions on CCC clusters discussed above. The three clusters that do not occur have to be specifically identified and ruled out. To distinguish between clusters that are ruled out by general phonotactic statements, and ones that have to be specifically identified and ruled out, we shall call the former **illicit clusters** and the latter **potential clusters**. Illicit clusters never occur, and never could occur in the language. They are not permitted by general phonotactic rules of the language in question. Potential clusters (and words) could but do not occur. They are permitted by the general phonotactic rules of the language in question but are excluded by specific statements.

Repeat the previous exercise but with initial CC clusters. List any generalisations concerning the nature of CC clusters, for example nasal + fricative clusters are illicit. Identify any illicit clusters and potential clusters.

Answer:

Only the following initial CC clusters occur in English:

p + l, r, j	b + l, r, j
t + r, j, w	d + r, j, w
k + l, r, j, w	g + l, r, j, w
m + j	n + j
l + j	
f + l, r, j	v + j
θ + r, j, w	s + l, j, w, p, t, k, m, n, f
ʃ + r	h + j

Stops, both oral and nasal, and fricatives are followed by approximants. (Only /k/ and /g/ may be followed by any of the four approximants. All other stops and fricatives may be followed by a subset of the approximants.) The only exception to this is /s/. It may be followed by one of the voiceless stops, /m/ or /n/, or /f/, as well as by three of the approximants. Except for clusters beginning with /s/, there is an opening of the oral cavity as we move from initial to final consonant in most initial CC clusters.

In our discussion we have concentrated on initial consonant clusters. However, phonotactics, as defined above, define the admissible syllable types of a language. Therefore, the phonotactic rules of a language should include statements concerning syllable-final clusters, and which vowels may combine with which consonants or consonant clusters. For example, no word in English may begin with /ŋ/, or with any of the following /ðʊ θɔi zʌ/ or /jɑi/. Furthermore, none of /j w h/ or /e æ ʌ ɒ/ may occur in syllable-final position in English. As with initial consonant clusters, there are limits on the possible combinations of consonants in word-final clusters, for example, there are no /gb vŋ nð mdʒ/ final clusters. There are also restrictions on the vowels with which those consonants and clusters may combine, for example, /mf/ occurs only after /ʌ/, while /ŋ/ may only occur after /ɪ æ ʌ ɒ/.

Through defining the set of permissible syllable types in a language, phonotactics determine the range of permissible words. Consequently, our notion of illicit and potential clusters, introduced above, may be extended to words. Illicit words never occur, and never could occur in the language. They are not permitted by general phonotactic rules of the language in question. Potential words could but do not occur. They are permitted by the general phonotactic rules of the language in question but are excluded by specific statements. For example, neither /θliːmdʒ/ nor /kjɒhw/ are words of English. Nor could they ever be. Both violate the phonotactics of English. However, both /vjuːlz/ and /skwɔːmθ/ could be words of English. They both conform to the phonotactics of English. It just happens that neither of these potential combinations actually occurs in English.

3.3.3 *Allophonic rules*

In our discussion of phonemes and allophones (section 3.2), we claimed that allophones are the predictable realisations of phonemes, and as such their occurrence can be expressed formally by a rule. These rules that link an abstract phoneme to its allophonic realisations are called allophonic rules.

allophonic rule

The function of the rules may be illustrated by the following diagram:

INPUT   OUTPUT

Phonemic Form   →Acted on by→   Phonetic Representation
(Abstract Unit)   Allophonic Rule(s)   (What speakers produce)

The form of allophonic rules may be best illustrated by an example:

(Context)

/t/   →   [tʲ]   /   ___j

(Input)   (Output)   (Conditioning factor)

This rule tells us that the phoneme /t/ is realised by its palatalised allophone when it occurs before a palatal approximant. Like all allophonic rules, this rule may be divided into two halves, which are separated from each other by a slash – /. We shall refer to the first half, on the left side of the slash, as the process side. On the process side of the rule we find the input segment to the rule and its output – in this case /t/ and [tʲ]. The part of the rule to the right of the slash specifies the context in which the rule operates and gives the conditioning factor. In this example the allophone occurs before a palatal approximant, which is the conditioning factor.

The process side of any allophonic rule is basically:

/X/ → [Y] /

that is, phoneme X is realised as allophone Y.

The context of a rule may be quite complex, and there are three basic possibilities. First, the conditioning factor may occur to the right of the input phoneme:

/ ___A

This possibility is illustrated by the palatalisation of /t/ discussed above.

Secondly the conditioning factor may precede the input:

/ A___

As an example, consider the realisation of /t/ in *bathtap*. In this sequence /t/ may be dentalised under the influence of the preceding dental. We can capture this in the following rule:

$$/t/ \rightarrow [\underline{t}] / \theta \underline{\quad\quad}$$

Thirdly, the input phoneme occurs between two conditioning factors:

$$/ A \underline{\quad\quad} B$$

In some varieties of English /t/ and /d/ are realised between vowels as an alveolar tap – [ɾ]. If we take /t/ as our input, then the rule for this process would be:

$$/t/ \rightarrow [ɾ] / V \underline{\quad\quad} V \text{ (where V = any vowel)}$$

In each of the examples above, the process applies in a single context. If a process applies in two (or more) contexts do we write two rules or can we still write a single rule?

Consider our dentalised and unreleased allophones of /t/. /t/ is dentalised when it is followed by a dental fricative, for example in *eighth*. However, /t/ is also dentalised if it is word-final and the next word begins with a dental fricative, for example in *not think*. Dentalisation occurs both within a word and over word boundaries. This gives us two rules:

$$/t/ \rightarrow [\underline{t}] / \underline{\quad\quad} \theta \qquad /t/ \rightarrow [\underline{t}] / \underline{\quad\quad} \#\theta$$

$$(\# = \text{word boundary})$$

In both of these rules the process is the same: only the context is different. We can collapse these two rules into one by isolating the common material – in this case the process and part of the environment, and then by placing the non-overlapping part of the contexts inside curved brackets or parentheses:

$$/t/ \rightarrow [\underline{t}] / \underline{\quad\quad} (\#)\theta$$

The material inside the brackets is optional. It may or may not be present. The rule states that /t/ is realised by its dentalised allophone when it is followed by a voiceless dental fricative, and when it is followed by a word boundary *and* a voiceless dental fricative.

Now consider the unreleased /t/. /t/ is unreleased when it is followed by another stop, for example /d/, but let us say that it is also unreleased in word-final position. This would give us two rules:

$$/t/ \rightarrow [t^\urcorner] / \underline{\quad\quad} d \qquad /t/ \rightarrow [t^\urcorner] / \underline{\quad\quad} \#$$

In both of these rules the process is the same: only the context is different. We can collapse these two rules into one by isolating the common material – in this case the process, and then by placing the non-overlapping part of the contexts inside braces:

$$/t/ \rightarrow [t^\neg] / \underline{\quad} \begin{Bmatrix} d \\ \# \end{Bmatrix}$$

The braces indicate a disjunction – /t/ is unreleased before either /d/ *or* a word boundary. The braces tell us that the rule will apply only if one of the contexts inside the braces is met.

The environment half of every allophonic rule is an account of the distribution of a particular allophone. As the allophones of a phoneme are in complementary distribution, that is, no two allophones of a phoneme occur in the same environment, then for any phoneme, the environment half of each allophonic rule for a particular phoneme must be different. If this were not the case, we would have parallel distribution, the potential for contrast, and the sounds in question would be phonemic rather than allophonic.

Exercise 3.6

Return to your solutions to Exercises 3.2 to 3.5. For each pair of allophones you identified in the data in these exercises, select one member as the underlying or phonemic form, and write an allophonic rule to derive the other member of the pair.

* * * * * * * * * *

3.4 Allophonic processes

Having introduced the notion and formalism of allophonic rules, let us consider a number of allophonic processes in English.

3.4.1 *Aspiration*

In English one allophone of the voiceless stops is aspirated. Although the environment in which aspirated stops occur is more complex than that of [tʲ], it is possible to write a rule which predicts where these allophones will occur. Concentrating on the voiceless alveolar stop /t/, consider the following words:

*t*en

s*t*em

The /t/ in *ten* is aspirated, whereas in *stem* it is not. You can test this for yourselves. Put your hand close to your mouth and utter both words. You should feel a small puff of air on your hand when you release the /t/ in *ten* but not in *stem*. Based on these two words, it would appear that for /t/ to be aspirated it must appear in initial position in a word. We might posit as our rule that /t/ is realised as [tʰ] if it occurs in initial position in a word. Formally, this would be stated as:

/t/ → [tʰ] / #____

However, now consider *attack*. This contains [tʰ] but not in initial position. This violates our initial hypothesis. How might we rescue our hypothesis? We could simply add the new environment to our rule. However, that would suggest that aspiration of initial and non-initial stops is unrelated. It is unlikely that the same process would be triggered by two unrelated environments. Any solution should attempt to capture whatever is common to both the non-word-initial aspirated stop and the word-initial ones. What do the stops in *ten* and *attack* share? It could be the case that /t/ is aspirated only when followed by a front vowel. However, words like *top* and *atop* with aspirated stops show that this is not the case. If we were to divide *attack* into syllables, we would find that it contains two syllables, with the dividing line falling between the initial vowel and the first consonant. Now although [tʰ] in *attack* does not occur word-initially, it does occur syllable-initially. Given that *ten* is a single or monosyllabic word, we can now see that syllable-initial position is the common factor, and revise our initial rule. A voiceless stop is aspirated if it occurs in syllable-initial position. Formally this gives:

/t/ → [tʰ] / .____   (. indicates a syllable boundary)

Finally, consider *tautology*. This word contains two occurrences of /t/ in syllable-initial position. For some of you both *t*s are aspirated. However, for others only one *t*, the second, is aspirated. The situation where only one /t/ is aspirated violates our hypothesis. This time we must discover why one syllable-initial stop is aspirated but not the other. Transcribe *tautology* and divide it into syllables. Repeat the word paying attention to the effort you put into pronouncing each syllable. Do you put more effort into one syllable, which is more prominent than the others? If so which one? You should find that you put more effort into the second syllable. This increase of effort which is reflected in increased prominence, is called 'stress'. It is the stop at the beginning of this stressed syllable which is aspirated. We can now conclude that a voiceless stop is aspirated when it occurs in the initial position of a stressed syllable. Formally, this is stated as:

/t/ → [tʰ] / .____V
                   [+ stress]

In the above exercise we were presented with some data, and on the basis of this data we set up a hypothesis concerning the aspiration of voiceless stops in English. When this database was expanded we saw that our initial hypothesis was no longer valid, and revised it to take account of the additional data. A further expansion of the database led to revision of the second hypothesis and rule. The setting up of a hypothesis which can be tested against the data is a common approach to problem solving and analysis of language. We did not attempt to arrive at an overall solution in a single step but set out an initial hypothesis which was gradually revised and refined.

3.4.2 *Assimilation*

In speech the sounds of a language do not occur in isolation but in strings of variable length. When placed in a string, sounds may be influenced by their neighbours. They may acquire some of their neighbours' characteristics, and in doing so become more like their **assimilation**   neighbours. Assimilation is the name we give to the process where one segment becomes more like (or identical to) another segment, or two segments become more like each other.

Consider the words *happen* and *input*. If pronounced carefully and transcribed, we would probably get:

   [hæpən] *happen*   [ɪnpʊt] *input*

However, in a more natural speech style we might find:

   [hæpm] *happen*   [ɪmpʊt] *input*

In both examples the alveolar nasal, /n/, becomes more like the bi-labial stop, /p/, by becoming a bi-labial nasal, [m]. Furthermore, in both examples the bi-labial stop triggers the assimilation, and the alveolar nasal is the segment which changes. All assimilation processes involve at least one segment which is changed, and one which is the source of the change. We shall refer to the segment which is changed as the 'target', and the segment which influences the target as the 'source'.

Although all assimilation processes involve a source and a target, what may vary is the position of the source in relation to the target. Where the source comes before the target the direction of influence is from left to right, or forwards through the word. This is called 'progressive assimilation' because the influence progresses forwards through the word. This direction of assimilation is also referred to as 'perseverative assimilation' – it preserves some aspect of a segment, beyond the segment from which it originates. Our first example, *happen*, is an example of progressive assimilation, which may be expressed by the following rule:

$$/n/ \rightarrow [m] / p^{(source)} \underline{\quad} {}^{(target)}$$

/n/ is realised as [m] when it is preceded by /p/.

'Regressive assimilation' is where the source comes after or to the right of the target, and the direction of influence is from right to left, or backwards through the word. This type of assimilation may also be called 'anticipatory assimilation' because a segment is altered in a way which anticipates a phonetic property of a segment which comes later in the word. *Input* is an example of regressive assimilation. The rule for this regressive assimilation is:

$$/n/ \rightarrow [m] / \underline{\quad} {}^{(target)} p^{(source)}$$

/n/ is realised as [m] when it is followed by /p/.

3.4.2.1 *Assimilation types*
In discussing assimilation, not only do we identify the direction of the assimilation, but it is also useful to establish a list of assimilation types. The most common types of assimilation are: place, voice, nasalisation, and lip attitude.

place, voice, nasalisation
lip attitude

3.4.2.2 *Place*
The above examples involve assimilation of place – in both examples an alveolar nasal assimilated to a bi-labial stop. The dentalised, palatalised, and retroflex allophones of /t/ we discussed above are all examples of assimilation of place.

In the discussion of *input*, although the alveolar nasal is realised as a labial nasal this is not reflected in the spelling.

3.4.2.3 *Voice*
A second assimilation type involves phonation, or voice. In assimilations of voice, a sound becomes more like its neighbours by 'agreeing' in voice. Voiceless sounds become voiced, and voiced ones may become voiceless. We call the first type voicing, and the second type devoicing. As with assimilations of place, assimilations of voice may be either progressive or regressive.

voicing, devoicing

Transcribe the following words. Do not be misled by the spelling system but pay particular attention to what you say.

town's, book's, people's, Pat's

You should have transcribed these words as:

[tɑunz bʊks piːpəlz pæts]

In the transcribed versions, the possessive marker 's has two versions – [s] and [z]. If we take the voiceless version as the phonemic form, /n/ and /l/ as the source, and /s/ as the target, then we have progressive assimilation of voice.

> **Now consider the following words:**
>
> small, slap, slush, trap, class, crush

If we were to transcribe these words phonemically we would probably transcribe them as:

/smɔːl slæp slʌʃ træp klɑːs krʌʃ/

However, if we were to listen carefully to a recording of these items we would find that the second consonant is either voiceless or only partially voiced. The voiced sound has assimilated to the initial voiceless one by becoming either fully or partially voiceless. Using the diacritic [̥] to indicate that a sound which is normally voiced has been devoiced, we may represent this in a phonetic version of our transcription, giving:

[sm̥ɔːl sl̥æp sl̥ʌʃ tr̥æp kl̥ɑːs kr̥ʌʃ]

These are examples of progressive assimilation, with the initial consonant being the source and the following sonorants being the target. We can also find examples of regressive devoicing.

If we were to transcribe the following sequences phonemically and then phonetically:

have to   used to

we would have:

/hæv tə/ and /juːzd tə/

and:

[hæf tə] and [juːs tə]

Again we have examples of devoicing. In this case we have regressive assimilation, with /t/ the source, and /v/ and /d/ the targets.

3.4.2.4 *Nasalisation*

In the discussion of articulation, we pointed out that the velum or soft palate could be either raised or lowered. When it is raised, velic closure occurs and air flows from the lungs out through the oral cavity. However, when the velum is lowered the nasal cavity is open to the flow of air from the lungs. Air can now flow out through the nasal cavity, giving nasal sounds. In English the velum is usually lowered for only the three nasal stops – /m n ŋ/. However, the position of the velum is not dependent on the other processes and may be lowered during the production of other segments. 'Nasalisation' occurs when the velum is lowered during the production of a segment which is not normally nasal. The most common occurrence of nasalisation in English is regressive nasalisation of vowels in vowel–nasal sequences. For example:

/kɒŋgres/ *congress* → [kʰ ɒ̃ŋgres]

In this example, the nasal is the source and the vowel is the target. The property of nasalisation is transferred from the source leftwards to the target giving regressive nasalisation. This may be represented by the following rule, where V represents any vowel, N any nasal, with the diacritic ～ to indicate nasalisation:

V → Ṽ/ ____N

Whereas such nasalised vowels in English are allophones of oral vowels, French has a set of phonemic nasalised vowels. After vowel nasalisation occurred in French the nasal was deleted phonemically, although not in the spelling, giving sets of minimal pairs:

/pɛ̃/ *pain* 'bread'   /pe/ *paix* 'peace'

3.4.2.5 *Lip attitude*

'Lip attitude' refers to the position of the lips during the articulation of a sound. During the articulation of back rounded vowels, the lips are, of course, rounded. This lip rounding, represented by the diacritic ʷ, may spread to adjacent consonants. This gives:

/kʊl/ *cool* → [kʷʰʊl]   /loub/ *lobe* → [lʷoub]

3.4.2.6 *Fusion*

Fusion is a type of assimilation where two segments assimilate to each **fusion** other. The outcome of this assimilation is a third distinct segment which combines properties of the two assimilating segments. For example, in careful speech, *caught you* and *would you* would be realised as: [kʰɔːt juː] and [wʊd juː], but in normal conversation they are more likely to be realised as: [kʰɔːtʃə] and [wʊdʒə]. In both examples the alveolar stop and following palatal approximant fuse to give the voiceless and voiced post-alveolar affricates [tʃ] and [dʒ]. The voice, place, and manner of articulation of the two input segments are combined to form a third segment. The voiced quality of the fused segment is decided by the voice quality of the first consonant. The place of articulation is mid-way between alveolar and palatal, and the manner of articulation of both the input segments is reflected in the fused segment, which is both a stop and a continuant.

As well as these assimilatory processes, there are a number of other processes which affect segments in context.

3.4.3   Elision

Consider the following list of words. Read each word aloud and then transcribe what you say, remembering to concentrate on what you say and not what you read.

handsome, windmill, handkerchief, mostly, kindness, attempts

elision

In your transcription you may have omitted some of the consonants which you might have expected to be present. For example, you may have omitted the /d/ in *handsome, windmill, handkerchief,* and *kindness,* the /t/ in *mostly,* and the second one in *attempts.* We call the deletion of a segment normally present in the stream of speech elision. Elision is more common in less formal and more casual speech styles. In careful speech most of the consonants which were elided in the above examples would be present.

The most frequently elided consonants in English are /t/ and /d/. For example:

West Cliff	/west klɪf/ →	[wes klɪf]
thousand points	/θɑuznd pɔints/ →	[θɑuzn pɔints]

The elision of a segment may allow an assimilation to occur. For example:

handbag /hændbæg/ → hænbæg → [hæmbæg]

As well as consonants, vowels may also be elided. This is most obvious in the various contractions found in English, for example *I am* → *I'm,* *she is* → *she's,* and *do not* → *don't.* Vowel elision also occurs in other words, for example: *bottle* /bɒtəl/ → [bɒtl̩], *police* /pɒliːs/ → [pliːs], and *geography* /dʒiːɒgræfɪ/ → [dʒɒgræfɪ]. The small diacritic line in [bɒtl̩] indicates that the [l] is a syllabic consonant, a one consonant syllable.

These are some of the more obvious examples of elision. If you were to transcribe phonetically a passage of informal conversation you would find a far greater range of both consonant and vowel elision than the few examples discussed above.

Elision of segments is not confined to contemporary English but also occurred in the past. In many cases the elision of both consonants and vowels has taken place but the orthography has not been adjusted to take account of the 'new' pronunciation, and still retains symbols (silent letters) which reflect the earlier pronunciation. For example: *wright, knee, gnaw, thistle, fasten, walk,* and *lamb* all contain symbols for consonants which are no longer pronounced even in careful speech. *Gloucester, Salisbury, evening, written,* and *time* all contain vowel symbols to which no sound value is assigned.

3.4.4 *Insertion*

In the previous section we saw that segments which are present in careful speech may be elided in more casual speech styles. It is also possible for segments not normally present in careful speech styles to be inserted. The term for such insertions is epenthesis. Both consonant and vowel epenthesis occur in English. In some dialects of English schwa [ə] is inserted between two consonants. For example: [fɪləm] *film*, [æθəli:t] *athlete*, [ærəm] *arm*, and [gɪrəl] *girl*. Consonant epenthesis is most frequent, in English, between nasal–fricative and nasal–stop sequences such as: /ns/ and /mt/, giving [mɪnts] *mince/mints* and [drempt] *dreamt*. These insertions arise from timing errors. The velum closes before the oral consonant is formed, and this results in an epenthetic oral stop, with the same place of articulation as the nasal.

epenthesis

3.5 Allophones

Having discussed some of the more common allophonic processes in English, let us look at some of the more common allophones of consonants. In the following discussion, it will become apparent that the various processes tend to affect classes of segments rather than individual segments. This is not to deny that some processes may only affect one or two members of a class, for example only the alveolar stops – /t/ and /d/ – are dentalised before the dental fricatives. Consequently, we shall structure our discussion around groups and processes rather than individual segments.

3.5.1 *Stops*

There are a number of processes which affect the class of stops as a whole. All stops occur with nasal release when followed by a nasal. If the stop–nasal sequence is homorganic (both have the same place of articulation) then the complete closure in the oral cavity is not released and the air escapes through the nasal cavity when the velum is lowered. For example:

[tɒpⁿmoust]

If the stop–nasal sequence is not homorganic, then the oral stop is not normally released until the articulation of the following nasal is complete. For example:

[bɪgⁿmaus]

Although there is a difference between the homorganic and non-homorganic sequences, the term 'nasal release' applies to both.

With homorganic stop–lateral sequences we get lateral release. The stop is released by the lowering of the sides of the tongue for the following lateral, for example *bottle*, *throttle*, *atlas*, *at last*, and *coddle*. No other articulatory movement is involved. If the stop–lateral sequence is not homorganic then it is usual for tongue tip contact to occur before the stop is released. Although an additional articulation is involved, the air escapes over the sides of the tongue. The non-homorganic stop–lateral **lateral escape** cases are examples of lateral escape, for example *please*, *black*, *quick lime*, and *big lake* all involve lateral escape.

We discovered in the first section of this chapter that /t/ was unreleased when followed by another stop. This applies to all stops, not just when they are followed by another stop but also when they occur in final position. With the voiced stops there may be some devoicing if the following stop is voiceless. Taking /p/ and /b/, these allophones are illustrated below:

[p˺] [rɪp˺]   [b˺] [rɪb˺keidʒ]

3.5.1.1 *Voiceless stops*
Aspiration is the one process which affects only the voiceless stops. Voiceless stops are aspirated, as we discovered in section 3.4.1, in initial position of a stressed syllable and immediately preceding the vowel. In our discussion we looked only at /t/, but the same process under the same conditions applies to the other voiceless stops as well, for example the /p/ in *post* and the /k/ in *keep* will both be aspirated.

3.5.1.2 *Voiced stops*
Devoicing is the main process which affects voiced but not voiceless stops. Voiced stops are partially devoiced when followed by a voiceless consonant, and in utterance-initial and utterance-final positions, that is when either preceded or followed by silence. As we noted above, when a voiced stop occurs in final position, or is followed by a word beginning

with a voiceless consonant, then it will be unreleased, as well as partially devoiced. Taking /d/ as an example, we have:

deep [d̥i:p˺], *trod* [trɒd̥˺], *board claims* [bɔ:d̥˺kleimz]

3.5.2 *Voiced fricatives*

These tend to devoice in utterance-initial or final position, or when followed by a voiceless consonant:

view [v̥ju:], *cave* [keiv̥], *we've found* [wi:v̥ faund]

3.5.3 *Sonorants*

As with voiced stops and fricatives, devoicing is the main process which affects sonorants. All sonorants devoice within a word if preceded by a voiceless consonant:

smile [sm̥ɑil]	*snow* [sn̥ou]	*cringe* [kr̥ɪndʒ]
play [pl̥ei]	*refuse* [rəfju:z]	*quick* [kw̥ɪk]

If /r/ is preceded by either /t/ or /d/, then it tends to be realised as a fricative rather than as an approximant. In the former combination devoicing also occurs.

When /j/ and /w/ follow a voiceless consonant, then they are realised as a voiceless fricatives. /j/ is realised as a voiceless palatal fricative – [ç], and /w/ as a voiceless labio-velar fricative – [ʍ]. In section 2.2.2.3.2. we said that the glides – /j/ and /w/ – were phonetically like vowels, but behaved like consonants. These allophones are clearly consonantal, that is they are voiceless and fricative – and illustrate further the dual nature of the glides. (See also section 3.7.2.)

Apart from a voiceless allophone, /l/ has two other major allophones. The first is articulated with the blade of the tongue and the alveolar ridge. We call this allophone 'clear l'. It occurs before vowels:

leap   [li:p]   silly   [sɪlɪ]

This allophone also occurs if /l/ is in word-final position and the next word begins with a vowel:

fill in   [fɪl ɪn]

The other is a velarised alveolar lateral, and occurs after a vowel or before a consonant:

fall   [fɔ:ɫ]   help   [heɫp]

We call this allophone 'dark l'.

3.5.4 Vowels

In section 2.2.3.3.5 we stated that vowels in English may be either long or short. /ɪ e æ ʌ ɒ/ are all short, while the remaining monophthongs and all diphthongs are long. However, the precise length of any vowel depends on its environment. Vowels followed by a voiceless consonant are shorter than those followed by a voiced consonant or in word-final position. In the following examples the vowels in the words in the first column are shorter than those in the second or third columns:

beat	bead	bee
bit	bid	
base	beige	bay
bet	bed	

Taking /i:/ as an illustrative example we might transcribe the words in the first line as follows:

[bit   bi:d   bi:]

3.6 Derivations

From our discussion of some of the common allophonic processes and allophones of English, it should be apparent that although allophonic rules apply to individual phonemes, these phonemes do not occur in isolation but in the context of a phonological or underlying representation. Consequently, while allophonic rules do link phonemes to allophones, they also relate underlying representations to surface ones. For most phonologists surface representations (consisting of allophones) are derived from underlying ones (consisting of phonemes) thus giving a derived form, through the application of allophonic rules. We usually refer to the process of deriving (or determining) the pronunciation of an underlying representation as a derivation.

surface representation

derived form

derivation

As an illustrative example of a derivation, let us consider *congress* and *ten past (eight)*:

	Underlying Representation
	/kɒngres/
Aspiration	kʰɒngres
Nasalisation	kʰɒ̃ngres
Vowel Lengthening	kʰɒ̃:ngres
Surface Representation	[kʰɒ̃:ngres]

	Underlying Representation
	/ten pɑːst/
Aspiration	tʰen pɑːst
Assimilation	tʰem pɑːst
Nasalisation	tʰẽm pɑːst
Vowel Lengthening	tʰẽːm pɑːst
Surface Representation	[tʰẽːm pɑːst]

In the first example /k/ is aspirated and the following vowel is nasalised and lengthened. In the second example /t/ is aspirated, /n/ assimilates to /p/, and /e/ is nasalized and lengthened.

3.7 Features

So far in our discussion of phonology we have established two different but related units – phonemes and allophones. Although both units may be described in articulatory terms, for example the phoneme /t/ may be defined by a three-term label (voiceless, alveolar, stop), many phonologists have considered phonemes to be indivisible. They were the smallest units with which many phonologists worked. However, other phonologists proposed that phonemes were simply cover symbols, and could be decomposed into smaller units, which they called distinctive features. For these phonologists the fundamental or primitive unit of phonology was no longer the phoneme but the distinctive feature. They did not adopt this position without sound arguments.

distinctive feature

3.7.1 *The necessity of features*

In section 3.4.1 we analysed the distribution of [tʰ], found that its distribution was predictable, and wrote a rule which derived it from /t/. Let us now consider the remaining English voiceless stops /p/ and /k/.

Consider the following two sets of data:

(a)	occur	(b)	preposterous
	concussion		pull
	acquire		spanner
	caught		oppose

For both sets, identify all occurrences of /k/ and /p/. Which occurrences are realised by the aspirated allophones [kʰ] and [pʰ]? Can you write the rules which predict the occurrence of these allophones?

Although the input and output of the two rules required here differ from that in the discussion of aspiration in section 3.4.1, the process of aspiration and the conditioning environment in which the rule operates are identical:

$$/t/ \rightarrow [t^h] \: / \: .\underline{\quad\quad} V$$
$$[+ \text{stress}]$$

$$/p/ \rightarrow [p^h] \: / \: .\underline{\quad\quad} V$$
$$[+ \text{stress}]$$

$$/k/ \rightarrow [k^h] \: / \: .\underline{\quad\quad} V$$
$$[+ \text{stress}]$$

Although these three rules may capture accurately what happens, they fail to capture a general point of English phonology: all voiceless stops are aspirated when they are the only consonant before a stressed vowel. Phonological rules tend to apply to classes of related phonemes, rather than to classes of unrelated ones. The members of these classes are related by virtue of sharing one or more aspects of their description. In the above example the members of the class share two features – they are voiceless stops. If a formalism is to be of any use then it must be able to capture succinctly any such generalisations concerning the classes of phonemes which participate in rules. Clearly the notation fails to do this.

One solution to this problem lies in our discussion of phonetics. Although we use symbols such as /p/, /z/, and /n/, these symbols are simply an abbreviation for a set of phonetic properties. Back in section 2.2.2.3.2 we assigned each consonantal phoneme of English a three- or four-term label of phonetic features, for example /t/ is a voiceless alveolar stop. It may be possible to use these features rather than symbols to identify segments. This would certainly allow us to reduce the above three rules to one:

$$[\text{voiceless stop}] \rightarrow [\text{aspirated}] \: / \: .\underline{\quad\quad} V$$
$$[+ \text{stress}]$$

Already we can see that there is a sound argument for abandoning the notion that phonemes are indivisible, and seeing them as simply cover labels for sets of features.

Although such a system appears to provide a solution for the above example, it is somewhat simplistic, and soon runs into problems. In English the regular expression of the plural morpheme is *s*. This morpheme is realised in three different ways by speakers of English – /s/, /z/, and /əz/. Each realisation is called an 'allomorph' from the Greek allo 'other' and morph 'form'. (See Chapter 5 for a discussion of the terms *morpheme* and *allomorph*.) Given any noun, a speaker of English will always choose the correct allomorph of the plural morpheme. Therefore, it should be possible to write a rule which will correctly predict the realisation of the plural morpheme for any noun.

> Draw up three columns – one for each allomorph of the plural – and then put each of the following nouns into one of the three columns according to which version it takes:
>
> *dog, cat, church, judge, book, zoo, base, bee, pod, tap, game, tone, brush, bruise, day, cuff, cub, move, month, lathe, pang*

You will probably have got a set of answers like this:

/s/   tap, cat, book, cuff, month

/z/   cub, pod, dog, move, lathe, game, tone, pang, day, zoo, bee

/əz/   base, bruise, brush, church, judge

> Can you identify the factor which determines which version occurs with which noun? You should pay particular attention to the final sound in each noun.

The final sound in the nouns which occur with /s/ is always voiceless. It is either a stop or a labio-dental or dental fricative. The nouns which occur with /z/ always end in a voiced sound – a vowel, voiced stop, nasal stop, or a voiced labio-dental or dental fricative. Those nouns which occur with /əz/ always end in a fricative, which may be either voiced or voiceless and is either alveolar or post-alveolar, or one of the two affricates. The choice is conditioned by the phonological properties of the final segment of the noun. This conditioning is a type of assimilation and is referred to as 'phonological conditioning'. **phonological conditioning**

Each of the three classes is quite complex and cannot be easily identified. The first class, for example, consists of all voiceless stops and some voiceless fricatives. It is impossible, given the phonetic features introduced in sections 2.1.1 and 2.2.2.3.2 above, to provide a more concise description of this group of sounds. If we wish to capture these three classes, then we require a more comprehensive system of features. **features**

3.7.2   *A set of distinctive features for English*

There are a number of issues which must be taken into account when deciding how many features, and which ones, are necessary to provide an adequate description of a language. First, as we noted above,

natural class

phonological rules apply to classes of phonetically related segments (or natural classes, of which we shall say more in section 3.7.11, below), rather than to classes of unrelated segments. Any feature system must be devised so that it is easier to capture natural classes than unnatural ones. Secondly, we must have sufficient features to allow us to specify uniquely all the phonemes in a language. In other words our features must allow us to capture all distinctive oppositions in a language. This requirement gives rise to the term 'distinctive feature'. Ideally our features should also allow us to distinguish one allophone from another. The features discussed below are sufficient for English but there are many languages which would not be covered by this set. Thirdly, we should be able to relate each feature to a clearly identifiable phonetic property. This property will usually be an articulatory one, but occasionally it may be acoustic.

feature matrix

Each segment in a language may be defined by a list of features. If we accept that segments are to be defined in terms of features then a symbol such as /p/ will be no more than a cover term for a list of distinctive features. These lists of features are usually arranged, as we shall see below, in columns, which are called feature matrices. Finally, features are often thought of as being binary. In the description of any segment the property associated with each feature will be either present or absent. If it is present this will be signalled by a plus (+), and a minus (−) will signal absence.

sonorant
obstruent

Distinctive features may be divided into various groups. There are those features which allow us to identify the major classes of sounds – vowels and consonants – and to distinguish between the sonorant and obstruent consonants. There are also features which define place of articulation, manner of articulation, and voicing. We shall look at each of these groupings.

3.7.3   *Classificatory features*

These features allow us to distinguish between the two major classes of sounds in a language – vowels and consonants. Furthermore, within the class of consonants we must also be able to distinguish the obstruent consonants (stops, fricatives, and affricates) from the sonorant ones (approximants and nasals), and to separate the glides from the liquids. This may be achieved by the introduction of three features – [±syllabic], [±consonantal], and [±obstruent].

syllabic

Segments that function as the peak or nucleus of a syllable are [+syllabic]. Therefore, vowels are always [+syllabic]. Consonants are [−syllabic]. The only exception to this are syllabic consonants, which we shall discuss in section 4.1.3.

In the production of a consonantal sound, one of the active articulators (the lower lip or tongue) obstructs the flow of air at some point in the vocal tract. Stops, fricatives, affricates, nasals, and liquids are [+consonantal], while vowels and glides, which involve a free flow of air through the oral cavity, are [−consonantal].

Obstruents are a subset of consonantal sounds. Oral stops, fricatives, and affricates are all [+obstruent]. These sounds involve a radical obstruction of the air flow. For stops and affricates, the flow is completely obstructed, while in the production of fricatives the air flow is impeded to the extent that an audible hiss is produced. All other sounds are [−obstruent].

These three features are distributed over the classes identified above as follows:

	Obstruents	Nasals	Liquids	Glides	Vowels
syll	−	−	−	−	+
cons	+	+	+	−	−
obs	+	−	−	−	−

There are two points to note about this table. First, the glides, that is [j] and [w], are [−syll, −cons, −obs]. In section 2.2.2.3.2 we claimed that glides were phonetically like vowels, but still classified as consonants. The above feature specification captures this claim. Like vowels, the glides are [−cons], that is, they are produced with a free flow of air through the oral cavity. However, like consonants (and unlike vowels), the glides are [−syll], that is they cannot function as the nucleus of a syllable. Secondly, these three features are not sufficient to uniquely identify the above five classes. Nasals and liquids have identical feature specifications. Clearly, we require an additional feature to allow us to distinguish between these two classes.

3.7.4 Nasals

To distinguish between nasals and non-nasals the feature [±nasal] is introduced. All nasal stops in English are [+nasal], while all other segments are [−nasal]. In our discussion of manner of articulation (see section 2.2.2.3.2), we pointed out that the velum could be moved independently of all other speech production processes. Consequently, [+nasal] is not restricted to stops, but may occur with any other features. This allows for the occurrence of nasalisation as an allophonic process.

3.7.5 Place of articulation features

These features may be divided into two sets – tongue body features and place features. The first set defines the position of the tongue in the oral cavity in relation to a neutral position, while the second specifies an area of the oral cavity.

3.7.6   *Tongue body features*

As stated above these features define the position of the tongue in relation to a neutral or 'resting' position. If you stop articulating and allow your articulators to return to their rest position, your vocal cords will remain open, your velum will be lowered, and your mouth will most likely close. However, your tongue does not simply lie on the floor of your mouth. In its rest position, it remains partially raised. The rest position for the tongue is close to that of the final vowel in *sofa*. This position is taken as the rest or neutral position for the tongue.

The tongue body features are 'high', 'low', and 'back'.

1. High.   If the tongue is raised above the rest position the sound produced is assigned the feature high. Palatal and velar consonants, and high vowels, are all [+high], while labial and dental consonants, and non-high vowels, are all [−high].

2. Low sounds are those produced with tongue lowered from the rest position. The only segments, in English, which are [+low] are the low vowels. All other segments are [−low].

3. Back sounds are articulated with the tongue retracted from the rest position. Back vowels and velars are all [+back], while all other segments are [−back].

The features high and low define three classes: [+high, −low], [−high, −low], and [−high, +low]. Since [+high] implies [−low], and [+low] implies [−high], the first and third of our classes can be referred to as [+high] and [+low] respectively. While segments can be [−low, −high], that is mid, no segment can be [+high, +low]. This would imply a segment in which the tongue is both simultaneously raised and lowered from the rest position. This is impossible.

Together these three features define the following segments:

	iː	e	æ	ɑː	ɒ	ɔː	uː
high	+	−	−	−	−	−	+
low	−	−	+	+	+	−	−
back	−	−	−	+	+	+	+

	p	θ	t	ʃ	j	k	h
high	−	−	−	+	+	+	−
low	−	−	−	−	−	−	−
back	−	−	−	−	−	+	−

You may have noticed that the above feature matrices fail to distinguish between some segments. The low back rounded and unrounded vowels have identical descriptions, as do the labial, dental, and alveolar consonants. It is obvious that further features are required to allow us to distinguish between these classes.

3.7.7 *Further articulatory features*

Our first problem can be easily solved by the introduction of the feature [+round]. All rounded vowels and /w/ are [+round]. This now gives: **round**

	iː	e	æ	ɑː	ɒ	ɔː	uː
high	+	−	−	−	−	−	+
low	−	−	+	+	+	−	−
back	−	−	−	+	+	+	+
round	−	−	−	−	+	+	+

The problem of the labial, dental, and alveolar consonants is not so easily resolved and requires two additional features – anterior and coro-   **anterior, coronal**
nal. These features apply only to consonants.

1. Anterior.   In English, labials, labio-dentals, dentals, and alveolars are [+anterior]. These sounds all involve, in their articulation, an obstruction to the flow of air in the area in front of the post-alveolar region. Any consonant made with such an articulation will be [+anterior]. All other consonants are [−anterior].

2. Coronal.   Dentals, alveolars, post-alveolars and palatals are coronal. These sounds are articulated with the blade of the tongue raised from the neutral position, which was identified in the discussion of the features high and low above. All other consonants are [−coronal].

If we add these new features to the feature matrix introduced above we get:

	p	θ	t	ʃ	j	k	h
high	−	−	−	+	+	+	−
low	−	−	−	−	−	−	−
back	−	−	−	−	−	+	−
anterior	+	+	+	−	−	−	−
coronal	−	+	+	+	+	−	−

One further articulatory feature is required. On the basis of the features given above, provide feature matrices for /l/ and /r/.

Both these segments are approximants, and therefore will be [+cons, −obs]. Furthermore, they are both alveolar approximants and are [+ant, +cor]. It would appear that both segments have the same feature specification and we cannot distinguish between them. To avoid this situation the feature [+lateral] is required. /l/ is [+lateral], and all other segments in English are [−lateral].

3.7.8 *Manner features*

Having identified and defined a set of features for the major classes of segment types and place of articulation, it is necessary to introduce a set of manner of articulation features. Two features are required.

continuant

[+continuant]   All articulations which involve a complete closure in the oral cavity are [−cont]. Oral and nasal stops, and affricates, are all, therefore, [−cont], while fricatives, approximants, and vowels are [+cont].

delayed release

[+delayed release]   This feature is required to differentiate between stops and affricates. Affricates are articulated with a complete closure, which is gradually released causing the fricative phase of the affricate.

3.7.9 *Source features*

These features refer to the acoustic output of a segment. As with the manner features two are required for English.

[+voice]   This feature requires little discussion. Needless to say, all voiced segments are [+voice], and all voiceless segments are [−voice].

strident

[+strident]   This is an acoustic feature. Strident sounds are characterised by high-frequency noise such as you hear when compressed air escapes from a puncture. Contrast [s] and [θ] in English. [s] is [+strident], while [θ] is [−strident]. The labio-dental, alveolar and palato-alveolar fricatives, and the affricates in English are [+strid]. All other English segments are [−strid].

Table 3.3 provides complete feature matrices for all the consonant phonemes of English.

Table 3.3

	p	b	t	d	k	g	f	v	θ	ð	s	z	ʃ	ʒ	h	tʃ	dʒ	l	r	j	w	m	n	ŋ
syll	−	−	−	−	−	−	−	−	−	−	−	−	−	−	−	−	−	−	−	−	−	−	−	−
cons	+	+	+	+	+	+	+	+	+	+	+	+	+	+	+	+	+	+	+	−	−	+	+	+
obs	+	+	+	+	+	+	+	+	+	+	+	+	+	+	−	+	+	−	−	−	−	−	−	−
voice	−	+	−	+	−	+	−	+	−	+	−	+	−	+	−	−	+	+	+	+	+	+	+	+
nasal	−	−	−	−	−	−	−	−	−	−	−	−	−	−	−	−	−	−	−	−	−	+	+	+
cont	−	−	−	−	−	−	+	+	+	+	+	+	+	+	+	−	−	+	+	+	+	−	−	−
del rel	−	−	−	−	−	−	−	−	−	−	−	−	−	−	−	+	+	−	−	−	−	−	−	−
strid	−	−	−	−	−	−	+	+	−	−	+	+	+	+	−	+	+	−	−	−	−	−	−	−
ant	+	+	+	+	−	−	+	+	+	+	+	+	−	−	−	−	−	+	+	−	−	+	+	−
cor	−	−	+	+	−	−	−	−	+	+	+	+	+	+	−	+	+	+	+	+	−	−	+	−
high	−	−	−	−	+	+	−	−	−	−	−	−	+	+	−	+	+	−	−	+	+	−	−	+
low	−	−	−	−	−	−	−	−	−	−	−	−	−	−	−	−	−	−	−	−	−	−	−	−
back	−	−	−	−	+	+	−	−	−	−	−	−	−	−	−	−	−	−	−	−	+	−	−	+
lateral	−	−	−	−	−	−	−	−	−	−	−	−	−	−	−	−	−	+	−	−	−	−	−	−

3.7.10   *Feature matrices and redundancy*

In section 3.7.6 above in our discussion of the features [+high] and [+low], we claimed that there was an implicational relationship between these two features. [+high] implies [−low], and [+low] implies [−high]. Therefore, if a segment is [+high], we do not need to include [−low]. The value of the feature low is implied by the value of the feature high. Similarly, if a segment is [+low], we do not have to include [−high]. To include either [−low] when a segment is [+high] or [−high] when a segment is [+low] would be redundant.

This implicational relationship (and its linked redundancies) does not just occur with the features [±high] and [±low]. There are a number of other cases. For example, [+obs] implies [+cons], [+nas] implies [+voi] and [−lat], and [+syll] also implies [+voi].

One consequence of the implicational relationships is that they allow us to reduce the number of features in a matrix. For example, the matrix for /n/ can now be reduced from its full entry

$$
\begin{bmatrix}
-\text{syll} \\
+\text{cons} \\
-\text{obs} \\
+\text{voi} \\
+\text{nas} \\
-\text{cont} \\
-\text{del rel} \\
-\text{stri} \\
+\text{ant} \\
+\text{cor} \\
-\text{high} \\
-\text{low} \\
-\text{back} \\
-\text{lat}
\end{bmatrix}
\quad \text{to} \quad
\begin{bmatrix}
+\text{nas} \\
+\text{ant} \\
+\text{cor}
\end{bmatrix}
$$

We know from above that [+nasal] implies [+voice], but if we look at Table 3.3 we can see that all nasals are also [+cons], [−obs], [−cont], [−del rel], [−stri] and [−lat]. Therefore, we may omit all of these from our matrix. Furthermore, segments that are [+ant, +cor] are also [−high, −low, −back]. Again we may omit these features from our matrix.

Some of the implicational relationships are universal, that is they apply in all languages. For example, the relationship between [+high] and [−low] is universal. There is no language in which any segment may be [+high, +low]. However, the relationship between, for example, [+nasal] and [+voice] is not universal. It is possible for nasals to be voiceless: for example, Hopi, an Uto-Aztecan language, has voiceless nasals.

3.7.11   *Natural classes*

In section 3.7.2, above, we claimed that one of the requirements of a feature system is that it be able to capture natural classes. In particular the feature system should be such that it is easier to capture natural classes than non-natural ones. Before discussing the ability of the feature system we have outlined above to capture natural classes, it may prove useful to define, in more detail, what we mean by a natural class.

First, a natural class is a group of two or more segments which share one or more phonetic properties. For example, the English voiceless stops /p t k/ form a natural class. They share two phonetic properties, that is they are all voiceless and they are all stops. No other segments in English share both of these properties.

Secondly, the relationship between the features which identify a natural class is always one of conjunction, that is voiceless fricatives must be both [−voice] and [+continuant]. The relationship between the features which identify a natural class can never include disjunction, that is a class of segments which are [+cont], and either [+high] or [+voice] is not a natural class.

Thirdly, the members of a natural class show similar behaviour in identical phonetic environments. As we discussed above, the voiceless stops are all realised by an aspirated allophone when they are the only consonant to occur before a stressed vowel, and they may be either unreleased or realised with glottal reinforcement when they occur in syllable-final position after a stressed vowel. In other words, a natural class tends to behave like a unit.

Given these criteria we can see that, unlike /p t k/, /s d g f m j i/ do not form a natural class. We cannot find any single phonetic property or group of properties which will identify only these segments and exclude all others. Secondly, the relationship between the features required to identify this class would be disjunctive, for example the members of this class are either [+cons] − /s d g f m / or [−cons] − /i j/. Finally, we are unlikely to find any rule which refers to this group of segments. /s d g f m j i/ is an unnatural class.

As we discussed above, /p t k/ form a natural class, and this class is defined by the features [–voice, –cont, –del rel]. By adding or removing features, we can reduce or enlarge this class. For example, if we add the feature [–coronal] we are left with /p/ and /k/. However, if we remove the feature [–voice] then the voiced stops are now included, giving /p b t d k g/. If we remove [–del rel] then the voiced and voiceless affricates are now included. The more features we use to define the class, the smaller the class will be, and the fewer features we use, the larger the class will be. We can say that the size of a natural class is in inverse proportion to the number of features required to define that class.

Finally, the class of voiceless stops is actually the intersection (or conjunction) of three classes: the class of voiceless segments, the class of non-delayed release segments (everything except affricates), and the class of non-continuants (stops and affricates). These three classes are given below:

/p t k tʃ f θ s ʃ/

/p b t d k g f v θ ð s z ʃ ʒ l r j w m n ŋ/

/p b t d k g tʃ dʒ m n ŋ/

The only segments which are common to all three classes, that is the only segments which are [–voice] and [–delayed release] and [–continuant], are the voiceless stops: /p t k/.

The notions of membership of classes or sets and intersection of sets will be familiar to those of you who have studied algebra.

Exercise 3.7

Return to the allophonic rules you wrote for exercise 3.6. Using the features introduced in this unit attempt to re-write your rules using features. For 3.2, 3.3, and 3.4 you should be able to write a single rule which covers all alternations, rather than a rule for each alternating pair.

In writing your rules remember that you do not have to list all the features for any given segment or class of segments. You should omit wherever possible redundant features, as we discussed in section 3.7.10. Furthermore, on the process side of the rule, you need only list in the output those features whose values change. For example, if a rule nasalises vowels, then the output should be only [+nasal]:

[+syllabic] → [+nasal] / ____[+nasal]

We do not include [+syllabic] in the output, as it does not change, and [+nasal] is not included in the input, as we assume that the vowels are [–nasal]

3.7.12   *The plural revisited*

Having introduced a set of features for English and defined those features, we are now in a position to solve the problem of the allomorphs of the English plural. In our discussion above we observed that there were three allomorphs of the English plural morpheme – /s/, /z/, and /əz/. Which allomorph occurs with a noun depends on the final sound of the noun. The final sound in the nouns which occur with /s/ is always voiceless. It is either a stop or a labio-dental or dental fricative. The nouns which occur with /z/ always end in a voiced sound – a vowel, voiced stop, nasal stop, or a voiced labio-dental or dental fricative. Those nouns which occur with /əz/ always end in a fricative, which may be either voiced or voiceless, and is either alveolar or post-alveolar, or one of the two affricates. As was pointed out in the discussion of this exercise, each of the classes which conditions the realisation of the plural morpheme is quite complex and could not be easily identified. However, the set of features introduced above allows each class to be easily and uniquely identified.

Using the features introduced above, identify the three classes of sounds which condition the form of the English plural morpheme. It may be useful to set out the sounds which occurred at the ends of the nouns in the exercise in section 3.7.1, above, and provide a feature matrix for each sound. Having done this, check each matrix to see what features the sounds in each class have in common.

Your answer should look like Table 3.4.

Given that the sounds which occur with /s/ are all voiceless and those which occur with /z/ are all voiced, the feature [±voice] will be required. The problem is to exclude those sounds which occur with /əz/. To exclude /s z ʃ ʒ tʃ dʒ/, it is necessary to find a feature or features which

Table 3.4

	p	b	t	d	k	g	f	v	θ	ð	s	z	ʃ	tʃ	dʒ	m	n	ŋ	iː	uː	ei
syll	−	−	−	−	−	−	−	−	−	−	−	−	−	−	−	−	−	−	+	+	+
cons	+	+	+	+	+	+	+	+	+	+	+	+	+	+	+	+	+	+	−	−	−
obs	+	+	+	+	+	+	+	+	+	+	+	+	+	+	+	−	−	−	−	−	−
voice	−	+	−	+	−	+	−	+	−	+	−	+	−	+	+	+	+	+	+	+	+
nasal	−	−	−	−	−	−	−	−	−	−	−	−	−	−	−	+	+	+	−	−	−
cont	−	−	−	−	−	−	+	+	+	+	+	+	+	−	−	−	−	−	+	+	+
del rel	−	−	−	−	−	−	−	−	−	−	−	−	−	+	+	−	−	−	−	−	−
strid	−	−	−	−	−	−	+	+	−	−	+	+	+	+	+	−	−	−	−	−	−
ant	+	+	+	+	−	−	+	+	+	+	+	+	−	−	−	+	+	−	−	−	−
cor	−	−	+	+	−	−	−	−	+	+	+	+	+	+	+	−	+	−	−	−	−

are shared by the members of this class but not by any of the other sounds involved. We usually say that it is necessary to uniquely specify or identify the sound or sounds involved. If we look at our feature matrix we can see that these sounds all share the features [+strident, +coronal]. Furthermore, none of the sounds involved in conditioning of the other two allomorphs is [+strident +coronal]. We can use these features to uniquely identify the class of sounds which occur with the /əz/ allomorph. We can now write a rule which predicts the form of the plural morpheme:

$$z \rightarrow \begin{cases} \text{əz} & / \text{ [+strid +cor]} \\ \text{[-voice]} / \text{ [-voice]} \end{cases} \# \underline{\quad} \#$$

There are three points to note about this rule.

First, we have chosen one of the three allomorphs as the underlying representation of the morpheme plural. With allomorphs we select one as the underlying representation, and derive the allomorphs from it by rule. In this case we have chosen /z/.

/z/ has the widest distribution. It occurs after all voiced sounds, except the coronal stridents – /z ʒ dʒ/. The other two allomorphs occur after much more restricted sets of sounds – /s/ after /p t k f θ/ and /əz/ after /s ʃ tʃ z ʒ dʒ/. It is not unusual for the allomorph with the widest distribution to be chosen as the underlying representation.

Furthermore, the occurrence of /əz/ and /s/ is determined by the phonotactics. There are no word-final /sz ʃz tʃz zz ʒz dʒz/ clusters in English. The addition of /z/ to any noun ending in a coronal strident would result in one of the above clusters. Therefore, /ə/ is inserted before /z/, and the phonotactics are satisfied. All word-final obstruent (stop, fricative, and affricate) clusters in English agree in voice. Therefore, /z/ cannot occur after /p t k f θ/, but /s/ can. By devoicing /z/ the phonotactics are once again satisfied.

Secondly, having selected /z/ as the underlying form of the plural morpheme, it is not necessary to specify it in the output of the rule. If neither of the contexts specified in the rule is met, then the form of the plural will be /z/.

Thirdly, the two parts of this rule are disjunctively ordered (see p. 68 above). Either the first or the second part applies but not both. If the first line applies successfully, then the second line does not apply. Furthermore, the first line must be ordered before the second, otherwise we will not derive the correct forms. For example, if the second part were to be ordered before the first then all nouns that end with a voiceless consonant would receive the /s/ allomorph. We know that this is not the case. *Bus*, *brush*, and *church* all end with a voiceless consonant but occur with /əz/ and not /s/in their plural form.

The introduction of distinctive features has allowed us to capture succinctly the three classes of sounds which condition the form of the English plural morpheme. Without distinctive features we would simply have to list the classes of sounds involved, as we did in section 3.5.1, above. Although listing the classes would work, it fails to highlight, especially in the case of the coronal stridents – /s ʃ tʃ z ʒ dʒ/ – that the sounds involved have anything in common.

Consider the following data:

cat*'s*	cut*s*	clapp*ed*
dog*'s*	call*s*	cann*ed*
judge*'s*	brush*es*	want*ed*

Each of the italicised suffixes performs a particular function. *'s* was introduced in section 3.4.2.3. It is attached to nouns and marks the possessive. The *(e)s* in the second column and *ed* in the third are attached to verbs. The former marks the third person singular present tense, while the latter is the marker of the regular past tense.

(a) List other examples of nouns and verbs with these suffixes.

(b) Like the plural, each suffix is a morpheme. How many allomorphs can you identify for each morpheme?

(c) Is each realisation phonologically conditioned?

(d) Using the features introduced above, write a rule which will correctly predict the form of each allomorph.

Each morpheme has three allomorphs. The allomorphs of the possessive and the third person singular present tense are identical to those of the plural. Furthermore, the conditioning factors, and the explanation for the occurrence, are also identical to those of the plural.

The past tense also has three allomorphs – /əd/, /t/ and /d/. Like the allomorphs discussed above, these are phonologically conditioned. The first occurs if the stem ends in either /t/ or /d/, the second if it ends in any voiceless segment except /t/, and the third if it ends in any voiced segment except /d/. As with the plural, the occurrence of the three allomorphs may be expressed through a set of rules:

$$d \rightarrow \begin{Bmatrix} \text{əd} & / \text{ [–cont +ant +cor]} \\ \text{[–voice]} & / \text{ [–voice]} \end{Bmatrix} \# \_\_ \#$$

As with the plural rule, we have chosen one of the three allomorphs as representing the underlying form of the past tense. Of the three allomorphs of the past tense, /d/ has the widest distribution. It occurs after vowels, and all voiced consonants except /d/. An explanation for the form of the other two allomorphs may be found in the phonotactics.

There are no final /dd dt tt td/ clusters. Therefore /ə/ is inserted before /d/, and the phonotactics are satisfied.

We have already noted that all word-final obstruent clusters agree in voice. Therefore, if the verb stem ends with a voiceless obstruent, except /t/, then the form of the past tense will be /t/.

Having chosen /d/ as the underlying form of the past tense, we do not have to specify it in the output of the rule. If neither of the contexts specified in the rule is met then the form of the past tense will be /d/.

The parts of this rule are disjunctively ordered, and the first line must apply before the second, if we are to derive the correct forms.

We have introduced two different units in our discussion of English phonology: the phoneme, and distinctive features, which are smaller than the phoneme. Although we have argued for a unit smaller than the phoneme, we have not discussed the possibility that there may be units which are larger than a single phoneme. In the next chapter we shall discuss units larger than the phoneme, and features which may apply to more than a single segment.

Further exercises

Exercise 3.8

Consider the data below, which are based on Italian, and then answer the questions that follow:

[mina]	*mina*	'mine'	[nido]	*nido*	'nest'
[muffa]	*muffa*	'mould'	[notʃe]	*noce*	'nut tree'
[lima]	*lima*	'file'	[cane]	*cane*	'dog'
[limone]	*limone*	'lemon'	[denaro]	*denaro*	'money'
[lombo]	*lombo*	'loin'	[andare]	*andare*	'go'
[pompa]	*pompa*	'pump'	[tondo]	*tondo*	'round'
[liŋgwa]	*lingua*	'tongue'	[tʃiŋkwe]	*cinque*	'five'
[fuŋgo]	*fungo*	'mushroom'	[baŋko]	*banco*	'bench'

How many different nasal sounds are there in the above data?

Are all the nasal sounds phonemic? You will need to set up a distribution table.

If one of the nasals is not phonemic, but an allophone of one of the other nasals, then write a rule to derive the allophones.

Exercise 3.9

Consider the following pairs of words:

possible	impossible	probable	improbable
opportune	inopportune	decisive	indecisive
edible	inedible	tangible	intangible
literate	illiterate	legal	illegal
reversible	irreversible	responsible	irresponsible

What is the difference in meaning between the members of each pair?

List the prefixes which are added to the first member of each pair to derive the second.

If each prefix has the same meaning then it is likely that they are allomorphs of a single morpheme.

Are the allomorphs phonologically conditioned? If so select one allomorph as the underlying representation of this morpheme, and write a rule to derive the other allomorphs.

4 Syllables and suprasegmentals

In the previous chapter we concentrated on segmental phonology. We did not discuss any unit larger than the phoneme, or any aspect of phonology which may apply to more than a single segment. In this chapter we shall look at the syllable – a unit which may be larger than a single segment –and various suprasegmental aspects of phonology. Suprasegmentals are, as their name suggests, features which apply to units larger than a single segment.

4.1 Syllables

Although the discussion of phonotactics above (see section 3.3.2) introduced the term syllable, no attempt was made to define this notion. Most speakers of English, although probably unable to define the term syllable, have some intuitive notion of how many syllables a given word contains.

syllable

Transcribe each of the following words, divide them into syllables by inserting the syllable boundary marker – . – and list the number of syllables. For example:

divide   2   /də.vɑid/

phonetic, linguistics, member, wombat, data, ancestral, aardvark, communal, extra, monopoly, quickly, taboo

Your answers are probably like this:

3	/fə.ne.tɪk/	3	/lɪŋ.gwɪs.tɪks/
2	/mem.bə/	2	/wɒm.bæt/
2	/dei.tə/	3	/æn.ses.trəl/
2	/ɑ:d.vɑ:k/	3	/kɒm.jə.nəl/
2	/ek.strə/	4	/mə.nɒ.pə.lɪ/
2	/kwɪ.klɪ/	2	/tə.bu:/

While it is unlikely that we will have disagreed on the number of syllables each word contains, you may disagree, for some words, with our placement of the boundaries. For example, you may have /æn.se.strəl/, /kɒ.mjən.əl/, /kwɪk.lɪ/ or /eks.trə/. All of these alternatives are acceptable. For other words, for example *aardvark*, *wombat*, and *member*, the only possible syllabifications are those given above. Neither /me.mbə/ nor /memb.ə/ is acceptable. Any account of the syllable should explain why, for some words, there is only one possible syllabification but for others alternative syllabifications are possible.

4.1.1 *Syllable boundaries and phonotactics*

The number of syllables in any given word would appear, at least from the data considered above, to be related to the number of vowel sounds (monophthongs and diphthongs) the word contains. If a word contains two vowel sounds, for example *exclude*, then it contains two syllables. Clearly there is a principled means for arriving at the number of syllables in a word. There is also a principled means by which we can identify those words which have alternative syllabifications and what those alternatives are.

Consider the word *member*, which we transcribed as /membə/. *Member* may only be syllabified as /mem.bə/, and not as either /me.mbə/ or /memb.ə/. We may arrive at an understanding of why this is so if we consider the cluster /mb/. In our discussion of the phonotactics of English (section 3.3.2, above), we identified the possible word-initial clusters of English. The list of possible word-initial CC clusters does not include /mb/. This is an illicit cluster, and no word or syllable may begin with this cluster. Consequently, *member* cannot be syllabified as /me.mbə/, as the second syllable would then begin with an illicit cluster. Although we did not identify or discuss the permissible word-final clusters, no English word may end with /mb/. It is both an illicit initial and an illicit final cluster. For /mb/ the only possibility is to place the syllable boundary between the two consonants.

We may use the phonotactics of the language as a principled basis for determining where syllable boundaries occur in bi- and polysyllabic words. Implicit in this approach is the claim that the phonotactic restrictions apply not to words but to syllables. If a cluster cannot occur at either the beginning or the end of a word, then it cannot either begin or end a syllable. Any consonants that occur between two vowels will be assigned to a vowel so as to produce permissible word-initial or final clusters. Although this is illustrated by *member*, consider, as a further example, *stalwart*. This word also contains two syllables, with the boundary occurring between /l/ and /w/. We know the boundary must occur between these two segments because there are no words which either begin or end with /lw/. Therefore, no syllable may either begin or end with this cluster.

These are unambiguous examples. It is clear where, given the phonotactics of English, the boundaries must occur. There are, however, a large number of cases for which it is not so clear where the syllable boundary should occur. As an illustrative example consider *extra*. Transcribed phonemically, we have /ekstrə/. If we have one syllable per vowel, then this word contains two syllables. As /k/, /ks/, and /kst/ are all possible word final clusters, the syllable boundary may be placed in any of these positions. The problem of where to place the boundary is complicated further when we take the second syllable into consideration. /r/, /tr/, and /str/ are all possible word-initial clusters, and therefore the boundary may be placed in any of these three positions. These positions coincide with the possible positions for the end of the preceding syllable:

/ek.strə/   /eks.trə/   /ekst.rə/

Some consonants may belong to more than one syllable. We refer to such consonants as ambisyllabic. In the above example, /s/ and /t/ are **ambisyllabic** ambisyllabic as they may belong to either the first or the second syllable. Individual speakers may differ on which of the three possible positions they choose, but all are possible.

4.1.2 *Syllable structure*

In our discussion of the syllable, we have assumed, so far, that a syllable consists of a vowel and initial and final consonant clusters. Of these three constituents only the vowel is obligatory. All syllables must contain a vocalic nucleus. The initial and final consonant clusters are optional. This means that the simplest syllable will be a vowel, for example *eye* or *a*. Such syllables are represented as V. The next simplest syllable types are consonant–vowel (CV) or vowel–consonant (VC), for example *me*, *he*, *go*, *on*, *at* and *an*. Many languages have only either V or CV syllables, for example Maori. We discussed the largest syllable-initial clusters in English in section 3.3.2, above. These clusters contain three consonants, the first of which is always /s/, the second a voiceless stop /p t k/, and the third is an approximant /r l j w/. The largest syllable-final cluster in English contains four consonants, for example sixths – /ksθs/, and, as with the syllable-initial clusters, the range of possible combinations is severely limited.

4.1.3 *Nucleus, rhyme, onset and coda*

As we discussed above, all syllables must contain a vocalic element, and this is called the nucleus. The optional initial consonant or consonants **nucleus** are called the onset, while the optional final consonant or consonants **onset** are called the coda. Together the nucleus and coda form the rhyme. We **coda, rhyme**

Σ is the Greek letter sigma and is used to represent the whole syllable.

Figure 4.1

can now represent the structure of the syllable as a tree. Consider as an example *streets*, as shown in Figure 4.1. The onset and coda constituents are self-explanatory. They represent initial and final consonants or clusters. However, the inclusion of the rhyme requires some further explanation.

The rhyme constituent consists of both the vocalic nucleus and the coda. There are a number of arguments for grouping these constituents together. First, in poetry the rhyme arises from the use of syllables whose nucleus and coda are identical but onsets differ. It is the nucleus and coda of the final word of one line which rhyme with the nucleus and coda of the final word of a later line, for example:

> The furl of fresh-leaved dogrose down
> His cheeks the forth-and-flaunting sun
> Had swarthed about with lion-brown
> Before the spring was done.

> (Gerard Manley Hopkins)

Here the nucleus and coda of *down* rhymes with that of *brown*, and that of *sun* rhymes with that of *done*. The onset plays no role in these rhymes. The rhyme in poetry is carried by the rhyme constituent of the syllable. When the initial constituent of two or more syllables is identical, we refer to the resulting effect as alliteration, for example:

> Doom is dark and deeper than any sea-dingle

> (W. H. Auden)

Secondly, we saw above that in the stream of speech some segments are elided (see section 3.4.3). It is usually consonants which are elided, but vowels, especially short ones, may also be elided. Schwa – /ə/ – is especially susceptible to elision. For example, in a word like *single*, the schwa of the final syllable may be elided:

single /sɪŋgəl/ → [sɪŋgl]

When this vowel is elided, the final syllable no longer contains an obligatory nucleus. However, the syllable does not cease to exist, but a new nucleus is found. In this example, /l/ becomes the new nucleus. This section is indicated in the transcription by placing a small dot, beneath the /l/, to indicate that it is now the nucleus:

[sɪŋgl̩]

You may recall that we used this symbol in section 3.4.3.

We call consonants which may become the nucleus of a syllable syllabic consonants. In English, /l m n/ are the only consonants which may become the nucleus of a syllable. Not only is the number of syllabic con-   **syllabic consonant** sonants limited, but also these consonants must be part of the coda of the syllable. Consonants which become the nucleus of a syllable whose vocalic nucleus has been elided are never taken from the onset. This suggests that the relationship between the nucleus and coda differs from that between the onset and the nucleus. The nucleus and the coda are more directly related to each other. This more direct relationship is reflected in a structure of the syllable which groups these two constituents together as the rhyme.

Thirdly, the rhyme plays a role in stress placement in English. In all bi- and polysyllabic words, one syllable will always be more prominent than the others. We call this prominent syllable the stressed syllable.

Identify the stressed syllable in each of the following words by placing a single quotation mark at its beginning:

> monopoly, politics, wombat, become, dogma, algebra, phoneme, window, butcher, bromide, digital, promise

Speakers of English, when presented with a word they have not previously seen or heard, are usually able to assign it the correct stress pattern. We can conclude from this that there must be a set of principles or rules which allows speakers to assign stress to the appropriate syllable of a word. Given that stress placement is quite complex, there will be (and are) exceptions to any such set of principles or rules.

Monosyllabic words pose no problems since there is only one syllable the speaker can stress. However, in more complex cases a number of factors influence the placement of stress. These factors include word class membership, word structure, and the composition of the rhyme constituent.

Consider the following list of verbs and nouns. For each member of the list, provide a transcription, identify the stressed syllable by placing a single quotation mark before the stressed syllable, and draw syllable trees for each syllable.

ballot, exclude, attract, annoy, divide, abstract(v), enter, target, delight(n), money, abstract(n), canteen, incline, linguist, machine

Answer:

/'bælət eks'klu:d ə'trækt ə'nɔi də'vaid əb'strækt 'entə 'ta:gət
də'lait 'mʌnɪ 'æbstrækt kæn'ti:n ɪn'klain 'lɪŋgwɪst mə'ʃi:n/

If we consider the verbs first, we can see that the stress may fall on either the first or the second syllable. In discussions of stress it is normal to refer to syllables by counting back from the end of the word. In a bisyllabic word the second syllable is the ultimate or final syllable and the first is the penultimate. The antepenultimate is the initial syllable of the three-syllable word. This is illustrated by considering, as an example, *rhododendron*, as shown in Figure 4.2.

To determine the rule for stress placement, we should consider the rhyme section of the stressed syllable and compare it with the rhyme of the unstressed syllable. Furthermore, stress placement rules usually apply to the final syllable first, so in your comparison compare the rhymes of stressed and unstressed final syllables.

The rhyme constituent of those final syllables which are stressed contains either a diphthong – /də'vaid/, a long vowel – /eks'klu:d/, or a short vowel followed by a coda of two consonants – /əb'strækt/. The rhymes which contain either a long vowel or a diphthong may also contain a coda of one or more consonants, for example, /eks'klu:*d*/ and /də'vai*d*/. These consonants do not play a role in stress placement in these cases. However, if the rhyme contains a short vowel, it will only accept stress if it also contains a coda of two or more consonants. These rhymes are traditionally referred to as being 'heavy'.

Rhymes which consist of either a short vowel or a short vowel plus a single consonant are called 'light', for example /'entə/. So if the rhyme

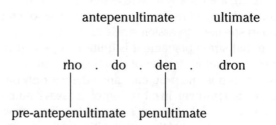

Figure 4.2

constituent of the final syllable of a bisyllabic verb is heavy it will accept stress. If it is not, then it rejects stress which then falls on the penultimate syllable irrespective of its weight.

In our introductory discussion to stress placement, we noted that word class membership, as well as the structure of the rhyme, plays a role in stress placement. If we now turn to the nouns, we see that they differ from verbs with respect to which rhyme types accept stress. Stress falls on a final syllable which contains either a long vowel or a diphthong. If the final syllable contains a short vowel and two or more consonants, then unlike the verbs it rejects stress. The notion of a heavy syllable is more restricted with nouns. This difference accounts for the different stress placement on noun–verb pairs such as *abstract, conduct, frequent*, and *protest*. In each pair the verb is stressed on the final syllable, while the noun is stressed on the penultimate.

One final point concerning the structure of the syllable concerns the distribution of sound types through the syllable. The nucleus is always either a vowel or a syllabic consonant, which in English is always a sonorant (either an approximant or a nasal). As we move out from the nucleus, we find that the sounds in consonant clusters become gradually less sonorant. In any cluster approximants and nasals, if present, occur closer to the nucleus than obstruents. The less vowel-like a sound is, the further from the nucleus it occurs.

4.2 Suprasegmental features of English

In our discussions of English phonetics and phonology we have concentrated on the description of individual segments – consonants and vowels. We have also discussed a number of processes which affect these individual segments, for example assimilation, elision, and aspiration. These individual segments may combine with each other to form larger units, for example syllables and words. There are a number of phonological features which extend or spread over more than a single segment. We call these features prosodies or suprasegmentals. Stress, pitch, and intonation are all suprasegmental features.

prosody, suprasegmental
stress, pitch, intonation

4.2.1 *Pitch*

In section 2.2.2.2 we discussed the contribution of the phonatory process to speech production. This process introduces voice into speech through the activity of the vocal cords. The rate at which the vocal cords may vibrate is not fixed but can be deliberately varied by the speaker.

Taking the syllable [ju:], try saying this with your normal pitch, a low pitch, high pitch, a rising and a falling pitch. This demonstrates that pitch is controlled by the speaker.

The faster the vocal cords vibrate, the higher the pitch of a sound, and the slower the rate of vibration, the lower the pitch will be. We can increase or decrease the rate at which our vocal cords vibrate in two ways. First, we can vary the pressure of the air coming out of the lungs. The greater the pressure, the higher the pitch, and vice versa. Secondly, any change in the tension of the vocal cords will result in a change of pitch. An increase in the tension of the vocal cords will raise the pitch of the voice.

All speakers have a pitch span, which ranges from the lowest note they can produce to the highest. In normal speech production, speakers do not make use of their entire pitch span, but only a middle portion. Movements out of this middle portion are often associated with particular emotional states or attitudes towards the topic of discussion. For example, if a speaker is happy, nervous, excited, or enthusiastic about the topic of discussion, then he or she will make more use of the upper portion of their pitch span. Use of the lower portion may occur when the speaker is sad, bored or unenthusiastic about the topic of discussion.

4.2.2 *Intonation*

Consider the following sentence:

The doctor has been called.

Say it once as a statement, and a second time as if it were a question. Paying particular attention to the end of the sentence, do you notice any difference in the pitch of your voice between the two?

The pitch of your voice should have dropped on *called* when you uttered the sentence as a statement but risen when you uttered it as if it were a question. These variations in pitch contribute to our understanding of the utterance as a whole. Our response to the above sentence uttered with a falling pitch on the final word would differ from that to the same sentence uttered with a rise in pitch on the final word. These two pitch movements are not unique to this example but recur across the language. We call these recurrent changes in pitch movement 'intonation'. Intonation is another suprasegmental feature.

Intonation involves a limited number of recurrent pitch movements or patterns. Each pitch pattern may be used to convey the speaker's attitude to the topic of conversation, or to the hearer, or the speaker's personality, or to signal grammatical features such as whether the utterance is a question. We shall call these pitch patterns tones. We can identify, for English, three basic tones: (a) a fall from high to low, indicated by ˋ; (b) a rise from low to high, indicated by ˊ; and (c) a monotone, indicated by ˉ. The terms high and low are relative. There is no absolute value attached to these terms. What is important is that the finishing point is lower than the start, and not the value of either point.

tone

Each of the tones introduced above may be associated with a typical meaning. A fall typically signals 'finality'. The speaker has concluded his or her contribution, or does not wish to say or hear any more on the topic being discussed. For example:

A   Did you see the documentary on sheep last night?

B   ˋNo (and I'm not interested).

A rise in the pitch is associated with 'questioning' or a desire to say or hear more. For example:

A   Did you see the documentary on sheep last night?

B   ˊNo (but I'm interested).

The monotone is unnatural and is associated with routine. For example:

A   Have you ever been refused car insurance?

B   ˉNo.

A   Have you ever been charged with a traffic violation, except parking?

B   ˉNo.

There are two further tones, which are combinations of the rise and fall tones. These tones are the fall–rise, indicated by ˇ, and the rise-fall indicated by ˆ. The fall–rise signals 'limited agreement' or 'agreement with reservation'. For example:

A   Do you like my new shoes?

B   ˇYes.

Speaker A would expect B to continue and explain why he/she has reservations, and what they are. The rise–fall is associated with strong feelings of either approval or surprise. For example:

A   Do you like my new shoes?

B   ˆYes.

These tones do not change the meaning of the word with which they are associated, but change the meaning of the utterance as a whole. In the above examples, *no* retains the same lexical meaning no matter which tone the speaker uses. However, the tones modify the meaning of the utterance, as is illustrated by either the fall and rise examples, or the fall–rise and rise–fall examples.

The use of tone in English differs from that in languages such as Thai, Chinese, and Vietnamese. In these languages, unlike English, tone does change the meaning of a word. For example, in Thai the meaning of /naa/ changes with the tone: /naa/ plus a high tone means 'young maternal aunt or uncle', but when uttered with a mid tone it means 'rice paddy'. Tone in Thai is phonemic. To change the tone of a Thai word results in a different word, just as changing the initial /t/ of English /tɪp/ to /d/ results in a different word.

4.2.2.1   *Tone groups and tonic syllables*

Conversation does not consist of one-word utterances. Draw two lines to represent the minimum and maximum pitch of your own voice, and then try to draw a line, as illustrated by the first example, in Figure 4.3, to represent your intonation for the following sentences:

I	s a w	J a n e	yesterday

Figure 4.3

(a)   All the people are coming.

(b)   Are all the people coming?

(c)   I decided yesterday I didn't want to go.

Your answers might look like the drawings in Figure 4.4.

We can see from these examples that major changes in pitch do not occur on all the syllables of an utterance. There is only a single tone in each of the first two examples. This tone falls on the first syllable of *coming*, which is the last stressed syllable of the utterance. In the third example there are two tones. The first falls on the final syllable of

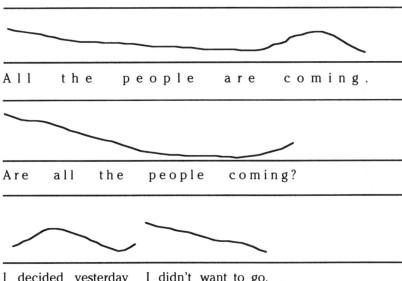

All   the   people   are   coming.

Are   all   the   people   coming?

I   decided   yesterday   I   didn't   want   to   go.

Figure 4.4

yesterday, while the second occurs on *go*. The distribution of tones in continuous speech has led to the establishment of a unit which is generally larger than a single syllable. We call this unit the tone group. **tone group** Although tone groups are usually larger than a single-syllable, both single syllable and multi-syllable tone groups are possible.

To clarify the notion 'tone group', let us consider some examples.

Consider both the intonation contour assigned to the first example in the previous exercise, and those assigned to B's answers to A's questions. What do all of these tone groups have in common?

All of these tone groups contain one of the tones we identified above in section 4.2.2. Tone groups must contain a syllable on which a major change of pitch occurs. This syllable is called the tonic syllable and is **tonic syllable** the only obligatory member of a tone group. The simplest tone group will consist only of a tonic syllable, while larger tone groups will contain a tonic syllable and a number of other syllables on which no major change of pitch occurs. The pitch may change from one syllable to the next, but it remains constant throughout the production of these syllables. The obligatory tonic syllable is the only syllable in the tone group where the pitch changes during its production.

The structure of the tone group proposed above parallels that which we proposed for the syllable. Both syllables and tone groups must contain an obligatory element. In the case of the syllable it is the vocalic nucleus, and for the tone group it is the tonic syllable. All other constituents (onset, and coda or non-tonic syllables) are optional.

In any tone group, we can identify the tonic syllable through its possession of the following properties. First, it carries the major pitch change, which will be one of the tones introduced above. Secondly, it will always be a stressed syllable, but it is more prominent than other stressed syllables. This additional prominence is called 'tonic stress'.

4.2.2.2 Tone groups and continuous speech

Any stretch of continuous conversation will consist of a number of tone groups. Although we have established a basic structure for tone groups, we have not discussed any criteria which would allow us to place boundaries between adjacent tone groups. We may use grammatical, semantic, and phonetic criteria to delimit tone groups.

Tone group boundaries tend to occur at major grammatical boundaries, for example those between phrases about which we will have more to say in Chapter 7. This is illustrated by the examples in Figures 4.5 and 4.6, where the vertical stroke indicates a tone group boundary.

There are two tone groups in each of these examples. In the first example the boundary falls between the two clauses, while in the second it falls between phrases but not in the middle of them. The tone groups coincide with grammatical constituents, and also have meaning. If the boundary were to fall between *alligator* and *eyed*, then the tone group would cut across grammatical constituents, and produce a tone group

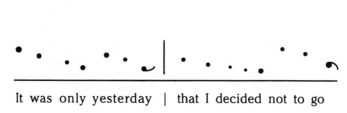

It was only yesterday | that I decided not to go

Figure 4.5

The large evil   alligator | eyed the spectators

Figure 4.6

which was semantically anomalous. This tendency for tone group boundaries to coincide with major grammatical boundaries gives tone groups both grammatical and semantic coherence.

One possible phonetic marker of tone group boundaries is the pause. Furthermore, pauses may coincide with major phrase boundaries. The occurrence of a pause at a major phrase boundary suggests strongly that this is also the location of a tone group boundary. However, not all units that are bounded by pauses are tone groups. As tone groups must contain a tonic syllable, which is always stressed, then any unstressed syllable bounded by pauses cannot be a tone group.

Furthermore, it is also the case that an intonation contour which goes from one pause to the next is not necessarily a single tone group. Consider, for example, the third sentence in the exercise in section 4.2.2, above. Even if this sentence were uttered without any internal pauses, it would contain two tone groups. In most people's intonation there will be a break in the continuity of the intonation after *yesterday*. This break in continuity suggests that a boundary occurs at this point. Support for the placing of a tone group boundary in this position comes from the behaviour of the pitch of the voice. After the tonic syllable, which falls on the final syllable of *yesterday*, and is uttered with a falling tone, there is a slight step up in pitch to the next syllable, which is unstressed. This change of pitch between a stressed and an unstressed syllable usually indicates a tone group boundary.

Finally, the tonic syllable is often the stressed syllable of the final lexical word in a tone group. Having identified the tonic syllable, the tone group boundary may be placed after the tonic and any associated unstressed syllables. These associated syllables may be part of a syntactic constituent, or if the tonic does not fall on the final syllable of a word, then the boundary will occur after the remaining (unstressed) syllables.

Despite these guidelines, there are often cases where it is impossible to make a principled decision on the placement of tone group boundaries. This is especially the case in spontaneous conversation, where hesitation phenomena and other planning difficulties result in various anomalies. The problems posed by spontaneous conversation, and solutions to these problems, are discussed in Brown, Currie and Kenworthy (1980).

4.2.2.3 *The functions of intonation*

We can identify three functions for intonation: (a) attitudinal function, (b) accentual function, and (c) grammatical function. Let us look at each of these in more detail.

attitudinal function
accentual function
grammatical function

We may use intonation to indicate our attitude or emotions towards the topic being discussed. This involves not just intonation but also pitch placement, tempo, voice quality, and facial expressions.

The tonic syllable is usually the stressed syllable of the final lexical word in the tone group. However, for contrastive purposes, it is possible to place the tonic syllable on any word. This is illustrated by the following, where the italics indicate the tonic syllable:

(a)   He was wearing a blue *suit*.

(b)   (He wasn't wearing a *grey* suit.) He was wearing a *blue* suit.

In (a) the tonic syllable would normally fall on *suit*. However, if it were to fall on *blue*, this would imply a contrast, as illustrated by the (b) example. Similarly, prepositions are normally unstressed, and placement of tonic stress on a preposition again implies a contrast, which is illustrated by the following:

Place the book on the *table*.

Place the book *on* the table.   (Not under or next to it.)

For purposes of emphasis, the tonic may be placed on any syllable. For example:

(a)   This is really *dull*.

(b)   This is *really* dull.

(a)   You mustn't run so *quickly*.

(b)   You *mustn't* run so quickly.

The (a) examples are non-contrastive, while the (b) ones are contrastive.
    The tonic syllable may be located earlier within a tone group if the later information is given. For example:

Here's the *book* you asked me to buy.

The request to buy the book is not new, and therefore, the tonic is located earlier in the tone group.
    In our discussion of tone group boundaries, we claimed that these boundaries normally coincide with the boundaries between major grammatical units. One consequence of this is that intonation may be used to disambiguate structures which, when written, are ambiguous. For example:

Those shareholders who bought quickly reaped the benefits.

There are two possible interpretations to this sentence:

(a)   Benefits were reaped by those shareholders who bought quickly.

(b)   Benefits were reaped quickly by those shareholders who bought.

There are two possible ways of uttering this sentence. The first corresponds to the first interpretation, and the second to the second interpretation. These two possibilities are given below:

| Those shareholders who bought *quickly* | reaped the *ben*efits |

| Those shareholders who *bought* | quickly reaped the *ben*efits |

The first interpretation would have the tone group boundary between *quickly* and *reaped*, with the tonic falling on *quickly*. The second possibility has the boundary falling between *bought* and *quickly*, with the tonic falling on *bought*.

4.3 Stress

In our discussion of the syllable and intonation, we introduced the term 'stress' and discussed stress placement, but we did not provide a definition nor did we discuss stress as a phenomenon. We said that stressed syllables tend to be more prominent but did not discuss what contributed to this prominence. Prominence of sounds is relative. There is no absolute measure of prominence. Sounds are only prominent in relation to another sound. Length, loudness, pitch and quality all contribute to a speaker's perception of a syllable as prominent.

Length   The length of a vowel contributes to prominence. Syllables containing long vowels tend to be more prominent than those which contain short vowels, even when they are unstressed.

Loudness   Hearers often perceive stressed syllables as louder than unstressed ones. This is a direct result of speech production factors such as greater muscular effort in forcing air between the vocal cords, which in turn vibrate more vigorously. This increased activity is ultimately perceived as an increase in loudness. Some linguists refer to loudness as intensity.

Pitch   As we saw in section 4.2.1, this term is applied to the rate of vibration of the vocal cords. If the pitch changes on a syllable then that syllable will be perceived as prominent. This is often called 'pitch prominence'. It does not matter whether the pitch moves up or down, what counts is that it moves.

Quality   The quality of a sound also contributes to its prominence. In general vowels are more prominent than consonants, but within each group there is a hierarchy. The more open a vowel is, the more prominent it is. /ɑ:/ is more prominent than either /i:/ or /u:/. Approximants and nasals are more prominent than fricatives, which are more prominent than stops.

While all of these factors contribute to the prominence of syllables, some are more important than others in determining stress. It would seem logical that loudness is a major contributor to prominence, but this is not the case. As we discussed above, some sounds are more prominent, that is they sound louder, than others by virtue of their quality. While it is true that stressed syllables tend to be louder (or more intense) than unstressed ones, pitch movement is the most obvious cue to prominence for the hearer.

Of the remaining three factors, length contributes quite strongly to prominence. Quality also plays a role but to a lesser extent than either pitch movement or length. Although stressed syllables tend to be louder than unstressed ones, loudness by itself as a marker of prominence is the least effective of the four contributory factors. In general, a stressed syllable will tend to be marked by a change in pitch and, in comparison with unstressed ones, to be longer and louder. Stress is the result of the cumulation of two or more of these properties on a single syllable.

4.3.1 *Levels of stress*

Some longer words have more than one stressed syllable. For example, the following words have two stressed syllables: *'mini'mize, 'circu'late, 'explan'ation*, and *'deri'vation*. Not only do these words have two stressed syllables, but when uttered in isolation, there would also appear to be a difference in the degree of stress. In the first two examples, the first stressed syllable appears to be more prominent than the second, while in the third example this position is reversed. We call the more prominent of the two stresses the primary stress and the lesser the secondary stress. For example, primary stress falls on the initial (or antepenultimate) syllable of *minimize*, while secondary stress falls on the final (or ultimate) syllable. We indicate primary stress with a raised mark and secondary stress, where it occurs, with a low mark. For example:

'mini,mize   'circu,late   ,expla'nation   ,deri'vation

4.3.2 *Stress in connected speech – rhythm*

In isolation all English words have at least one stress. However, in connected speech certain words are commonly unstressed. For example, *the, a, be, have, he, she, it, and, but, in, to, on,* and *at* are usually unstressed. Bi- and polysyllabic words will contain at least one unstressed syllable. Consequently, in connected speech there will be a large number of unstressed syllables, and a smaller number of stressed ones. Alternations between stressed and unstressed syllables provide connected speech with its rhythm.

rhythm

Read the following sentences aloud and tap with a finger on each stressed syllable:

What did you hope to discover by that test?

What's the problem with all these people?

What's the difference between a free and a bound morph?

Mark the beginning of each stressed syllable and count the number of syllables between each stress, and note the regularity with which you tap each stressed syllable. Does the number of unstressed syllables between each stressed one vary or remain constant? Does the rate at which you tap the stressed syllables remain constant or does it change?

Answers:

'What did you 'hope to dis'cover by that 'test?

'What's the 'problem with 'all these 'people?

'What's the 'difference between a 'free and a 'bound 'morph?

The number of unstressed syllables between each stressed one varies: 2, 2, 3 in the first; 1, 2, 1 in the second; and 1, 4, 2, 1 in the third. However, the rate at which you tap does not vary. There is a regular beat in each of the above sentences. Stressed syllables in English occur at regular time intervals. This leads us to say that English is stressed timed, that is the **stressed timed** period of time between each stressed syllable, irrespective of the number of intervening unstressed syllables, is roughly equal. Each stressed syllable and the unstressed ones which follow it are grouped together to form a metrical unit we call the foot. All utterances may be **foot** divided up into feet. We can illustrate this using one of the above sentences as an example:

|What's the |difference between a |free and a| bound |morph?

If stressed syllables occur at approximately regular intervals, then each foot, irrespective of the number of syllables it contains, should be of approximately equal length. To ensure that, for example, a foot of five syllables is of the same duration as of two syllables, various phonological processes operate on the unstressed syllables. For example, consonants in unstressed syllables may be elided:

'postmaster [pousmɑːstə]

Unstressed vowels may be reduced, usually to [ə], or [ɪ]. We can see vowel reduction most readily in cases where we have the same stem with different word endings added. With the addition of further syllables the stress shifts (usually towards the end of the word), and the syllable which was formerly stressed has its vowel reduced:

de'rive [dəraiv], de'rivative [dərɪvətɪv], deri'vation [derɪveiʃən]

You will notice that the stressed syllable has the full phonemic value, the one we would expect from the spelling. When the stress is removed the vowel is weakened. Sometimes instead of reducing, vowels can disappear altogether. When this happens the syllable is left without a vowel, and then, as we noted in section 4.1.3, one of the syllabic consonants, if present, takes over the function of the syllable. For example:

bottom [bɒtm̩],   thicken [θɪkn̩],   fiddle [fɪdl̩]

In some cases no syllabic consonant is present, and elision of the vowel may leave us with a 'syllable' which violates the phonotactics of English. For example:

should [ʃd],   there is [ðz]

Although we said above that stressed syllables tend to occur at regular intervals, this is only a tendency. Speakers may, and do, vary the rhythmical patterns of their speech. If a speaker were to use a single rhythmical pattern, he or she would sound monotonous, and hearers would soon lose interest in what was being said. To avoid sounding monotonous, speakers vary the rhythmical patterns they use. Such variations are most obvious in poetry. In the following extract, W. H. Auden controls the rhythmical pattern and creates a rhythm which echoes the sound of a train:

NIGHT MAIL

This is the night mail crossing the border,
Bringing the cheque and the postal order,

Letters for the rich, letters for the poor,
The shop at the corner, the girl next door.

Pulling up Beattock, a steady climb:
The gradient's against her, but she's on time.

Past cotton-grass and moorland boulder,
Shovelling white steam over her shoulder,

Snorting noisily, she passes
Silent miles of wind-bent grasses.

Finally, syllables which are stressed are more prominent not just in their loudness but also in the way the phonemes in the syllable are perceived.

In poetry, for example, sound patterns of stressed syllables are more important than those of unstressed ones. For example, a line of poetry which contains alliterating consonants at the beginning of stressed syllables will sound a lot more 'noisy' than one which has those consonants at the end of lightly stressed syllables. For example, compare:

*p*lay *p*ool with a *b*ig, *b*ad *c*annon*b*all

with:

o*b*servation is a sim*p*le necessi*t*y.

Further exercises

Exercise 4.1

Transcribe into phonetic script, and then provide syllable trees for the following monosyllabic words. Remember that the only obligatory elements in a syllable are the rhyme and the nucleus. Both the onset and the coda are optional.

groan, keep, dog, through, ooze, pain, thought, wipe, egg, lamb

Exercise 4.2

Consider the rhythmical patterns of the following poem. How does the rhythmical pattern contribute to the images created by the words?

INVERSNAID

This darksome burn, horseback brown,
His rollrock highroad roaring down,
In coop and in comb the fleece of his foam
Flutes and low to the lake falls home.

A windpuff-bonnet of fáwn-fróth
Turns and twindles over the broth
Of a pool so pitchblack, féll-frówning,
It rounds and rounds Despair to drowning.

Degged with dew, dappled with dew
Are the groins of the braes that the brook
      treads through,
Wiry heathpacks, flitches of fern,
And the beadbonny ash that sits over the burn.

What would the world be, once bereft
Of wet and of wilderness? Let them be left,
O let them be left, wildness and wet;
Long live the weeds and the wilderness yet.

(G. M. Hopkins)

Exercise 4.3

Look at the following verse of poetry and see how stress has highlighted some of the phonemes, and ask what effect this has had on the sound of the poem.

THE MOODS

Time drops in decay,
Like a candle burnt out,
And the mountains and woods
Have their day, have their day;
What one in the rout
Of the fire-born moods
Has fallen away?

(W. B. Yeats)

Glossary

Accent Accent refers to variation in pronunciation between speakers (or groups of speakers) of the same language. The variation may have either a social or a geographic base, and may be systemic, distributional, realisational, or selectional. *See also* **Dialect**.

Active articulator The articulator that moves during the production of a speech sound. In English the tongue and the lips are the active articulators.

Affricate Affricate is a manner of articulation. It involves a complete closure in the oral cavity followed by a slow release, which results in friction, for example the initial and final sounds in *judge* /dʒ/ are affricates.

Allophone An allophone is the phonetic realisation of a phoneme. The allophones of a phoneme are in complementary distribution, phonetically similar, and are predictable. Being predictable, allophones are rule governed, that is we can write a rule to account for the occurrence of each allophone.

Allophonic rule   Allophonic rules link the abstract phonemes to their phonetically real allophones (or underlying representations to surface ones).

Alveolar   This is a place of articulation. Alveolar sounds are produced by the tip/blade of the tongue articulating with the alveolar ridge, which lies behind the upper front teeth.

Ambisyllabic   We label a consonant or group of consonants which belong to more than one syllable ambisyllabic, for example in *extra* the /s/ and /t/ may belong to either the first or the second syllable – /ek.strə/, /eks.trə/, or /ekst.rə/.

Anterior   Anterior is one of the set of distinctive features. In English bi-labials, labio-dentals, dentals, and alveolars are [+anterior]. These sounds all involve, in their articulation, an obstruction to the flow of air in the area in front of the post-alveolar region. Any consonant made with such an articulation will be [+anterior]. All other consonants are [−anterior].

Approximant   Approximant is a manner of articulation. During the production of an approximant, the active and passive articulators come close to one another but not quite close enough to produce audible friction. [j] is an example of an approximant.

Articulation   Articulation is one of the three speech production processes. It can be divided into place of articulation (where an articulation occurs), and manner (what type of articulation). *See also* **Initiation** *and* **Phonation**.

Articulator   A part of the oral cavity that is directly involved in making a speech sound.

Aspiration   Aspiration is a short puff of breath which occurs between the release of a stop and the onset of voicing. In English the voiceless stops are aspirated when they are the only onset consonant in a stressed syllable.

Assimilation   The process by which one segment becomes more like another, or two segments become more like each other.

Back   Back is one of the place of articulation features. It is a member of the set of tongue body features. Back sounds are articulated with the tongue retracted from the rest position. Back vowels and velars are [+back], while all other segments are [−back].

Central   In the articulation of central sounds the tongue forms an air-tight seal with the upper molars and gums. This forces the airstream over the centre of the tongue. In English all sounds except /l/ are central. The articulation of some vowel sounds may also be referred to as central. Central vowels are articulated with the middle section of the tongue. In English, /ʌ/, /ɜ:/ and /ə/ are all central vowels.

Coda   In syllable structure the rhyme constituent consists of an obligatory nucleus and an optional coda. The optional coda consists of any post-vocalic consonants, for example, in *text* /kst/ constitute the coda.

Complementary distribution   Sounds which only ever occur in different (or mutually exclusive) environments are in complementary distribution. If the sounds in question are phonetically similar then it is more than likely that they are allophones of the same phoneme. For example, the palatalised allophone of /t/ only occurs before the palatal approximant, whereas the dentalised allophone only ever occurs next to a dental. These two sounds are in complementary distribution – we never find the palatalised allophone before a dental. Furthermore, they are phonetically similar. Therefore, they are allophones of the phoneme /t/.

Consonant   This is one of the major classes of sounds. Consonants occur at the margins of syllables (in the onset and coda) and not normally in the nucleus. They involve some obstruction (complete or partial) of the flow of air through the vocal tract, and therefore are usually defined in articulatory terms, that is voiced/voiceless, place of articulation, and manner of articulation.

Consonantal   Consonantal is one of the three classificatory distinctive features. (The others are syllabic and obstruent). These features allow us to distinguish between the two major classes of sounds in a language – vowels and consonants. Consonantal sounds are defined by stricture. All sounds which involve the presence of an obstruction in the oral tract are [+consonantal]. Stops, fricatives, affricates, nasals, and liquids are [+consonantal], while vowels and glides, which involve a free flow of air through the oral cavity, are [−consonantal].

Continuant   Continuant is a member of the set of manner features. All articulations which involve a stricture of complete closure are [−cont]. Oral and nasal stops, and affricates, are all, therefore, [−cont], while fricatives, approximants, and vowels are [+cont].

Contrastive distribution   Contrastive distribution involves two or more sounds which occur in identical environments and for which at least one minimal pair can be found, for example /p/ and /t/ occur in contrastive distribution in the words *pan* and *tan* – /pæn/ and /tæn/.

Coronal   Coronal is a member of the set of articulatory features. Only dentals, alveolars, post-alveolars, and palatals are coronal. These sounds are articulated with the blade of the tongue raised from the neutral position, which is identified in the discussion of the features high and low. All other consonants are [−coronal].

Defective distribution   This term is used to describe any phoneme which appears in some environments but not in others, for example /h/ appears only in syllable-initial position, whereas /ŋ/ appears only in syllable-final position.

Delayed release This is a manner of articulation feature. It is required to differentiate between stops and affricates. Affricates are articulated with a stricture of complete closure, which is gradually released causing the fricative phase of the affricate.

Dental Dental is a place of articulation involving the tip of the tongue and the front incisors. In English, /θ/ and /ð/ are both dental, while in French, /t/ and /d/ are dental and not alveolar as they are in English. We call the assimilation of a segment to the dental place of articulation dentalisation.

Derivation For most phonologists, surface representations (consisting of allophones) are derived from underlying ones (consisting of phonemes), through the application of allophonic rules. We usually refer to the process of deriving (or determining) the pronunciation of an underlying representation as a derivation.

Derived form Any representation to which one or more allophonic rules have been applied.

Devoicing Devoicing is an assimilatory process whereby a normally voiced segment is realised as voiceless. Devoicing may be either partial or full. In full devoicing, a segment which is normally voiced remains voiceless throughout its entire production. In a partial devoicing, the onset of voicing is delayed.

Dialect The term dialect refers to differences in pronunciation, syntax, morphology, and vocabulary, between speakers or groups of speakers. As with accent these differences may have either a social or a geographical basis. *See also* **Accent**.

Diphthong A vowel of continually changing quality within one syllable is a diphthong. The change in quality may be caused by a movement of the tongue and/or lips. The vowels in *house*, *high*, and *toy* are all diphthongs.

Distinctive feature Distinctive features are the fundamental units of phonology. They are smaller than phonemes, which are composed of sets of features. The features are usually binary (they have two values, + or −). We use the term distinctive because the features are primarily intended to capture only the phonological (or distinctive) oppositions in any language, and not necessarily the phonetic realisation of these oppositions.

Distributional difference This is one of the four ways in which dialects may differ. The dialects in question have the same set of phonemes, but the distribution of certain phonemes may differ between the dialects in question, for example all dialects of English possess a voiced alveolar central approximant – /r/, but in southern British English /r/ is restricted to pre-vocalic position only, while in Ulster

English it has a full distribution. It occurs before vowels, consonants, and pauses. *See also* **Realisational**, **Selectional** *and* **Systemic differences**.

Elision   Elision is the deletion of a segment normally present in the stream of speech.

Epenthesis   Epenthesis is the insertion of segments not normally present in careful speech.

Feature matrix   A feature matrix is a column of features which specify a single segment.

Features   *See* **Distinctive features**.

Flap   *See* **Tap**.

Foot   The foot is a metrical unit consisting of a stressed syllable and all unstressed syllables up to but not including the next stressed syllable.

Free variation   We refer to the suspension of phonemic contrast in isolated examples as free variation. For example, although /i:/ and /ai/ contrast in English (and are therefore phonemes), in [i:ðə] vs [aiðə] the contrast is suspended. The substitution of /ai/ for /i:/ (or vice versa) does not in this case result in a different word.

Fricative   Fricative is a manner of articulation. In the production of a fricative, the active articulator comes sufficiently close to the passive one to impede the flow of air but not to stop it completely. As the airstream is squeezed through the narrow gap between the articulators it becomes turbulent, and an audible hiss is produced. [f v s z] are all fricatives.

Front vowel   In the articulation of front vowels the tongue is not retracted in the oral cavity. [i:] is an example of a front vowel.

Fusion   Fusion is a process whereby two segments fuse together to form a third segment which shares features of the two input segments. For example, in English, /t/ and /j/ often fuse together to form [tʃ].

Glide   Glides are a subset of approximants. The glides are also called semi-vowels. Phonetically glides are very short vowels, but phonologically they behave like consonants.

Hard palate   The hard palate is a bone that separates the oral cavity from the nasal cavity. It runs from the alveolar ridge to the beginning of the velum or soft palate. Sounds for which an active articulator moves towards or articulates with the hard palate are palatal.

High   High is one of the set of distinctive features. Like back and low it is a tongue body feature. If the tongue is raised above the rest position the sound produced is assigned the feature high. Palatal and velar consonants, and high vowels, are all [+high], while labial and dental consonants, and non-high vowels are all [−high].

Homorganic   Sequences of consonants which share the same place of articulation are homorganic, for example /n/ and /t/ in *dent* /dent/.

Illicit cluster   Illicit clusters are those consonant clusters which are ruled out by the general phonotactic rules of the language.

Initiation   Initiation is one of the three speech production processes. Initiation involves the creation of an airstream, which may then be modified by the articulatory and/or phonatory processes. *See also* **Articulation** *and* **Phonation**.

Intonation   Intonation is a suprasegmental feature. It involves a limited number of recurrent pitch movements or patterns. Each pitch pattern may be used to convey the speaker's attitude to the topic of conversation, or to the hearer, or the speaker's personality, or to signal grammatical features such as whether a sentence is a question.

Labial   Labial is a place of articulation. Any sound involving the lips in its articulation is labial. In English there are six labial sounds: two labial stops – /p b/; one labial nasal /m/; two labio-dental fricatives – /f v/; and a labio-velar approximant – /w/.

Larynx   The larynx is positioned at the top of the trachea (windpipe). It is a box-like construction consisting of cartilage. The protuberance known as the 'Adam's apple' is the top of the larynx. The vocal cords are located inside the larynx just below the level of the Adam's apple.

Lateral   If the tongue forms an air-tight seal at some point in the centre of the vocal tract, then escaping air will pass round this obstruction and out over the sides of the tongue. The manner of articulation involved is described as lateral, for example the initial sound in *lateral* is a lateral. The feature [±lateral] is used to distinguish laterals from non-laterals (centrals).

Lateral escape   In non-homorganic stop–lateral clusters the airstream trapped by the stop escapes over the sides of the tongue.

Lateral release   Lateral release occurs in homorganic stop–lateral sequences. The stop is released by the lowering of the sides of the tongue.

Liquid   Liquid consonants, in English /l/ and /r/, are a subset of approximants. Unlike glides, liquids are phonetically consonants and they behave phonologically like consonants.

Low   Low is one of the set of tongue body features. Low sounds are those produced with tongue lowered from the rest position. The only segments, in English, which are [+low] are the low vowels. All other segments are [−low].

Mid vowel   A mid vowel is articulated with the tongue departing little from its rest position. Mid vowels are articulated between the position of high vowels and low vowels. [e] is a mid vowel.

Minimal pair test   The minimal pair test is a simple and effective means for identifying the phonemes of any language. The test uses the notion of minimal contrast through the minimal pairs to identify phonemes.

Minimal pair   Two words which differ in one and only one sound are a minimal pair, e.g *pit* and *pot*, or *pip* and *pit*.

Monophthong   A monophthong is a vowel the quality of which remains relatively unchanged throughout its production, for example /ɪ/ and /æ/ are both monophthongs.

Nasal   Nasal is a manner of articulation. The term is usually applied to sounds that involve a complete obstruction in the oral cavity, that is a stop, but for which the velum is in the lowered position. This allows air to escape through the nasal cavity. The position of the velum is independent of all other speech production processes. Consequently, although we find only voiced nasal stops in English, it is possible for nasals to be voiceless, and for any segment to be articulated with the velum in the lowered position. In this latter case we describe the sound as being nasalised, for example the vowel sound in the French word *bon* – /b�õ/ – is nasalised. Nasalisation is signalled through the placing of ~ over the nasalised sound.

Nasal release   Oral stops may be released either by releasing the closure in the oral cavity or by lowering the velum. We refer to the second possibility as nasal release.

Natural class   A group of two or more segments which share one or more phonetic features.

Nucleus   The nucleus is the obligatory constituent of a syllable. It must be either a vowel or one of the few consonants which may function as the nucleus in the absence of a vowel. In English, only /l m/ and /n/ may function as a syllable nucleus.

Obstruent   This is one of the three classificatory features. The other two are consonantal and syllabic. Obstruents are a subset of the class of consonants. All obstruents involve a radical obstruction of the air flow at some point in the vocal tract. Consequently, oral stops, fricatives and affricates are [+obstruent]. Nasals, liquids, glides, and vowels are [−obstruent]. Non-obstruents are also referred to as sonorants.

Onset   This term refers to the optional initial consonant or consonants of a syllable, for example in *string* /strɪŋ/ the onset is /str/.

Orthography   Orthography is the writing system of a language.

Palatal   Palatal is a place of articulation. Palatal sounds involve the front of the tongue and the hard palate. The sound at the beginning of *yacht* is palatal. Assimilation of a segment towards the palate is palatalisation.

Parallel distribution   Two or more sounds are in parallel distribution when they occur in identical environments.

Passive articulator   In the articulation of a speech sound an active articulator moves towards a passive one. Passive articulators do not move. In English the passive articulators are the teeth and the points on the roof of the mouth.

Pharynx   This is part of the vocal tract. It extends from behind the velum to the larynx.

Phonation   Phonation is one of the three speech production processes. Phonation involves the modification of the air stream from the lungs by the vocal cords. The main phonation types in English are voiced and voiceless. *See also* **Articulation** *and* **Initiation**.

Phoneme   A single sound segment which is contrastive in a language.

Phonemic system   A list of the phonemes of a language or dialect.

Phonetic similarity   For two or more sounds to be considered allophones of a single phoneme they must not only be in complementary distribution, but also phonetically similar to each other.

Phonetics   Phonetics is the scientific study of the production, perception, and analysis of speech sounds.

Phonological conditioning   If the distribution of allomorphs is determined by phonological factors then we say that the allomorphs are phonologically conditioned.

Phonology   Phonology is the study of the function and organisation of sounds in a particular language, or in language in general. A phonological analysis includes: the identification of distinctive units (phonemes or features), the assigning of an underlying or phonological representation to all the items in the lexicon, a list of all the rules which link underlying representations to surface ones, a statement of the phonotactics, and prosodic features.

Phonotactics   Phonotactics are a list of restrictions on the distribution of segments, possible combinations of segments into clusters, and admissible syllable types.

Pitch   Pitch, a suprasegmental, is the property of a sound which allows a hearer to judge it as either high or low. It is related to the frequency at which the vocal cords vibrate.

Potential cluster Potential clusters are consonant clusters which are not ruled out by the general phonotactic restrictions of the language, and have to be specifically identified and ruled out. *See* **Illicit clusters**.

Prosody   *See* **Suprasegmental**.

Realisational difference This is one of the four ways in which dialects of a language may differ. Two dialects may possess the same number of phonemic oppositions but differ in the phonetic realisation of particular phonemes. For example both southern British English and New Zealand English possess an opposition between the vowels in *bit* and *bet*. However, in New Zealand English the vowel in *bit* is more central than its counterpart in southern British English, while the vowel in *bet* is realised slightly higher. *See also* **Distributional**, **Selectional** *and* **Systemic differences**.

Rhotic A rhotic dialect of English has the phoneme /r/ fully distributed, i.e. before vowels, consonants and pauses. Scottish English is fully rhotic whereas Australian English is not.

Rhyme The rhyme is an obligatory constituent of a syllable. It consists of an obligatory nucleus and an optional coda. *See also* **Coda**, **Nucleus**, *and* **Syllabic consonant**.

Rhythm Rhythm can be defined as the regular occurrence of an event. In language, rhythmical patterns arise from the alternation between stressed and unstressed syllables, and the regular occurrence of stressed syllables.

Round Round is a distinctive feature which refers to the position of the lips in the articulation of a sound. In English the vowels /ɒ ɔː uː/ and the labio-velar approximant /w/ are [+round].

Selectional difference This is one of the four ways in which dialects of a language may differ. With selectional differences, two dialects have the same set of phonemic contrasts but particular words select different phonemes in each dialect. Again this is best illustrated with an example. The vowels /iː/ and /ɪ/ occur in both British and New Zealand English. However, for example in *cloudy*, speakers of British English select /ɪ/ as the final vowel, while New Zealand English speakers select /iː/. *See also* **Distributional**, **Realisational**, *and* **Systemic differences**.

Soft palate *See* **Velum.**

Sonorant In articulatory terms, sonorants are approximants, nasals, and vowels, and non-sonorants are stops, fricatives, and affricates.

Stop Stop refers to a manner of articulation. For all stops an air-tight seal is formed at some point in the vocal tract. This completely obstructs (or stops) the flow of air from the lungs. In English, [p b t d k g m n] and [ŋ] all involve an air-tight seal in their production, and therefore, are all stops.

Stress In an utterance, some syllables appear more prominent in relation to their neighbours. We refer to this relative prominence as stress. Length, loudness, pitch, and quality all contribute to a speaker's perception of a syllable as prominent or stressed.

Stress timed   A kind of rhythm which English has where the length of time between stressed syllables is roughly equal no matter how many unstressed syllables come between the stressed syllables.

Strident   This is an acoustic feature. Strident sounds are characterised by high-frequency noise. These sounds are often referred to as sibilants. Contrast [s] and [θ] in English. [s] is a sibilant and is, therefore, [+strident], while [θ], which is not a sibilant, is [−strident]. The labiodental, alveolar and post-alveolar fricatives, and the affricates in English are [+strid]. All other segments are [−strid].

Suprasegmental   Suprasegmentals are those aspects of speech production which involve more than a single segment. Stress, tone and intonation are all suprasegmental features. Another term for these features is **prosody**.

Surface representation   The term surface representation refers to a phonetic word form, of which the constituent parts are phonetically real allophones.

Syllabic   Syllabic is one of the three classificatory distinctive features. The other two are obstruent and consonantal. Only those sounds that function as the nucleus of a syllable are syllabic. As vowels are always the nucleus of a syllable, they are [+syllabic]. All consonants, with the exception of the syllabic consonants, are [−syllabic].

Syllabic consonant   A syllabic consonant is any consonant which is functioning as the obligatory nucleus of a syllable. In English only /l m/ and /n/ may function as the nucleus of a syllable.

Syllable   The syllable is a phonological unit which may be larger than a single segment. It contains an obligatory nucleus, and optional initial and final consonant clusters. The syllable types and consonant clusters (if any) permitted in a language are defined by the phonotactic rules of the language.

Systemic difference   This is one of the four ways in which dialects may differ. Dialects which differ systemically have different phonemic systems, for example Scottish English has a voiceless velar fricative, /x/, which other dialects lack. *See also* **Distributional**, **Realisational**, *and* **Selectional differences**.

Tap   Tap and flap are manners of articulation. In the articulation of taps and flaps, the active articulator makes a single fast contact with the passive one. In many US dialects of English the alveolar stops are articulated as taps when they occur between two vowels, for example the *t* in *phonetic* would be a voiced alveolar tap − [ɾ].

Tone   Tone is the term used to refer to pitch movements. In some languages tone is phonemic, that is it is used to distinguish words, for example in Thai the meaning of /naa/ changes with the tone: /naa/

plus a high tone means 'young maternal aunt or uncle', but when uttered with a mid tone it means 'rice paddy'. In English, tones are the major changes in pitch which occur on a tonic syllable. Each pitch pattern or tone is associated with a typical meaning.

Tone group   A tone group may consist of a single syllable or a number of syllables over which an intonation contour extends. All tone groups contain an obligatory tonic syllable.

Tonic syllable   The tonic syllable is the obligatory element in a tone group. The tonic syllable will be stressed but more prominent than other stressed syllables in the tone group. We call this additional prominence tonic stress. It also carries the major change of pitch, which will be one of the intonation tones found in the language.

Trill   Trill is a manner of articulation. For trills the active articulator is positioned so that the airstream flowing over it causes it to vibrate rapidly against the passive one. The vocal tract is alternately open and closed. In some dialects of Scottish English the sound at the beginning of *rabbit* is a voiced alveolar trill.

Underlying representation   An underlying representation is the phonemic representation of a sound or word. It is an abstract representation, and is also referred to as the lexical or dictionary form.

Uvula   The uvula is the pendulum-like end of the velum. It is a place of articulation and any sound involving the uvula as the passive articulator is uvular.

Velum   The velum is a muscle that separates the nasal and oral cavities. It may be raised to form a seal with the pharynx closing off the nasal cavity. This is called velic closure. Any sound involving the velum as a passive articulator is velar. In English the sounds at the beginning of *call* and *golf*, and the sound at the end of *hang*, are velar. We refer to the assimilation of a sound to the velum as velarisation.

Voice   Voice refers to the buzzing sound created by the vibration of the vocal cords. Any sound for whose production the vocal cords vibrate is voiced, for example /b d g m n ŋ v ð z ʒ dʒ l r w j/. Sounds produced without the vocal cords vibrating are voiceless, for example /p t k f s ʃ tʃ/. As well as a phonetic aspect of speech production, voice also occurs as a distinctive feature. All voiced segments are [+voice], and all voiceless segments are [−voice].

Voicing   This is an assimilation process whereby a normally voiceless sound is realised as voiced under the influence of a neighbouring voiced sound.

Vowel   Vowels function as the nucleus of a syllable. They are usually defined through reference to tongue position on vertical and horizontal axes, and lip position, rather than through place and type of stricture.

Further reading

Brown, G., *Listening to Spoken English* (London: Longman, 1977).

Brown, G., Currie, K. L., and Kenworthy, J., *Questions of Intonation* (London: Croom Helm, 1980).

Carr, P., *Phonology* (London: Macmillan, 1993).

Catford, J. C., *A Practical Introduction to Phonetics* (Oxford: Oxford University Press, 1988).

Chambers, J. K., and Trudgill, P., *Dialectology* (Cambridge: Cambridge University Press, 1980).

Chomsky, N., and Halle, M., *The Sound Pattern of English* (New York: Harper Row, 1968).

Cruttenden, A., *Intonation* (Cambridge: Cambridge University Press, 1986).

Crystal, D., *The English Tone of Voice* (London: Edward Arnold, 1975).

Durand, J., *Generative and Non-Linear Phonology* (London: Longman, 1990).

Francis, W. N., *Dialectology: An Introduction* (London: Longman, 1983).

Geigerich, H., *English Phonology: An Introduction* (Cambridge: Cambridge University Press, 1992).

Gimson, A. C., *An Introduction to the Pronunciation of English,* 4th edn (London: Edward Arnold, 1989).

Halliday, M. A. K., *A Course in Spoken English Intonation* (Oxford: Oxford University Press, 1970).

Hawkins, P., *Introducing Phonology* (London: Routledge, 1992).

Kreidler, C. W., *The Pronunciation of English: A Coursebook in Phonology* (Oxford: Blackwell, 1989).

Ladefoged, P., *A Course in Phonetics* (New York: Harcourt Brace Jovanovich, 1975).

Lass, R., *Phonology: An Introduction to Basic Concepts* (Cambridge: Cambridge University Press, 1984).

Macaulay, R. K. S., and Trevelyan, G. D., *Language, Social Class and Education: A Glasgow Study* (Edinburgh: Edinburgh University Press, 1977).

O'Connor, J. D., *Phonetics* (Harmondsworth: Pelican, 1973).

Roach, P., *English Phonetics and Phonology: A Practical Course* (Cambridge: Cambridge University Press, 1983).

PART II

Words

Introduction to Part II

Concepts

In this section you will be introduced to the formal properties of words, that is, their grammatical category and their internal structure. You will then look at the meanings of words and at various ways in which groups of words form vocabularies through being used by different speakers and for different uses, and how vocabularies may be added to or lose words.

Skills

By the end of the chapter you should be able to recognise the major syntactic categories: noun, verb, adjective, adverb and preposition. You should be able to determine the internal structure of words belonging to these categories, and be able to draw tree diagrams of their structure.

5 The form and function of words

Introduction: dictionaries and lexemes

When people think of what is central to their language, they often turn to its dictionary, the written repository of its words. This is in part because there is a widespread belief that words *are* the language. Although this is a half-truth it is certainly the case that one of the major tasks anyone has in learning a language is acquiring their own lexicon, their internalised store of words (to distinguish it from the written dictionary).

lexicon

We can get an initial idea of what knowing a word involves by looking at a dictionary entry. Dictionaries attempt to represent what a fully literate native speaker of a language knows about the words listed in the dictionary. Since you will be familiar with dictionaries, they are a useful place to start.

Examine the following simple dictionary entry taken from the *Oxford Dictionary of Current English*.

Sept, *n*. Clan, esp. in Ireland.

First comes the spelling of the word. In some dictionary entries the written spelling of the word is followed by a representation of its pronunciation in some form of phonetic script. These two forms of spelling, orthographic and phonetic, represent the word's *phonological form*.

While a word may have just one phonological form, this is not always the case. Look, for example, at *go* and *went*. Native speakers of English know that these are different forms of the same word. Because of cases such as this it is necessary to distinguish between the abstract item of vocabulary GO and the phonological or orthographic shapes which it can take. We can think of these shapes as the abstract vocabulary item's realisations (in sound or print). Linguists term such an abstract vocabulary word a lexeme, on analogy with phonemes which, as you found in the previous section, are also abstract units which have more concrete realisations in the form of allophones. It follows that a single lexeme can have a variety of word-form realisations.

lexeme

part of speech

grammatical category
syntactic category

semantic representation

Next in the dictionary entry for *sept* comes its part of speech label. For example, in the above word the letter n. is an abbreviation for noun. Every word in the dictionary has one of these labels. What it represents is the word's grammatical or syntactic category, indicated by a syntactic category label. The syntactic category label of a word is a kind of summary of its grammatical properties. In essence these properties determine the locations which the word can occupy in phrases. All words belong to a grammatical category, with a very small number of exceptions. These are words which are never part of a phrase or sentence. The word *yes* is a case in point. If you think of where the word *yes* is used in a sentence then you will find that it is never part of a phrase or a sentence. For example, *yes* is not a word that can function in phrases like **the old yes*, **has been yessing the grass*, **yes the lawns*. (Asterisks here indicate that these are ungrammatical phrases.) In fact it seems that *yes* is a one-word sentence. Therefore, it cannot have a syntactic category label, as it never functions as a sub-part of a phrase or sentence.

Third in the above dictionary entry comes a gloss for the meaning of the word. Most words have meanings which speakers can readily identify, such as the meaning of the word *horse*. So if you want to know the meaning of the word *sept* you look at this section of the dictionary entry, where you find a phrase or sentence or two which gives you the meaning of the word but expressed in different words. It should be noted, however, that just as *yes* does not have a grammatical category, not all words have easily definable meanings. This is clear when one looks up the meaning of a word like *of* in a phrase such as *the pursuit of happiness*. Other words, such as *this* and *a*, have important grammatical roles to play. However difficult it may be to pin down exactly what their meaning is, they clearly are not entirely meaningless. But the word *of* in the *pursuit of happiness* seems only to have a phonological form and grammatical category, and no meaning in any clear sense.

We can call the representation of the meanings or senses of a lexeme its semantic representation.

So a word, or, as we can now say, a lexeme, generally speaking, is a three-part symbol. It has a form or a number of forms, category and meaning arbitrarily linked together. In looking at lexemes in this part of the book we will be looking at all three of these aspects in turn.

The properties of lexemes we have just glanced at are strictly linguistic, that is they form part of the knowledge which speakers have of their native language. However, when we examine how words are used, they also appear to have a social aspect. Again using a dictionary for illustration, one sometimes finds words listed with indications as to how they should be used. For example, the abbreviation *vulg.*, short for *vulgar*, is often used to indicate that one should be careful about using such a word in polite company.

Furthermore, sets of words are often used by members of particular groups. This can be seen through the large number of specialist dictionaries which exist. There are dictionaries for foreign language learners, for biologists, dictionaries of slang and dictionaries of idioms. Later in this part of the book we will look at how words are used, and at the sub-lexicons, which contain various kinds of vocabularies for particular purposes.

5.1 Words and their grammatical categories: syntactic categories and inflection

5.1.1 *Introduction*

As we saw above, in a dictionary the words of a language are classified by grammatical category. In this section we will look at grammatical categories and how words may be assigned to particular categories. The reason for examining this property of words first is that the later section in this chapter, where we look at the internal structure of words, depends on being able to identify a word's grammatical category.

The speakers of a language recognise not only the words of their language, but also that words fit in different places in phrases and sentences. On the basis of where they fit, words can be classed into different categories. Speakers of English may not know the names of these categories or the principles by which words are assigned to categories, but they are aware that, for example, *wombat* and *stupid* are different in a rather basic way. If you are uncertain about this, try inserting each in turn in the following frame: a ____ idea. We will find that this difference is because they belong to different syntactic categories.

At this stage in our exploration of syntactic categories we have said only that syntactic categories indicate the function which words have in phrases and sentences. However, we have not said anything in detail about phrases and sentences themselves, and will not be looking at phrases and sentences seriously until Part III. Fortunately this does not prevent us from looking at syntactic categories in a preliminary way. It happens that particular syntactic categories of words often have characteristic grammatical endings which change the form of the word. We can use these as a partial way to identify at least some syntactic categories. We can also look at some of the functions of lexical categories as a way of supporting the analysis based on the word's grammatical endings.

Before looking at the specific grammatical categories of English lexemes we need to look in a little more detail at the way they change their form. Look, for example, at the lexeme TRY. Depending on how it is functioning it can take any of the following forms: *try, tries, tried, trying*, as in the following sentences: *The horse must try, The horse tries, The horse tried, The horse is trying*. We can call each of these forms a grammatical word form of the lexeme, since it is the grammar of English which requires the lexeme TRY to have these different forms in different syntactic contexts. The grammatical endings which create

inflection
stem

morphology

morphosyntactic category

morphosyntactic property

these different grammatical word forms are termed inflections. The form of the lexeme to which they are attached is termed the stem. The processes whereby words come to have internal structure such as a stem and inflection are morphological processes, the morphology of words having to do with their internal structure. Since inflections are associated with both the morphological structure of words and the syntactic functions of words, the categories for which words inflect are often called morphosyntactic categories. Tense, which accounts for the past-tense inflection *–ed* in *tri–ed*, is an example of a morphosyntactic category. Properties such as present tense or past tense are therefore morphosyntactic properties.

The categories which we will look at in this section are four major lexical categories: nouns, adjectives, verbs and adverbs. We will be looking at the morphosyntactic categories for which they inflect. At the section's conclusion we will briefly look at prepositions, although these do not have any characteristic grammatical endings.

5.1.2   *Nouns*

noun

Traditionally, a noun is a naming word; typically the name of a person, place, or thing. For example:

> *snake, rat, alligator, Fred, chainsaw, lawnmower*

are all nouns. For each of the above words we can find a set of objects to which the word is normally used to refer (although the name of a particular snake, rat, or alligator may be *Fred* or *Freda* for those with whom the animal is on intimate terms).

Consider the following nouns. Do they pose any problems for our definition of a noun?

anger, fame, cyclops, Zeus, Hamlet, Lilliput, furniture

It is impossible to point to an object in the physical world to which these words refer. Anger is a feeling and fame is an abstract quality; cyclops, and Zeus are both mythical beings; Hamlet is a fictional character, while Lilliput is a fictitious place. Furniture is not a person or a place or a thing either, or even a set of objects. In fact it isn't any particular thing but a class of things. Unlike alligators, where we can say of a particular alligator, 'That's an alligator,' we cannot say when pointing to a chair, 'That's a furniture.' So although their meaning may be useful in identifying some nouns, we must look elsewhere for some supporting facts about nouns if we are to become more familiar with them and be able to tell whether a particular word is a noun. To do that we will look at the inflections which nouns characteristically take.

Most nouns inflect for the morphosyntactic category of number and, as such, have a plural form like *–s* or *–es*. For example:

snapper	snappers
bee	bees
rosella	rosellas
box	boxes

Some nouns mark their plural in other ways, for example:

foot	feet
mouse	mice
louse	lice
child	children
ox	oxen

Other nouns never mark their plurals overtly:

sheep	sheep
deer	deer

while some nouns never occur without the plural marker, for example *scissors* and *trousers*. These are facts about the form of nouns. If a word has plural form, then it belongs to the category *noun*. (Note that the reverse does not follow: namely, that if a word has no plural form then it is not a noun.)

Notice that although words like *sheep* and *deer* do not take an ending to indicate that they are plural, they do have a plural form. It happens to be identical to their singular form. On the basis of this we can see the necessity to make a distinction between a lexeme and a grammatical word. There are two grammatical words with the word form *sheep*. One is the singular form of the lexeme SHEEP and the other the plural form. So SHEEP is a noun because it has a plural form.

grammatical word

We can also identify nouns by looking at the words that typically appear with them in a sentence or phrase. (Let us suppose for the time being that a phrase is a grammatically complete part of a sentence. We'll look at phrases in Part III.)

Most nouns appear with either *a(n)* or *the*, or refer to things that can be counted, for example:

a wombat	the wombat	three wombats
a barbecue	the barbecue	one barbecue

Consider the following list of nouns, and divide them into the following groups: nouns that can take *a(n)*, nouns that can take *the*, nouns that have a plural form, and nouns that refer to things that can be counted. Some nouns will appear in more than one group.

alligator, wombat, Pittsburg, video, lawnmower, butter, Fred.

Your answer should look like this:

	a(n)	the	plural	count
alligator	√	√	√	√
wombat	√	√	√	√
Pittsburg	×	×	×	×
video	√	√	√	√
lawnmower	√	√	√	√
butter	×	√	×	×
Fred	×	×	×	×

Notice that our nouns fall into three groups: those which appear in all four groups, those which appear in one group, and those which appear in none of the groups. The set which appear in all four groups are called **count noun, non-count noun** count nouns, those that appear in only one group are called non-count **proper noun** nouns, while those that appear in none of the groups are proper nouns. In English, proper nouns, typically the names of people and places, always begin with a capital letter. The nouns that appeared in all four groups, together with those that appeared in only one group, are called **common noun** common nouns.

In English, *a(n)* does not occur with mass nouns (that is, non-count nouns which refer to uncountable substances such as *putty*), and mass nouns do not have plurals.

The properties of nouns we have just looked at concern the way nouns are arranged in grammatical sequences with other categories of word. In **distribution** other words, nouns are nouns because of their distribution, i.e. where they come in grammatical sequences relative to where other words come.

So we have looked at nouns now from the perspective of both their form and a little of their function.

Exercise 5.1

Find the nouns in the following poem:

THE SICK ROSE

Oh rose, thou art sick!
The invisible worm,
That flies in the night
In the howling storm,

Has found out thy bed
Of crimson joy:
And his dark secret love
Does thy life destroy.

(William Blake)

* * * * * * * * *

5.1.3 *Adjectives*

Traditionally adjectives ascribe a property or quality to an object, for example: **adjective**

the *ripe* apple   the *evil* alligator

Adjectives may take two different endings, giving three forms, for example:

big   bigger   biggest
tall   taller   tallest

The adjective without the ending is called the standard form and represents the positive degree of comparison. The one with the *–er* ending is the comparative, and is used when we compare two objects for the same property. For example: **standard form** **positive** **comparative**

My dad is taller than your dad.

The *–est* ending is called the superlative (literally: raised above), and is used when we are comparing three or more objects for the same property. For example: **superlative**

Your dad may be taller than my dad but Raewyn's dad is the tallest.

Not all adjectives take the *–er* and *–est* endings; some use *more* and *most*. For example:

evil   more evil   most evil
incredible   more incredible   most incredible

comparison

The morphosyntactic category which has the morphosyntactic properties of comparative and superlative is called comparison. The unmarked form of the adjective shows the positive morphosyntactic property of this category. In other words, adjectives which show comparison show it in three forms: the simple positive form, the comparative form, and the superlative form.

Consider the following list of adjectives, and divide them into three groups: those which take the *-er* and *-est* endings, those which take *more* and *most*, and those which take neither of the above.

high, wide, dead, red, medical, ugly, narrow, absolute, painful, final

Answer:

	−er, −est	more, most	neither
high	√	×	×
wide	√	×	×
dead	×	×	√
red	√	×	×
medical	×	×	√
ugly	√	√	×
narrow	√	×	×
absolute	×	×	√
painful	×	√	×
final	×	×	√

gradable, non-gradable

Those adjectives that have comparative and superlative forms are called gradable, while those that do not are called non-gradable. What we mean by gradable is that there are degrees of the particular property rather than just the presence or absence of it. A medical bill cannot be more or less medical, at least as far as the English language is concerned.

As to their function, English adjectives may appear either before a noun or after a form of the verb *to be* (*am, is, are, was, were, being,* or *been*), for example:

the ripe apple	the apple is ripe
the evil alligator	the alligator is evil

Not all adjectives may appear in both of these positions. Some may only appear before nouns, while others may only appear after a form of the verb *to be*.

Consider the following list of adjectives. Which may appear only before a noun, which may appear only after the verb *to be*, and which may appear in both positions?

older, elder, hungry, ill, red, ugly, afraid, utter, incredible, loath.

Your answer might look like this:

	Before nouns		After *to be*	Both
older	√	√	√	
elder	√	×	×	
hungry	√	√	√	
ill	×	√	×	
red	√	√	√	
ugly	√	√	√	
afraid	×	√	×	
utter	√	×	×	
incredible	√	√	√	
loath	×	√	×	

Exercise 5.2

Find the adjectives in the following poem:

THE LILY

The modest Rose puts forth a thorn,
The humble Sheep a threat'ning horn;
While the Lily white shall in love delight,
Nor a thorn nor a threat stain her beauty bright.

(William Blake)

* * * * * * * * * *

Application
Below is a portion of a short story with its adjectives in italics. What would the description be like without the adjectives?

His name described him better than I can. He looked like a *great*, *stupid*, *smiling* bear. His *black matted* head bobbed forward and his *long* arms hung out as though he should have been on all fours and was only standing upright as a trick. His legs were *short* and *bowed*, ending in *strange*, *square* feet. He was dressed in *dark blue* denim, but his feet were *bare*; they didn't seem to be *crippled* or *deformed* in any way, but they were *square*, just as *wide* as they were *long*.

(John Steinbeck, 'Johnny Bear')

* * * * * * * * * *

If you remove the adjectives which come after forms of *to be*, the sentences become ungrammatical. When you remove all the adjectives which come before nouns, as well, there is virtually no description left.

5.1.4   *Verbs*

lexical verb
auxiliary verb

The grammatical class of verbs may be divided into two groups – lexical verbs and auxiliary verbs. The class of auxiliaries is quite small, and contains the following: *has, had, have, be, is, are, was, were, do, does, did, can, could, shall, should, will, would, may, might*, and *must*. We will look at these verbs in more detail in Part III. In this section we will concentrate on the class of lexical verbs.

Traditionally verbs are defined as denoting actions or states, for example *eat, drink, run, speak, forgive, understand, hate*. The first four of these verbs denote actions, that is, in doing these things we perform some physical action, while the final three denote states, that is, we can 'do' these things without performing any physical action.

English verb lexemes have more grammatical words associated with them than either nouns or adjectives. Each verb lexeme has five associated grammatical words. The changes in form associated with each grammatical word, listed below, are often brought about by adding an inflection to the verb.

V	V–s	V–ed	V–ing	V–en
call	calls	called	calling	called

Let us look at the morphosyntactic categories that give rise to these different grammatical words and word forms. The first category is tense. All English verbs can take tense and there are two tenses: past and present. The present tense form of CALL is *call* and the past tense form is *called*. You may ask what happens to the future in English. The future is not indicated by a word form but can be indicated by other means, such as the auxiliary verb *will* as in *will call*.

The next inflected form, the one ending in –*s*, indicates a number of morphosyntactic categories. It is found only if the verb to which it is attached is in the present tense, the noun in front of it in a simple two-word sentence must be singular and can be substituted for by *he*, *she*, or *it*, for example:

he, she, it, the postman, Mary/call*s* in the morning.

Such nouns are in what is termed the third person: not the speaker, who is the first person, or the person being addressed, the second person, but the person or thing spoken about, the third person. So here we have an inflection which indicates the state of not one morphosyntactic category but three: tense, number and person.

The V–ing and V–en forms are called participles. The V–ing form is the progressive participle and the V–en form is called the perfect participle. We will discuss the function of these participles in Part III. The simple form of verbs without any endings is called the infinitive. It is often introduced by the word *to*, for example, *to call*.

participle
progressive participle
perfect participle
infinitive

Verbs like *call* are regular, and regular verbs form the majority of verbs in English. For regular verbs the past tense form and the perfect participle form are identical. So how can we tell that these identical forms represent different grammatical words? In part because they have different functions in phrases and sentences, but also because, in the case of irregular verbs, the forms are different. There are about 200 irregular verbs:

V-stem	V–s	V–ed	V–ing	V–en
meet	meets	met	meeting	met
put	puts	put	putting	put
write	writes	wrote	writing	written
bring	brings	brought	bringing	brought

These verbs are all irregular in one way or another. All the verbs above, both regular and irregular, have regular V–s and progressive participle forms. The differences occur in the past tense and perfect participle.

These two forms of *meet* are identical, and are formed not by adding –*ed* to the stem, but by having a different vowel phoneme in the stem of the word. Other verbs that follow this pattern include *bleed* (*bled*) and *feed* (*fed*). *Write* and *bring* similarly change their stem vowels in the past tense (*wrote* and *brought*) and perfect participle forms (*written* and *brought*). Other verbs that also do this include; *sing*, *ring*, *ride*, and *strive*.

Put does not change at all in its past tense and perfect participle forms. *Hit* is another verb that follows this pattern.

We can now note that not all changes of word form are by way of inflection, that is the addition of an ending. Some morphosyntactic categories are realised in particular lexemes by changes to the stem of the lexeme.

If the verb *to concorde*, meaning 'to fly at supersonic speed', were to be added to the language would it follow the regular pattern or one of the irregular patterns? If there were more groups of irregular verbs, and these groups were larger, would this cause any problems for someone trying to learn English?

Any new verb would follow the regular pattern. In fact the classes of irregular verbs have been getting smaller over the centuries. If the irregular classes were more numerous, and larger, then this would make learning English more difficult. Rather than learning that the past tense and perfect participle forms of most verbs are formed by adding –*ed* to a base, we would have to remember which class a verb belonged to and how that class formed its past tense and perfect participle forms. It is interesting that young children frequently show how the regular form is used by using it on an irregular verb. For example, a child may say *I bringed my doggy*. For them, the regular forms allow them to use the past tense, while later they can and do learn all the exceptions.

Exercise 5.3

Find the verbs in the following poem:

NURSE'S SONG

When the voices of children are heard on the green
And whisp'rings are in the dale
The days of my youth rise fresh in my mind,
My face turns green and pale.

Then come home my children, the sun is gone down,
And the dews of night arise,
Your spring and your day are wasted in play,
And your winter and night in disguise.

(William Blake)

* * * * * * * * * *

5.1.5 *Adverbs*

adverb

The class of adverbs may be divided into two groups: degree, and general adverbs. Degree adverbs are a small group of words like *very*, *more*, and *most*. They must always appear with either an adjective or a general adverb, for example:

She runs very quickly.   *She runs very.

This sculpture is more beautiful.   *This sculpture is more.

General adverbs are a large class, and may appear without a degree adverb. For example:

She runs quickly.

Traditionally, adverbs tell us how (manner), where (place), or when (time) the action denoted by a verb occurs. For example:

She runs quickly.   How

The cat sat here.   Where

They left yesterday.   When

Adverbs have no inflected forms, although they do take comparison like adjectives, but by using the *more* and *most* forms, for example *more quickly, most quickly*.

Many of adverbs end with *–ly*, for example:

quickly, quietly, properly, instantly, seemingly, stupidly.

The sharp-eyed reader will notice that the *–ly* ending which forms adverbs is attached to adjectives. It is not an inflection since it does not relate to any morphosyntactic categories such as tense or number. We shall have more to say about such word-forming endings in the next section.

We will not provide an exercise for hunting adverbs. The easy cases all end in *–ly*, which makes such an exercise hardly worth doing. In other cases adjectives and adverbs behave in rather similar ways and so are often hard to tell apart, which makes such an exercise difficult.

5.1.6 *Prepositions*

The last major syntactic category we will look at in this chapter is preposition. Prepositions are words such as *in, out, on, by*, which often indicate locations in time or space, or direction.

preposition

While nouns, adjectives, verbs, and adverbs are members of open classes because the classes they belong to are very large, and while it is possible to add new items to any one of these open classes, prepositions are members of a closed class. Other closed classes of words are conjunctions, for example *and, but, because, or*; determiners, for example *a, an, the, these, those*; and the class of auxiliary verbs we looked at earlier in this chapter. It is not possible to add new members to the closed classes. In fact, there is no record of anyone ever adding a new conjunction to the language. Because the function of these words requires us to look more closely at the grammar of sentences we will leave discussing them until Part III, where we look at sentence structure.

open class

closed class, conjunction
determiner

Table 5.1

Syntactic category	Morphosyntactic categories	Morphosyntactic properties	Grammatical words	Regular inflections
Noun	Number	1. Singular 2. Plural	1. Singular form 2. Plural form	none –s
Verb	Tense	1. Past 2. Present	1. Past tense form 2. Non-3rd person singular present form	–ed no inflection
	Number	1. Singular 2. Plural	3. 3rd person singular present form	–s
	Person	1. First person 2. Second person 3. Third person	4. Progressive participle 5. Perfect participle	–ing –ed/–en
Adjective/Adverb	Comparison	1. Positive 2. Comparative 3. Superlative	1. Positive form 2. Comparative form 3. Superlative form	no inflection –er –est
Preposition	none	none	none	none

The morphosyntactic categories and properties of English lexemes and how they relate to inflections in English are summarised in Table 5.1.

Exercise 5.4

Identify the grammatical category of the italicised words in the following passage:

> The *witches hopped in* their *red* mini and *drove gently to* the convocation for an *evening* of fine *wines*, *entertaining* conversation and new spells.

* * * * * * * * *

5.2 Word formation

We assumed in the previous section that the lexemes we looked at were simple in not being made up themselves of other lexemes (although they were in many cases inflected). In this section we will look at complex lexemes which have other lexemes as component parts.

There are two main ways in which English lexemes may have other lexemes as constituents. Two lexemes may be put together to make a compound lexeme. For example, the lexeme BOOKSHELF consists, very obviously, of the lexeme BOOK followed by the lexeme SHELF. A lexeme can also have as constituents a single lexeme plus an ending. These endings are generally termed affixes. The grammatical endings we looked at in the previous section are inflectional affixes. The ones which are constituents of complex lexemes are derivational affixes since they derive one lexeme from another. Look, for instance, at the word GENTLENESS. This lexeme, again obviously, consists of the lexeme GENTLE followed by the affix *ness*. In the following two sections we will look first at compounding and then at derivation.

compound

affix

derivational affix

derivation

5.2.1 *Compounding*

When we looked at simple lexemes we saw that they had phonological, syntactic, and semantic properties. Compound lexemes too have all three sets of properties but, in their case, these properties are, in part, predictable in a way that they are not for simple lexemes. In general a compound lexeme has the segmental phonology of its component lexemes in that order. This seems very obvious but, as we shall see in the case of derivation, this isn't always the case. For example, when the lexeme ELECTRIC has the derivational affix *–ity* added to it it becomes *electricity*. You will know from the chapters on phonology that the phonological form of the constituent lexeme has been changed in a number of ways. Compounding does not make changes to the segmental phonology of the component lexemes.

The stress pattern of most compounds in English has the primary stress on the first word. For example, *income tax* has the primary stress on the *in* of *income* and not on the *tax*. *Whitewash* has primary stress on *white* and *soulsearching* has primary stress on *soul*. There is some debate as to whether this is always so. It certainly is generally the case.

As far as their syntactic properties go, compounds again have a rather simple, regular set of properties.

First they are always binary in structure. In other words they always consists of two and only two constituent lexemes. This means that a compound which has three or more constituents must have them in pairs. For example, *washingmachine manufacturer* consists of *washingmachine* and *manufacturer*, while *washingmachine* in turn consists of *washing* and *machine*. A simple tree diagram of such a word would show its binary structure, as in Figure 5.1

Compound words also usually have a head constituent. By a head constituent we mean one which determines the syntactic properties of the whole lexeme. For example, the compound lexeme LONGBOAT consists of an adjective, LONG, and a noun, BOAT. The compound lexeme LONGBOAT is a noun, and it is a noun because *boat* is a noun, that is, *boat* is the head

head

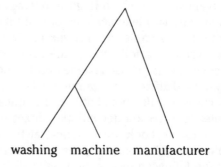

washing   machine   manufacturer

Figure 5.1

constituent of *longboat*. One interesting piece of support for the existence of heads comes from compound nouns which have two nouns as constituents. In such a case, how can you tell which is the head? Well if one of them has an irregular plural, then only if it is the head does the whole compound have that form of the plural. For example, *snowgoose* has the plural *snowgeese*, that is the form of the plural is the form that its head constituent, *goose*, takes and not the plural that the non-head constituent, *snow*, takes. In English the right-hand constituent of a compound is its head.

There are exceptions to the generalisation that compounds are syntactically headed. For example, *income* is a noun consisting of a preposition followed by a verb. Clearly neither of these constituents determine that the compound is a noun.

Compound words can belong to all the major syntactic categories we looked at in the previous section. Here are some examples of each:

Nouns: *signpost, sunlight, coatrack, bluebird, redwood, swearword, outhouse*

Verbs: *window shop, stargaze, outlive, undertake*

Adjectives: *icecold, hellbent, undersized*

Prepositions: *into, onto, upon*

Some of the constituent structures for compounds are very productive in the sense that speakers can make up new ones on the same pattern very readily. For example, a compound noun consisting of a noun plus noun, or adjective plus noun, is very easy to make up. In the computer industry new compounds like this are being created almost daily. For example, many of the following are now familiar words to anyone with a computer: *hard disk, floppy disk, hard drive, mousemat, screensaver, screendump*.

Those constituent patterns where compounding is very productive also allow compounds themselves to have compounds as constituents, as we saw when looking at the binary structure of compounds. For example, *floppy disk drive cleaner* has the compound noun *floppy disk* compounded with *drive* to create *floppy disk drive*. That compound noun in turn is compounded with *cleaner*.

On the other hand, new compound prepositions seem impossible to create. For example, **abovein* and **throughby* don't seem to be possible compound prepositions. You will recall that we said earlier that prepositions are a closed class. So it should not be possible to create new prepositions by compounding them.

As far as their meaning is concerned compound words are often headed in another way. If we look at a compound like *dinnersuit*, then a dinnersuit is a kind of suit, not a kind of dinner. Undereating is a variety of eating, and for something to be overgrown is for it to be grown in a special way. In other words, the lexeme which is the head of the compound from a syntactic point of view is also central to its meaning. The non-head modifies the meaning of the head, making it more specific in some way or other.

There are exceptions to semantic headedness. Redbacks, with which you became familiar in an earlier chapter, are a variety of Australian spider and not a variety of back.

This allows us to make an important distinction. *Redback* is a lexical **lexical item** item, in other words, it is listed in the lexicon of many (if not most) Australian speakers of English. Lexical items have a tendency to become specialised and idiosyncratic. That is why they must be listed in the lexicon since their idiosyncrasy is something speakers have to learn and cannot deduce. If we make up a new compound word, for instance *radiodog*, with the stress on the word *radio*, then we know that it is a noun because its head, *dog*, is a noun and we infer that a radiodog is a kind of dog. Further than that, we do not know what this noun designates. But the moment it became a lexical item, we would have to know more, for instance that it was the dog that a particular radio station used in order to bark the hours of the day before the reading of the hourly news bulletin. (Heaven forbid.)

Here again we have an important distinction between lexemes, which are abstract words that may or may not be lexical items. We would want to say that *radiodog* is a possible word of English but not a lexical item of English (although it may just have become one in the previous discussion.)

Exercise 5.5

Compounds are often frequent in modern technical areas where new vocabulary is being created. Find the compounds in the following passage:

A LaserWriter can print a document more quickly if the fonts used in the document are stored in the printer's memory or on a hard disk attached to the printer. Some LaserWriter printers come with built-in fonts, which are stored in the printer's read-only memory (ROM). You can transfer, or download, additional fonts to the printer's random access memory (RAM) or to a hard disk attached to the printer.

(Apple Computer, Inc., *System 7 Reference Manual*)

5.2.2   *Derivational affixation*

We have seen so far that although words in a dictionary are represented by sequences of letters and a grammatical category they may have more structure than the dictionary usually provides. Some are compounds consisting of two lexemes. Still others have affixes as constituents. Look, for example, at a word like *loveliness*. Its form is a sequence of sounds, but it can also be divided into three sections. It is made up of *love* plus *li* plus *ness*. One of these is a lexeme. The other two are affixes.

Divide the following words into these same kinds of building blocks.

movement, lowly, nationhood.

morpheme

You will almost certainly have got the following divisions: move-ment, low-ly, nation-hood. These minimal building blocks of lexemes are called morphemes. Why are morphemes and not phonemes the basic building blocks of complex lexemes?

A morpheme is usually realised (given form) as a speech sound or sequence of speech sounds just as a lexeme is, and it functions as part (or all) of a word. Morphemes also contribute to the meaning of a lexeme. For example, the word *girlhood* consists of two morphemes *girl* and *hood*. The *girl* part means 'young female person' and the *hood* bit means 'abstract property or state of being a...'. So the word *girlhood* means 'the abstract property or state of being a girl'. The property of having the meaning of a linguistic unit made up from the meanings of its structural parts is called 'compositionality' and a unit which has this

compositional

property is described as being compositional in its meaning.

Another property of morphemes which they share with lexemes is that the relationship between their form, that is the sounds of which they are constructed, and their meaning is arbitrary. Any sequence of speech sounds that the language allows can be a morpheme. There is nothing in the sequence of sounds that go to make up the morpheme *–hood* that makes it particularly suitable to be a morpheme, or the morpheme *–hood* in particular. The great Swiss linguist Ferdinand de Saussure termed this property of words and morphemes 'the arbitrariness of the sign'.

So morphemes are the basic building blocks of lexemes because they are essentially made the same way, that is, as symbols. Morphemes are building blocks of words just as lexemes are building blocks of phrases. The inflections which we looked at in section 5.1 are clearly morphemes, as are the derivational affixes which we will look at now.

The creation of new lexemes by the process of derivation involves word formation rules. These rules specify what happens in the process of using one lexeme to derive another. A word formation rule operates on a base, that is, a lexeme with all the properties lexemes have: form, **base** syntactic function, and meaning. It then specifies what happens to the base in the process of the derivation. The stem is the form of the base, **stem** that is its phonological shape, and that is how we have been using the term.

Let us look at an example. Take the nouns ending in –*ness*. The base for such nouns is a set of adjectives, for example: *happy*, *sad*, *cheerful*, *gentle*, *soft*, *prickly*. The word formation rule which derives the nouns *happiness*, *cheerfulness*, *gentleness*, *softness*, and *prickliness* from their respective bases only takes adjectives as a base, as we can see because the following are not possible English words: **shipness*, **slowliness*, **putness*, since these have a noun, adverb, and verb respectively as base and are therefore not well formed. Secondly, the word formation rule specifies that the meaning of the new word will be something like 'the state of being A', where A is the meaning of the base. So the meaning of *happiness* is something like 'the state of being happy'. Thirdly, the word formation rule specifies the form of the new lexeme by indicating that the new lexeme has the suffix –*ness* attached to the stem.

Things are not always so simple. Many word formation rules specify their bases more narrowly than this. Look, for example, at the suffix –*ee* in words such as *addressee* and *payee*. The base for this word formation rule is a set of verbs, and the meaning of the resulting lexeme is something like 'the one who is V-ed', the one who is addressed or paid. But this means that the verb which is the base for the word formation rule and to which the –*ee* suffix attaches must be the kind of verb which has both someone to do the V–ing and someone to whom the V–ing is done. It would, for example, not be possible to attach –*ee* to a verb like *breathe* because when breathing takes place no one gets breathed, nor to a verb like *mow* since what gets mowed is not a person. On the other hand, not all verbs which look as though they should be eligible permit this, in that the process denoted by the verb cannot be something like that denoted by *kiss* or *thump*. We do not get *kissee* or *thumpee*.

The suffix –*able*, by way of comparison, does attach to *mow* and *sing*, but not to *sit*. The reason for this is that there are at least things like grass and songs which get mowed and sung but nothing gets sat. The word formation rule for –*able* takes as its bases verbs which are not just actions but actions done to things or people. So people who might be loved are lovable; the things that could get mowed are mowable, and so on. Clearly things might also be kissable or thumpable.

The exact limitations on these particular word formation rules are not perhaps as significant as the fact that they involve rather delicate facts to do with the meaning of the base, and these facts must be accessible to the rules of word formation.

In other cases word formation rules specify that their base must belong to a sub-class of lexemes which came into the English language originally from another language. Look, for example, at the suffix *–ion* and the lexemes to which it attaches, like *decision*, *induction*, *conclusion* and *allusion*. The verb bases to which *–ion* is attached are *decide*, *induce*, *conclude*, and *allude*. All of them have Latin as their language of origin. Native English verbs like *break*, *run*, and *breathe* cannot take *–ion*, as you can work out for yourself. Another suffix which attaches to such Latin bases is *–ity*. Thus *domesticity*, *reciprocity* and *anonymity* are well-formed English words since their bases are foreign imports, but *hardity, *greyity and *loneity are not, because their bases are lexemes which have been part of English vocabulary for a very long time and were not 'borrowed' from other languages.

Word formation rules may also be sensitive to phonological properties of bases. The prefix *de–* with the meaning 'take off' seems typically to apply to monosyllabic bases as in *delouse*, *dehorn*, *degrease*.

A word formation rule may also be sensitive to what word formation process (if any) took place to create its base. For example, the suffix *–ity* happily attaches to bases ending in *–able*, for example *readable*, *readability*; *taxable*, *taxability*. But it is not happy to attach itself to lexemes ending in *–ful*, for example *thoughtful*, *thoughtfulity; *restful*, *restfulity. On the other hand, *–hood*, will not attach to any base which is anything but a single morpheme. For example *sisterhood*, *parenthood* and *priesthood* are well-formed but *blackbirdhood is not.

All this suggests that the processes of derivation are potentially sensitive to all of the following properties of bases: their phonological form, syntactic properties, semantic properties, their derivational source and even their historical provenance.

Their effects, you might imagine, would also include the same range of possible properties. We have already seen that derivational processes have the basic phonological effect of adding an affix, determining the syntactic category of the new lexeme and its meaning. But these are not the end of the matter.

Word formation rules which add derivational affixes may be divided into three groups. There are those which add stress-bearing affixes to their stems and those which cause the stress to shift, and those, like inflectional affixes, which have no influence on stress placement. You will recall that we looked at this phenomenon from a phonological point of view in Chapter 4. The first group includes: *–ee*, *–ese*, and *–esque*. All three suffixes take stress, for example:

pa'role – parol'ee, Su'dan – Sudan'ese, 'Roman – Roman'esque

The second group includes: *–eous*, *–y*, *–ial*, *–ion*, and *–ity*. The addition of one of these suffixes results in the stress shifting towards the suffix, for example:

'outrage – out'rageous, 'spectrograph – spec'trography,

'adverb – ad'verbial, 'renovate – reno'vation, e'lectric – elec'tricity

The third group does not have any influence on the placement of stress. This group includes: *–able*, *–age*, *–en*, *–ful*, *–ing*, *–like*, *–ment*, and *–wise*.

Word formation processes may also have phonological effects other than that affecting stress placement.

Look at the following bases and derived words:

commit	commission
submit	submission
admit	admission
revert	reversion
dominate	domination

Clearly the addition of the noun-forming suffix *–ion* has had more phonological effects on the base than just the addition of *–ion*, and don't let the spelling of the last example fool you. In each case the final phoneme of the base has undergone a change. This change is morpho-phonemic, that is it is a phonemic change caused by a morphological process. There are many such processes and they lead us to the concept of allomorphy. Just as a phoneme may have a variety of different phonetic realisations in different contexts so a morpheme may have different phonemic realisations in different contexts. We have already seen this in Chapter 3 when we saw that the plural in English has a variety of forms. Each of these: /s/, /z/, and /əz/, is an allomorph of the plural morpheme.

morpho-phonemic

allomorphy

Allomorphs may be stem allomorphs or affixal allomorphs depending on what has the variant forms. In the case of the stem to which the *–ion* affix attaches we are dealing with stem allomorphs whereas the plural forms are affixal allomorphs.

Exercise 5.6

Separate the affixes from the following words and divide them into inflectional and derivational subclasses:

singularities, neglectful, soils, deliberation, sacrifices, artificially.

* * * * * * * * * *

5.2.3 *Conversion*

There is a third word formation process which is rather difficult to deal with because nothing happens to the lexeme's form in the process. Look at the following pairs: [N drink], e.g. *Give me a drink*, [V drink], e.g. *She drank the water*; [N joke], e.g. *That's a good joke*, [V joke], e.g. *They joked about the Minister of Finance*; [N axe], e.g. *I have an axe for chopping firewood*, [V axe], e.g. *The Prime Minister decided to axe the Minister of Finance*. The noun *drink* and the verb *drink* have exactly the same form but differ in their syntactic category and consequentially also in their meaning. Because they differ in both their syntactic category and their meaning these pairs are pairs of different lexemes, and the process **conversion** which connects them is often termed conversion. Conversion is different from derivational affixation. There we can see the way in which the new lexeme has been derived from the base lexeme by the addition of an affix. The process has a directionality to it. But in the above pairs, since there is no change to the form, it is hard to say which of the pair is more basic. In some cases the meaning helps. Drinking is semantically more verb-like, while an axe is more noun-like. But in many cases it is not at all obvious.

Conversion is very common in English. Take most nouns and they can be converted to verbs. *Supermarket* could easily become a verb, for example *We are going to be supermarketting until 11 o'clock*. Conversion also happens with adjectives, as the following examples show: [A yellow], e.g. *a yellow tulip*, [V yellow], e.g. *The paper yellowed gradually*; [A dark], e.g. *a dark corner*, [N dark], e.g. *in the dark*.

5.3 Kinds of morphemes

Now that we have seen how inflections and derivational affixes function we can look at morphemes in a more general way so as to gain an understanding of some of their general properties.

5.3.1 *Bound and free morphemes*

Some morphemes which are parts of complex lexemes can be lexemes in their own right. In the lexemes *movement*, *lowly*, and *national* the morphemes *move*, *low*, and *nation* have this property. They are called **free morpheme** free morphemes. Those, like *–ment*, that can not stand on their own as **bound morpheme** lexemes, are termed bound morphemes.

Exercise 5.7

Divide the following morphemes into free and bound sets:

ation, nation, pre, post, angle, ible, infra, out.

* * * * * * * * *

5.3.2   *Stems and affixes*

A second classification of morphemes involves looking at the morphemes that are tacked on at the beginning or end of a word. It is a positional classification. Usually the stem is a free morpheme, as in the case of *lovely* where *love* is the stem of the word and a free morpheme. However, this is not always the case. For example, in the word *possible* the *ible* seems to be attached to the stem *poss*, which is itself bound. There are other cases, like the word *cranberry* where *cran* occurs nowhere but in this word and seems, therefore, to be a bound stem. The bound morphemes which are attached to a set of stems are collectively known as affixes, as you will recall.

Exercise 5.8

Separate the affixes from the stems in the following words:

trains, succeeded, lighter, predetermined, retroactive, confusions, instructional.

* * * * * * * * *

Affixes in English have two locations where they can be attached to stems. The obvious places are before and after the stem. In a word like *recreate*, the stem is *create* and the affix attached at its left-hand end is *re–*. Affixes which attach at the left-hand end of a stem are termed pre- **prefix** fixes. Affixes such as *–ation*, which are attached at the right-hand end of stems, are termed suffixes. It is one of the interesting properties of affixes **suffix** that a given affix is either a prefix or a suffix. It cannot be both. We can think of this property as being rather like a hook that the affix is provided with which is at one end only; a prefix hooking onto a stem at its right-hand end and a suffix hooking onto a stem at its left-hand end. Free stems, by contrast, have no hooks. We can see that this is the case by the fact that many stems will take both prefixes and suffixes.

   What about bound stems? Since they must be attached to either an affix or another stem to form a word, they too must come equipped with a hook. Look for example at the *cran* in *cranberry*. It clearly hooks onto a stem to its right.

5.3.3 *More on inflectional morphemes*

We have seen that there is an important distinction between derivation and inflection. In the case of derivation an affix is involved in creating a new lexeme whereas in the case of inflection the affix is the realisation of a set of morphosyntactic properties.

Inflections tend to appear regularly on almost all the words of a particular grammatical class, as we saw in the previous section. You will recall that almost all English nouns can take the morphosyntactic property *plural*, and this often appears in the form of a plural suffix. All English verbs can take a past tense and this morphosyntactic property is often represented in the form of a past-tense suffix.

All inflections in English are suffixes and if a word has an inflection attached to it then it will be the last morpheme in the word, since English only allows a single inflectional suffix to appear on any word. Inflections never attach to bound stems.

suppletive

In some cases, as we saw in the previous unit, verbs and nouns do not have regular forms of particular morphosyntactic categories but have what are termed suppletive forms, that is completely unpredictable ones. We saw suppletion in the earlier discussion in which we decided that word forms and lexemes had to be distinguished. The example we used was the past tense form of the lexeme GO, namely *went*. This form is suppletive.

What are the comparative and superlative forms of GOOD and BAD?

Answer:

They are *better* and *best*, and *worse* and *worst*. Their form is totally unpredictable on the basis of that of *good* and *bad*. Therefore, their formation cannot be rule-governed. They are therefore also suppletive forms.

syncretism

On the other hand, sometimes words which really are different in their inflectional morphology are identical in form. As we saw in section 5.1, the perfect participle in English is often indistinguishable in form from the past tense form. For instance, *Joanna has towed the boat* and *Joanna towed the boat* have identically inflected forms of the verb TOW. In the first sentence TOW has the perfect participle form and in the second it has the past tense form. We can tell this is so because, for other verbs, the two forms are different. For example, the verb BREAK in the following two sentences has different forms: *Joanna has broken the mower* and *Joanna broke the mower*. The situation where two different grammatical words have the same inflected form is termed syncretism. Someone who wants to speak English must learn these forms separately. They will therefore create difficulties for foreign-language learners of English.

Find five further English verbs which show syncretism between the past tense and past participle forms.

Remove all the inflectional affixes from the following passage:

The privileged man opened the packet, looked in, then, laying it down, went to the window. His rooms were the highest flat of a lofty building, and his glance could travel afar beyond the clear panes of glass, as though he were looking out of the lantern of a lighthouse.

(Joseph Conrad, *Lord Jim*)

Answer:

The privileged man open the packet, look in, then, lay it down, went to the window. His room were the high flat of a lofty building, and his glance could travel afar beyond the clear pane of glass, as though he were look out of the lantern of a lighthouse.

You can see from this exercise that two things have happened. First, the English sounds more telegraphic and quite ungrammatical. Also, the removal of some inflections, such as the plural, creates a different meaning and changes other things such as the fact that the word *were* is no longer the correct word to use if there is only one room. Other instances, such as the loss of the *ing* in *were looking*, make the sentence ungrammatical since *ing* is a necessary ending. You can see that inflectional affixes are an essential part of the language, even in a language which has as few of them as English does.

Exercise 5.9

More exercises on the structure of words

(a) Divide the following words into their constituent morphemes by placing a plus sign (+) between the morphemes, and indicate for each morpheme whether it is bound or free:

cleaning lady, anti-skidding device, mushroom, nationhood, deputise, derailments, predestination, internationalisation.

(b) Indicate for each of the following words, which have been divided up into morphemes, which are the affixes and for each affix, what is its associated stem.

involve+ment, in+support+able, sub+profess+or+ial, inter+sub+ject+iv+ity.

(c)   A number of morphemes in the following passage are italicised. For each, say whether it is bound or free; if bound, whether it is an inflection or a derivational affix.

> We are at once the most resilient, most resource*ful*, most rest*ive*, most receptive, most radical, most reaction*ary* people who ever liv*ed*. We have had time and the tide for every*thing* but those moments of thought necessary to reverse the prioriti*es* to cause us occasiona*lly* to look before leaping.

* * * * * * * * * *

5.4   Morphological properties

5.4.1   *Existing and non-existing, possible and impossible words*

If we look again at the distinction between inflectional and derivational affixes you will recall that adding an inflectional affix to a stem does not make a new lexeme. There is just the previous word with an affix added, whereas if we add a derivational affix to a stem then we have a new lexeme. That enables us to make two further distinctions which are important. There are words which we have stored in our brains as words, that is, words that we know. We have earlier called these lexical items. All native English speakers are likely to know the words *tree* and *sister*. They are words which exist in a native speaker's lexicon, the internalised store of words in his or her brain. Then there are words which do not exist in anyone's brain, perhaps – for example, the following word: *insultability*. There is no reason why this should not be a lexeme of English. It just doesn't seem to *be* a lexical item of English. So it is a possible but non-existing word. A word like *fmukg* is also non-existing, but it is impossible because its sequence of sounds is not possible in English. We looked at how such phonotactic constraints operate phonologically in Chapter 3.

Not all bases for word formation need to be existing words, that is lexical items. For example, adjectives ending in the suffix *–ly* can provide the base for the word formation rule which creates words ending in the suffix *–ness*, for example *friendliness*. So the number of lexemes in a language is infinite but the number of lexical items anyone actually has stored in their brain at one time is, of course, finite.

5.4.2   *Productivity*

Earlier we found that some affixes appear to attach to a limited set of bases.

How many lexemes can you find ending in *−hood*?

You will not have found more than two dozen. However, in theory it looks as though *−hood* is restricted to bases which are nouns and which are morphologically simple. So, again in theory, *−hood* should attach to base lexemes such as *soldier, friend, parson, nurse*, and many others. So as well as the potential set of lexemes of which a derivational morpheme might be a constituent, the actual set of lexical items that it is a constituent of may be much smaller. By contrast, *−ness*, attaches to adjectives and creates nouns. It is hard to find any adjective to which it cannot attach. It therefore appears that affixes may differ in their productivity.

derivational morpheme

productivity

Productivity can be looked at in a number of ways: *−hood* has a limited potential for creating new lexemes in that it will only attach to lexemes consisting of a single morpheme, and the lexeme must be a noun. However the set of such lexemes is quite large. But *−hood* does not form new lexemes from most of the set. In other words its productivity, given its potential, is quite small; *−ness*, however, is very productive given its potential.

Another way to look at productivity is to see how freely people use the affix in making new lexemes. If speakers commonly use the affix in coining new words, then the affix is productive.

Clearly productivity is a matter of degree. Some affixes may be highly productive, some middlingly so and some may be totally unproductive, that is, never used to create new lexemes. The prefix *a−* in such words as *astern, adrift*, and *asleep* is now completely unproductive, whereas the prefix *non−* can be quite freely attached to adjectives.

Applications

It is useful to be able to look at the morpheme structure of words because you can often get a good idea of a writer's style from looking at the structure of the words they use. When words of only one morpheme are used the style will appear to be very simple, whereas if words made up of a number of morphemes are used the style will appear to be more complex.

Exercise 5.10

Compare the extracts below by splitting words up into morphemes. Try and come to some conclusions about the authors' styles.

> I was away for two days at the posts. When I got home it was too late and I did not see Miss Barkley until the next evening. She was not in the garden and I had to wait in the office of the hospital until she came down.
>
> (Ernest Hemingway, *A Farewell to Arms*)

The author of these Essays is so sensible of their defects that he has repeatedly refused to let them appear in a form which might seem to indicate that he thought them worthy of a permanent place in English literature. Nor would he now give his consent to the republication of pieces so imperfect, if, by withholding his consent, he could make republication impossible.

(Thomas Babbington Macauley, *Critical and Historical Essays*)

I have allowed the Preface to the former edition of these Poems to stand almost without change, because I still believe it to be, in the main, true. I must not, however, be supposed insensible to the force of much that has been alleged against portions of it, or unaware that it contains many things incompletely stated. It leaves, too, untouched the question, how far, and in what manner the opinions there expressed respecting the choice of subjects apply to lyric poetry, that region of the poetical field which is chiefly cultivated at present. But neither have I time now to supply these deficiencies, nor is this the proper place for attempting it: on one or two points alone I wish to offer, in the briefest possible way, some explanation.

(Matthew Arnold, Preface to *Second Edition of Poems*)

* * * * * * * * * *

5.4.3   *Diagramming word structure*

Now that we have looked at both the functions of words and their internal structure we can put the work of the last two sections together to show the structure of words, and their function, in diagrams. If two lexemes are put together to form another lexeme then this is like a Chinese box arrangement with units existing within other units, as we saw in the case of *washing machine* earlier.

We can represent this structure by the use of tree diagrams, as we saw in Chapter 1. A tree diagram for *blackboard* would look like the one shown in Figure 5.2. What it shows is that we have one unit consisting of two sub-units, and these sub-units come in a fixed order.

Figure 5.2

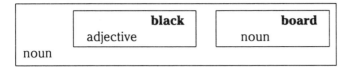

Figure 5.3

However, there is more to the structure of this word than just the fact that it consists of two units in a fixed order. We also know that each unit belongs to a lexical category, such as noun or verb. We can add this information into the Chinese box structure and it will look like Figure 5.3. The equivalent tree diagram would look like this: Figure 5.4

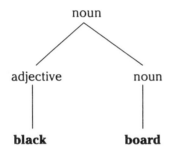

Figure 5.4

Both these representations are difficult to produce on a normal keyboard and so a third representation has been devised which essentially cuts the lines which join the ends of the boxes in the Chinese box representation and turns the ends into square brackets, so that the word *black-board* can be represented as shown in Figure 5.5. This representation is called, rather obviously, labelled bracketed notation.

labelled bracketed notation

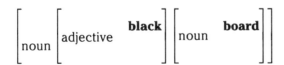

Figure 5.5

What about affixes? Since they are bound, bound in a particular direction, and are not themselves lexemes, their structure in the Chinese box representation looks like Figure 5.6. Notice that only the unit *school* has a syntactic category and so there is no labelled box around *pre*.

Figure 5.6

It follows that the tree diagram for this word will look like Figure 5.7. The labelled bracketed form will look like Figure 5.7.

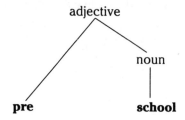

Figure 5.7

[adjective **pre**[noun **school**]]

So far each example has consisted of only two parts. It seems that words always consist of two parts, that is, two parts at a time. *Nationalisation* consists of *nationalise* plus *ation* tacked onto it. *Nationalise* in turn, consists of *national* plus *ise* tacked on the end of it, and so forth. So the structure of this word in tree notation looks like Figure 5.8. Or in labelled bracketed notation it looks like this:

[Noun[Verb[Adjective[Noun **nation**] **al**] **ise**] **ation**]

Exercise 5.11

Now try to represent the following words in both tree diagrams and labelled bracketed notation:

(a) bookworm

(b) singer

(c) mislay

(d) tax collector

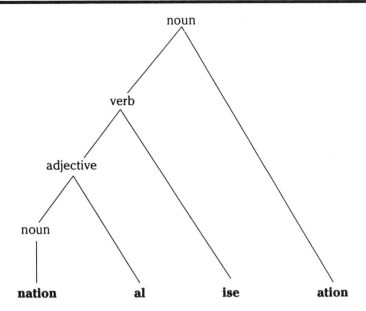

Figure 5.8

   (e)   physical sciences library

   (f)   unanalysable

   (g)   inexcusable

   (h)   internationalisation

* * * * * * * * * *

We have taken some time to introduce three different notations to represent the structure of words because each provides a different way of visualising the same facts about the structure of words: that words which have internal structure consist of units, which may or may not belong to syntactic categories and which come in a fixed order. In the case of words, such structures are relatively simple. When we look in Chapter 7 at the structure of sentences we will find that the structure of sentences can be represented in the same ways, but the syntactic categories are not just the by now familiar lexical categories which we introduced in section 5.1. It is well worth taking time over drawing both tree and labelled bracketed diagrams of word structure. Doing so will help you become familiar with visualising linguistic structure and representing it graphically.

Further exercises

Exercise 5.12

What is the grammatical category of the italicised words?

> Two *old* Daimlers were parked in a line *by* the traffic lights. One *of*
> them *seemed* to have lost its *headlight*s.

Exercise 5.13

In each of the following words, separate the affixes from their respective
stems. For each, decide whether it is a stem or an affix, bound or free, and
if it is an affix, whether it is derivational or inflectional:

> derivational, headstrong, unlikely, locater beacons.

Then draw tree diagrams of the structure of each word.

Exercise 5.14

Study the following passage and then answer the questions given below.
Take your examples from the passage.

> The crowd, in general more pleased with the bull even than with the
> peanut vendor, started to cheer. Newcomers gracefully jumped up on
> to fences, to appear standing there, marvellously balanced, on the top
> railings. Muscular hawkers lifted aloft, in one sinewy stretch of the
> forearm, heavy trays brimmed with multi-coloured fruits.
>
> (Malcolm Lowry, *Under the Volcano*)

(a) Identify two compound words, name the grammatical category
of the compound, and the grammatical categories of the elements that compose it.
(Example: *blackbird* is a noun, made up of adjective + noun.)

(b) Identify the class-changing derivational suffixes, name the grammatical category of the stem to which the suffix is attached and
the grammatical category of the derived word.

(c) Divide the following words into their component morphemes:

> *newcomers*, *marvellously*

(d) What kind of word-formation process links the noun *hawker* and
the verb *hawk*.

(e) Account for the pronunciation of the plural suffix in the words *railings, fruits, fences,* and *trays.*

(f) Identify another inflectional suffix (i.e. not the plural suffix) and explain its function or functions.

Exercise 5.15

Study the following passage and then answer the questions given below. *Take your examples from the passage.*

The dog swam ahead, fatuously important; the foals, nodding solemnly, swayed along behind up to their necks: sunlight sparkled on the calm water, which further downstream where the river narrowed broke into furious little waves, swirling and eddying close inshore against black rocks, giving an effect of wildness, almost of rapids; low over their heads an ecstatic lightning of strange birds manoeuvred, looping-the-loop and immelmanning at unbelievable speed, aerobatic as new-born dragonflies. The opposite shore was thickly wooded.

(Malcolm Lowry, *Under the Volcano*)

(a) Identify three compound words. For each one, name the grammatical category of the compound, and the grammatical category of the elements that compose it.
(Example: *watertight* is an adjective, made up of noun + adjective.)

(b) Divide the following words into their component morphemes, labelling each morpheme F (free), I (inflectional), or D (derivational):

    unbelievable   dragonflies

(c) What is the function of the suffix *–ly* in the words *fatuously, solemnly,* and *thickly?*

(d) Identify two other words containing (different) derivational suffixes, name the grammatical category of the stem to which the suffix is attached, and the grammatical category of the derived word.

(e) Describe the function of the suffix *–s* in *foals* and *waves,* and that of the suffix *–ed* in *swayed* and *sparkled.*

(f) Comment on the past tense forms *swam* and *broke.*

(g) The *Collins English Dictionary* contains the following entry:

Immelmann turn or *Immelmann...n.* an aircraft manoeuvre used to gain height while reversing the direction of flight. It consists of a halfloop followed by a half roll. [C20: named after Max *Immelmann* (1890–1916), German aviator.]

Comment on the word-formation processes which have led *firstly* to the inclusion of the above expressions in the Dictionary, and *secondly* to the author's use of the progressive participle form *immelmanning* in line 6.

Exercise 5.16

Look carefully at the choice of vocabulary. What differences in the styles of the two following passages can you discern and what do these differences suggest about the different narrators of the two stories?

> Mrs Clegg was quite a decent sort, but she had a glass eye that was cracked right down the middle, and it was funny the way she sort of looked out at you through the crack. Her old man was out of a job and that was why she was running the joint, though seeing she only had three rooms to let she said she wasn't making a fortune.
> When she'd fixed my bed up she took me down to the kitchen to give me the teapot, and her old man was reading the paper, and their little girl was saying pretty boy to a budgie that was answering her back. Though sometimes it would ring a little bell instead. Mr Clegg told me he'd been a cook on a boat but now he couldn't get a keel. It was hard, he said, because he liked being at sea, though I thought by the look of him it must have been only a coastal or even a scow he'd worked on. He was pretty red too, though he said he hadn't been until he'd had experience of being on relief.

> (Frank Sargeson, 'That Summer')

> It is perhaps an indication of the unusual features of my nature that for some days following the party, far from finding myself melted into a state of rapturous languor, I should find instead my mental capacities taxed by harder thinking than I had experienced during all that year. If I continued my association with Betty and the Gower-Johnsons, I foresaw that it would be elaborated to such a degree that my entire future might well be involved; and apart from minor advantages, such as benefiting from Betty's financial generosity, I saw my problem, if it was reduced to its bare, ineluctable elements, was nothing more or less than the same old problem which had first presented itself to me when I had finished with being a primary school boy: that is to say, the day-to-day activities of the environment I inhabited appeared not to be connected with what I conceived to be my major interests.

> (Frank Sargeson, *Memoirs of a Peon*)

6 Word meanings and vocabularies

6.1 The meaning of words

What does a word mean? What are meanings and how does a word mean more or less the same thing to anyone that knows it? We can start again by looking in the traditional place people look for meanings, a dictionary. As well as telling us the spelling of a word and its syntactic category, aspects of the nature of a word we have looked at in detail, dictionaries try to tell us the word's meaning or meanings. Let us look again at an example.

imposter, n. One who assumes a false character or personality; swindler.

Oxford Dictionary of Current English

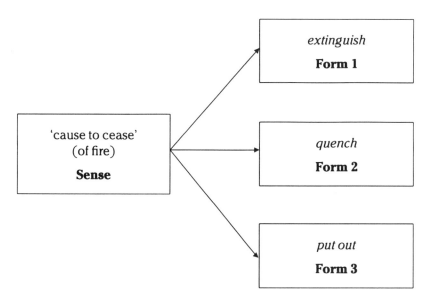

Figure 6.1 Synonymy: one meaning; multiple forms

This dictionary entry tells us that a word that is spelled *imposter* has a meaning given by other words. These words are not the meaning but have the same meaning as the word being defined. So here is a first important fact about word meanings. We can recognise sameness of meaning when we come across it just as we can recognise the sameness of two sounds which are allophones of the same phoneme when we hear them. When expressions share the same meaning they are 'synonymous'. Where one word or expression has the same meaning as another the two are called synonyms.

synonym

Which of the following words or expressions appear to have the same or very similar meanings; list them in pairs of letters:

(a) . effluent

(b) . knock over

(c) . sympathise

(d) boycott

(e) - outflow

(f) . construct

(g) show sympathy

(h) · the day after today

(i) · endure

(j) . build up

(k) · put up with

(l) . tomorrow

(m) · take a calculated guess at

(n) - estimate

Your answers should be:

(a), (e); (c), (g); (i), (k); (h), (l); (m), (n); (f), (j).

6.1.1 *Sameness and difference of sense*

The fact that this exercise proved to be so easy shows that we know the meanings of these words, and we, as speakers of English, share this knowledge.

If two words are synonymous then this allows us to make certain infer- ences. For example, if *car* and *automobile* are synonyms, then it follows from the fact that I am driving an automobile then I am driving a car, and conversely that if I am driving a car then I am driving an automobile, that is, if one is true then the other will be true and vice versa. The relationship where if one sentence is true, then the other is true is termed entailment. **entailment**

Exercise 6.1

Synonymy and entailment

In the following examples, what the first sentence expresses entails what the second expresses. Does the second sentence also entail the first? If it does, is this due to the synonymy of words or phrases in each sentence or not?

   (a)   Evelyn won the race. The race was won by Evelyn.

   (b)   Greg has hit the ball too hard. Greg has struck the ball too hard.

   (c)   My socks are both scarlet. My socks are both red.

   (d)   I bought some ripe tomatoes. I purchased some ripe tomatoes.

   (e)   My dog is bigger than your dog. Your dog is smaller than my dog.

   (f)   Her dad likes me a lot. Her father likes me a lot.

   (g)   This pencil belongs to Roger. Roger owns this pencil.

   (h)   Ken almost shot his foot. Ken nearly shot his foot.

   (i)   My neighbour owns a pistol. My neighbour owns a firearm.

* * * * * * * * * *

In the above dictionary entry for *imposter*, the word has only one mean- ing, but this is not always the case. Words often have different but related meanings. When this happens one can often see quite clearly how the meanings relate to one another. For example, the lexeme SIGHT has the general meaning of 'the capacity to see', as in *Jerry slowly regained his sight*, but also the more specialised meaning of a particular view, *The Grand Canyon is a magnificent sight*. The two meanings are obviously related. When this is the case the lexeme is said to be 'polysemous' and the property of having multiple meanings of this kind is called polysemy. **polysemy**

    Sometimes two quite different words accidentally have the same form. For example *sight* and *site* are both nouns and both have the identical phonological form. But native speakers know that these are two different lexemes and not one lexeme with two senses. Cases like that are called homonyms. Homonomy exists in both writing and speech. When two **homonym** words are spelled identically, for example *lead* as in what you take your dog for a walk on, and *lead*, the heavy metal, the result is homography, and when they are spoken identically, for example *soul* and *sole*, it is homophony.

It needs to be noted that it is not always clear whether one is dealing with polysemy or homonymy in a particular instance. A chair that people sit on and the position of being a professor in a university, that is, holding a chair, probably are not seen by most speakers as being related in meaning.

Exercise 6.2

Polysemy and homonymy

Are the senses of the italicised words related, i.e. is there one word with polysemous senses, or are these homonyms?

(a) The ship was *listing* badly.
     We are *listing* the requirements for the course.

(b) He gave her a diamond *ring*.
     His glass left a *ring* on the table.

(c) They came to a *fork* in the road.
     He placed the *fork* beside the knife on the plate.

(d) The dog tried to *lap* the water.
     The cat sat in my *lap*.

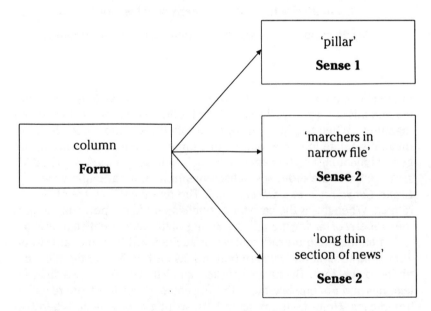

Figure 6.2 Polysemy: one form; multiple related meanings

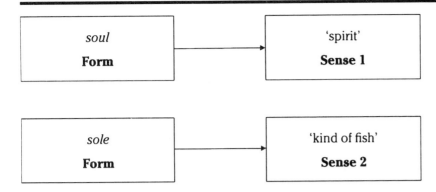

Figure 6.3 Homonymy: accidentally similar in form; unrelated meanings

(e) The dog had no *bark*.
Don't remove the *bark* from the tree.

(f) It is *hard* to play the violin.
Ebony is a *hard* wood.

* * * * * * * * *

Puns are made possible because words are polysemous or homonyms.   **Pun**

Exercise 6.3

Puns

Think of five jokes that rely on puns and then look up in a dictionary the words on which they are based, for an explanation of how the joke works. For example, Hamlet, in the play of the same name, calls Rosenkrantz and Guildenstern *recorders*, because they have been sent to record what he says and does. But he then accuses them of treating him like the musical instrument, the recorder. The source of the pun is the homonymy of the two words *recorder*.

* * * * * * * * *

6.1.2 *Oppositeness of sense*

While some words have senses which are the same as one another, other sets of words have senses which are 'opposite' to one another. The senses of words can be opposite in a number of quite distinct ways. Some of these are called antonyms. They are typically opposites near the ends   **antonym** of a scale, such as *hot* and *cold*. Their scale is the temperature scale.

Antonyms of this kind have many interesting properties. They are gradable which means that they can be modified by words like *very*, for example *very cold*, and can take comparative and superlative forms, as we saw in section 5.1, for example *hotter, hottest*. Gradability has to do with the fact that the position of the antonym on its scale is not an absolute but a relative one. Consequently an antonym's sense cannot be right at the end of the scale. If we can modify it then there are temperatures which are hotter than hot and colder than cold. It is also a consequence that there are positions in between. This can be seen clearly in the case of *hot* and *cold* by the fact that there is another antonym pair, *cool* and *warm*, which take up intermediate positions between *hot* and *cold*. It is an inherent feature of the meanings of gradable antonyms that this should be so.

When we look at the temperature scale on which *cold, cool, warm,* and *hot* indicate ranges of temperatures, we find that the scale is not precise. Each range has fuzzy edges so that we can't be sure where *hot* finishes and *warm* takes over. The range also depends on what is being talked about. A hot day has a different temperature range, when measured in degrees, from a hot drink.

A further property of gradable antonyms is that often one of the pair has two senses: one being its position on the scale and the other representing the whole scale. For example, if we ask how old someone is, we don't intend that to signify that the person is old. We can ask it of a week-old baby. This neutral sense is often termed the unmarked sense of the antonym. We can tell that only one of the pair has this unmarked sense because we can't ask how young someone is without that implying that they are young.

unmarked

Not all antonyms are gradable. For example, the pair *alive* and *dead*, as we saw in section 5.1, are not a matter of degree. Expressions like *half dead* can be used literally only if they mean that half of whatever it is, say a tree, is completely dead and the other half is alive. These are mutually exclusive opposites or complementary senses. Complementaries may have only two words in the set, like *boy* and *girl*, or they may be multiple, like *solid, liquid,* and *gas*, when they denote the only three states of matter in the set. Notice again that complementaries are not gradable except in a rather metaphorical sense. When we say that someone is very much a boy we are referring to some of the additional properties of boys and not the primary one of being a boy.

complementary senses

converse senses

Words with converse senses, such as *buy* and *sell*, or *husband* and *wife*, look as though they are opposite in sense but strictly speaking they are not, since they denote the same action or relationship but from a different perspective in that the person who is buying something from someone is having the someone sell something to them. If there is a married relationship then on one side of that there is a wife and on the other side there will be a husband.

These three kinds of sense relationship: antonymy, complementarity, and converseness all have repercussions for entailments. Antonyms can be involved in entailments in that if something has as a property one which is denoted by one of a pair of gradable antonymous senses then it does not have the other. For instance, if someone is old then they are not young. However, the entailment doesn't work the other way round. If someone is not young, it does not follow that they are old. With complementaries the situation is different. If someone is not married then they are single and if they are not single, then they are married. This is a direct consequence of the fact that complementary senses are mutually exclusive. Converses also have interesting entailment consequences. If A buys X from B, then it follows that B has sold X to A. But not all senses that look like converses work this way. If someone sends something to someone else then they don't necessarily receive it. That depends on the dependability of the postal service as well as the senses of the words *send* and *receive*.

Words with opposite senses enable us to discover some important facts about word meanings. The first is that word meanings can be broken down into smaller components. Look at *boy* and *girl*. Although their meanings are different, they still have a lot in common. Boys and girls are both young humans. They differ in only one aspect of their meaning, namely that girls are young female humans and boys are young male humans. So the meanings of these words consist of sub-components of meaning and the difference is in only one of these components. They have the others in common.

6.1.3 *Sense components*

Finding the component parts of the meanings of words is usually termed componential analysis. To discover what the components of a meaning of a word are, we can make use of a second fact we have also discovered with the aid of antonyms, and that is that antonyms belong to groups of words denoting related things. *Boy* and *girl* both denote children, *hot* and *cold* both denote temperatures. The word *child* and the word *temperature* are sometimes called the superordinates (or hypernyms) when we talk about their relation to the words 'under' them. These words which are included under a superordinate are termed hyponyms. You can check that a word is a superordinate of some other by putting them in sentences like this:

componential analysis

superordinate, hypernym

hyponym

'Hot' is a temperature.

'Cold' is a temperature.

but not

'Temperature' is a kind of cold.

A girl is a kind of child.

but not

A child is a kind of girl.

Exercise 6.4

Hyponymy

Arrange the words in each group so that every word is a hyponym of the word immediately before it.

    (a)   mouse, rodent, mammal

    (b)   house, building, bungalow, structure

    (c)   run, jog, move

    (d)   pistol, weapon, firearm, revolver

    (e)   person, uncle, relative

    (f)   dog, beast, beagle, hound

    (g)   pilfer, steal, take

* * * * * * * * * *

Exercise 6.5

Hyponymy

Arrange the following sets of words in a tree diagram to show which words are hyponyms of which. (Note that these tree diagrams do not show linear order, just hierachical order.)

    (a)   Bic, biro, fountain pen, pen

    (b)   station wagon, car, convertible, vehicle, bus, van

    (c)   shrub, tree, plant, poppy, rhododendron, flower, marigold

    (d)   steal, borrow, embezzle, get, burgle, buy

    (e)   sing, speak, croon, chat, vocalise, yodel

    (f)   denim, worsted, cotton, muslin, fabric, tweed, wool

    (g)   amble, run, sprint, locomote, stroll, jog, walk

* * * * * * * * * *

When senses are hyponymous, that can give rise to entailments. For example, it follows from the fact that something is a chair that it is an item of furniture. But it does not follow that, if something is an item of furniture then it will be a chair. As we have seen, not all entailments come about because of hyponymy but, when they do, it should be possible to determine the superordinate sense and the hyponymous sense which are responsible for the entailment by the fact that they are not reversible.

Exercise 6.6

Hyponymy and entailment

Does the first sentence entail the second? If is does, is this due to hyponymy or not?

(a) All dogs have fleas.   My dog has fleas.

(b) Bob killed Charles.   Charles is not alive.

(c) The bus is late.   The bus is very late.

(d) Alan planted marigolds.   Alan has planted flowers.

(e) Tom took a pig.   Tom stole a pig.

(f) Goldie ate the porridge.   Someone ate the porridge.

(g) I saw a human being.   I saw a person.

(h) Betty has not planted tulips.   Betty has not planted flowers.

(i) I am wearing black boots.   I am wearing black footwear.

(j) A tall pygmy came in.   A tall person came in.

(k) I ran home last night.   I went home last night.

(l) Bob killed Charles.   Bob murdered Charles.

(m) My socks are bright red.   My socks are red.

(n) My socks are almost dry.   My socks are dry.

* * * * * * * * *

When we look at all the co-hyponyms, senses which are both or all hyponyms of the same superordinate sense, we can often sort out some of their meaning components. For example, look at the other words denoting temperatures: freezing, frigid, cold, cool, tepid, luke-warm, warm, hot, boiling. Each of these means what it does because of what the others mean. Warm is a temperature between hot and cool, wherever they are. Cold is colder than cool, and so on. Groups of words that cover one territory are often described as covering a 'semantic domain' or semantic field. Some of these fields are rather simple, such as the scale we have just looked at, and some are very complex, such as the terms we use for members of our family or for vehicles.

co-hyponym

semantic field

Exercise 6.7

Semantic fields and components

Examine the following words. Sort out what sense components differentiate the senses of the various words:

rope, twine, cable, hawser, wire, string, thread, cord.

* * * * * * * * *

Exercise 6.8

Semantic fields and components

Find all the words that English makes available for us to use for members of a family, and see if you can work out how they relate to each other.

* * * * * * * * * *

Semantic domains and fields are an interesting source of information about the way a linguistic community thinks about a particular area. In current Western culture, its love affair with the internal combustion engine has given rise to a large number of hyponyms of the sense 'vehicle'. Not only that, many of these hyponyms, such as 'car' have hyponyms in turn, such as 'sedan', 'coupé', and so forth. Other societies have similarly complex fields to deal with, say, an item of staple diet such as taro.

If we return now to the dictionary, it will be clear that it often tries to give the meaning of a word in terms of its semantic components. When we read in the dictionary that *mother* means 'female parent', we have two of the major components of the word given in the form of the words which have that component as their sense. These components are relevant to some field – in this case, the field of kinship words.

But in many cases the semantic components of a word are relevant not just to the meaning of the individual word in its semantic field but also to the way the word functions with other words in sentences. This is true of the ways in which, for example, adjectives fit semantically with nouns, and the way verbs fit semantically with their noun phrase participants. Let us take, for example, a noun like *woman*. We know that one of the semantic components of this word is that of humanness, and that humans are animate, or alive. So we can talk about old women and young women since these adjectives can be used of things that are alive. We can talk of little men and big men because we can use these adjectives with concrete objects. But we could not talk literally of young and old comfort, or big and little sincerity. When we speak literally, the meanings of words restrict the other words with which they will semantically fit. Such restrictions are termed selectional restrictions. People can not eat gasses. You can sew only things that are sewable. Only female mammals can be pregnant. Only humans can pray.

selectional restrictions

Clearly many of these restrictions come about because of the way we conceive of the world as being, but that is not invariably so. For example, the verb *honour* seems to need the thing which is honoured to be a person or a human quality. We might say that the Nobel Prize committee honoured Nelson Mandella or that they honoured his courage. But it seems a bit odd to say that an architectural committee honoured a building. Here the selectional restriction seems to be rather more language-internal since there is nothing seriously incoherent about the idea of honouring a building.

Some breaches of selectional restrictions are minor, in that they don't do very serious violence to our view of the way things are. Others are egregious. For example, in a phrase like *the wind breathes in*, we can see our way through to how one might animate the wind so that it breathes. It is also a conventional way to treat the wind. However, if we say *the large boulder contemplated suicide*, then we are in more difficulty in that the selectional features on contemplating suicide are difficult to ascribe to boulders.

To summarise: synonyms cover the same bit of semantic territory, antonyms differ in meaning from each other by having one of their semantic components opposite to the other. Superordinates define semantic fields great or small, and within each field semantic components sort out the meaning of one word's semantic territory from that of the others in the field. We can also see these semantic components at work in the selectional restrictions that words have when they are put into sentences. What may look like, and in fact be, a perfectly grammatical sentence, may make little literal sense if the right semantic components are not meshed together.

Selectional restrictions are a factor in some sentences containing contradictions. Look at the following two sentences:

(a)   My male aunt bought a piano.

(b)   Babies are adults.

It is very easy to pick what causes the contradictions. In (a) the contradiction is in the words *male aunt*. Why is this? It is because one of the semantic components of the sense of the word *aunt* is the component 'female'. That clashes with the meaning of the adjective *male*. Similarly, it is part of the meaning of the word *baby* that babies are not adults.

Just as selecting incompatible semantic features can create contradictions, so selecting other ones can create semantic redundancy (tautology), as in the following two sentences: **semantic redundancy** **tautology**

(a)   Degas painted naked nudes.

(b)   I bought a male bull at the market.

It is a semantic component of the meaning of *nude* that it is a figure which is naked, as it is a semantic feature of the word *bull* that bulls are male. Thus significant semantic components of *nude* and *male* are redundant.

6.1.4   *Metaphor*

This brings us directly to metaphor. We are used to looking in poetry for metaphor but it is much more common than we think. A simple way to look at metaphor is to see it as a breaking down of the normal literal **metaphor** selectional restrictions that the semantic components of words have in a sentence. When we talk about, for instance, a window onto the future, we have to ignore some of the semantic components of the word *window* – for example, that it is a concrete object – and just take the fact that windows are things that allow us to look from an enclosed space outwards. The metaphor could also be seen the other way about, where the future is seen as something concrete that can be seen out of a window. The metaphor lies in the suppression of some of each word's semantic features.

personification

The figure of speech called personification is a special case. Here words that have the semantic component 'not human', have this suppressed so that these words are allowed to function in sentences as though they were human. *Freedom was at the helm of the ship of state*. Helmsmen are normally human. *Freedom*, the word, is allowed to perform an action normally reserved for words that have the semantic component 'human'. *The ship of state* too is a metaphor. In this metaphor the state is being seen as a ship with a captain and crew (presumably the government and its leader), and citizens, who might end up as metaphorical passengers. So the fact that states are not physical entities is being supressed in the metaphor.

The nature of metaphors is that they are literally false and therefore either baldly state a literal falsehood, or allow for the metaphor to be paraphrased by a literal falsehood. For example, if we describe someone as empty-headed, then this is literally untrue. The person does have things inside their head: a brain, bloodvessels, bones and so on. If we say that the car is a beast, then this is also literally false.

simile

Similes get one out of the falsehood by saying not that something is something that it is not, but rather that it is like something else, leaving the speaker to determine wherein the likeness lies. For example, we might say that a person acts as though there is nothing in their head, or that their car is like a beast. Using *as* or *like* in this way creates a simile.

Look at the vocabulary associated with a particular sport and see what metaphors and similes you can find.

The vocabulary of sport is often full of military metaphors. The word *captain* was originally a military rank, whose use was extended to sports teams. You will be able to find many more metaphors to do with sport. The metaphors tend to draw on an interesting and limited set of domains.

Exercise 6.9

The lexical semantics of political rhetoric

Look at this paragraph from the famous 'I have a dream' speech by Martin Luther King and see how he has used semantic fields and metaphors.

Fivescore years ago, a great American, in whose symbolic shadow we stand today, signed the Emancipation Proclamation. This momentous decree came as a great beacon light of hope to millions of Negro slaves who had been seared in the flames of withering injustice. It came as a joyous daybreak to end the long night of their captivity.

* * * * * * * * * *

6.1.5 *Word meanings in context*

So far you may have got the impression that word meanings are entirely stable collections of semantic components which only change in the case of metaphor. This is a half-truth. The meaning of a word given by its semantic components is more like a set of potential meanings. You were given some preliminary warning of this when we looked at the temperature field earlier in the chapter. A hot day and a hot iron are both hot but for a day to be hot is not the same as for an iron to be hot. It was said at the time that *hot* is a relative term, and it is relative not just to the other words on the temperature scale; what the whole scale denotes or what any meaning on it denotes depends on the context in which it is being used. Although terms on this scale retain the same relative positions, the scale changes its value for different types of things.

Furthermore, if all we had at our disposal to convey messages to one another were the meanings of individual words, we would be restricted in what we could say to as many messages as we had words in our vocabulary. But that isn't the case because we put words into sentences and combine the meanings of words into complex messages using the syntax of the language we happen to be speaking.

In their interaction with one another in grammatical sequences, the meanings of words undergo a number of changes. For instance, while words may be polysemous on their own, when placed in grammatical sequences some of their senses can be excluded. For example, the adjective *single* has a sense meaning 'only one'. It also has a sense of 'unmarried'. If we put *single* with the noun *book* then the possibility that *single* means unmarried is excluded by the semantic features of the sense of *book*.

There is something, therefore, which allows us to combine the meanings of words into the meanings of phrases, and this process is rule-governed.

Let us begin by looking at the meaning of a very simple phrase, *big car*, and let us suppose we know the senses *big* and *car*. *Car* has semantic components which might include: vehicle, internal combustion powered, for passengers, having wheels, driving on roads. *Big* has the sense component of: having physical dimensions larger than the norm. But, like temperatures, what constitutes big for a car is different from what constitutes big for an ant. It seems that to explain what such a simple

sense, denotation

phrase means we have to dive from the English language into the real world of cars and their relative sizes, and back into language again.

The reason for this muddle is that we have not yet made clear the distinction between the sense of a word and its denotation. What we have looked at so far as meaning – that is, basically, semantic components – gives words a denotation. The sense of the word *car* allows.it to denote the set of all possible cars, actual or imaginary. It does not specify the exact boundaries of the set. Look, for example, at the word *fruit* and the word *berry*. We know that apples, oranges, pears and bananas are fruit and that raspberries, strawberries, and gooseberries are berries, but what of tomatoes? We think of tomatoes as vegetables but can see them as either fruit or berries without it bothering us. (Think of the very small cherry tomatoes.)

Words in human languages usually do not denote well-defined sets of things, actions, and properties but sets whose boundaries are fuzzy. We may think this is very sloppy, but it actually allows words to denote things which do not seem clearly one thing or another. If we always had to be absolutely sure what it was we were talking about most of us would have to stop talking altogether.

Try holding a brief conversation with someone in which you have to define exactly what you mean for every noun you utter.

That should have been virtually impossible. Even if you felt you were doing quite a good job your conversation will have been much longer than normal.

But now to return to the phrase *big car*. It is clear that the senses of *big* and *car* are amalgamated somehow and thus the denotation of the phrase *big car* is a subset of that denoted by *car*. So, just as we saw earlier that some of the senses of words may be excluded when those senses are put alongside others in grammatical sequences, so other senses combine with those of neighbouring words to enable complex messages to be constructed from their component parts.

So far we have talked about words that have a fairly clear denotation, namely, of concrete objects. It is sometimes said that other words, like abstract nouns and nouns that denote internal states such as *pain*, are meaningless, that they are vague or useless. Strictly speaking, none of these statements is correct. Words like *courage* are harder to define than concrete nouns, because they denote social or cultural properties. Showing courage, roughly speaking, entails putting oneself at risk for some cause. Most people in English-speaking society would agree about that, so we know what the sense of the word is. What we might disagree about is whether a certain action by someone was courageous. But that is no different really from the problem of whether a bean bag can properly be referred to as a chair. The same goes for *pain*. I know what pain feels like and I assume other people do too even though an actor can simulate pain when he has not got it.

Words such as these can create communication breakdowns. On one side there are those who say that such and such an action is courageous, and on the other side are the other generation saying that such an action is not courageous but stupid. This is a disagreement about people's values that connect with language where sense makes denotation possible.

Similar areas of disagreement and breakdown come about because of what words denote in different speech communities. In the 1960s a big car in the United States was much bigger than a big car in Europe. So when someone from one side of the Atlantic told someone from the other side of it that they drove a big car, miscommunication about exactly what that involved could have resulted.

Let us return now to the way in which the senses of words combine. Recall that the set of entities denoted by *big car* was a subset of the entities denoted by *car*, just as the set of actions denoted by *run swiftly* is a subset of the actions denoted by *run*.

In some instances words come to be strongly associated with each other. When this happens their senses combine in a more idiosyncratic way than in the above examples.

> What actual colour are the following?
>
> white coffee, white wine, white sugar,
>
> black coffee, red wine, brown sugar;
>
> and how raw are raw meat and raw sugar?

Of the first three items only white sugar is actually white. White coffee is a muddy kind of colour and white wine is yellowish. Black coffee is dark brown, red wine is more red than anything else but not scarlet, and brown sugar really is brown. Raw meat denotes uncooked meat, not unprocessed meat, whereas raw sugar is rather less refined than some more refined sugars such as white and brown sugar. How does this come about? Coffee comes either with or without milk and these two states are really what *white coffee* and *black coffee* denote, just as white and red wine are the two generic kinds of wine. Imagine trying to sell light green wine (although some wines are light green)?

To cover this sort of situation the term collocation has been invented. **collocation** Collocations are linear associations of one word with another that give a rather special sense and denotation to one or both words, a meaning that the words have by virtue of being together in a lexicalised form. Some collocations are quite habitual. *Black tea, white wine, dry wine*, and so forth show how much we take the facts that the tea is not really black nor the wine either white or dry for granted.

6.1.6 *Reference*

reference

We have so far not said anything about words referring. This is a common way for people to talk about the meanings of words, that is, to say that words refer to things or actions; but linguists use the term 'reference' in a specialised way. Let is look at some examples.

What do the following phrases refer to:

the Taj Mahal, Alexander Graham Bell, Rover?

referring expression

Each of these phrases is a referring expression, that is, it has the potential to refer to someone or something or a group of people or things. But what does a referring expression actually refer to? It is tempting to think that the answer to that is simple. *The Taj Mahal* refers to a mausoleum in India. *Alexander Graham Bell* refers to the inventor of the telephone, and *Rover* refers to my dog. But the latter example clearly shows that this cannot be the case. *Rover* is not only the name of a particular dog, it is the name of many dogs. There are also, no doubt, a number of people whose name is Alexander Graham Bell, and there are a number of places called the Taj Mahal, as you can verify by looking up the Indian restaurants in many large cities. So words do not refer. Referring expressions can be used to refer but they only refer when a speaker is attempting to get a hearer (or hearers) to pick out an entity or set of entities on a particular occasion. For example, if I ask you whether you intend to go to the Taj Mahal, what *the Taj Mahal* refers to depends on whether I have just asked you to fetch a take-away Tandoori, or know you are going to India. This suggests that what a referring expression refers to is a matter of what the speaker intends the hearer to pick out, and the context in which the expression is used.

6.1.7 *Word associations and connotations*

pragmatics

associations
connotation

There are other aspects of meaning that are like referring in that they require us to look beyond the language and into the non-linguistic context where words are used. Such aspects of meaning are often termed pragmatic, and their study pragmatics. By way of illustration we will look at an example of pragmatics related to the sense of words. It is often said that there are no true synonyms because, although two words may denote the same range of things, they have different associations or connotations. Typically associations and connotations have to do with the positive and negative feelings people have towards things, properties, actions and the like. For example, if we feel badly disposed towards someone we might use words with negative connotations. An unreliable acquaintance will be called a rat because rats are animals which are not generally well thought of. We might term words with strong negative connotations 'snarl words' (or boo words) and words with positive connotations 'purr words' (or hurray words). In advertising it is typical to use purr words to accentuate the positive qualities of the product which is being advertised. You can hardly imagine a perfume advertisement which has the following slogan successfully selling the product even though the perfume may contain musk and attar of roses:

The stench of armpits and shrivelled petals.

Since connotations are based on social attitudes, they can reveal social attitudes.

Look at the negative connotations of metaphorical extensions of words referring to women, such as *cow*, *bitch*, etc. What does this tell you about social attitudes towards women? Repeat the exercise for words used to refer to men.

The majority of animal metaphors for women in English have negative connotations whereas the majority of animal metaphors for men have positive connotations. Look, for example, at the word *dog*. Used of a woman in North America it refers to a woman who is not considered good looking, and therefore has negative connotations, whereas referring to a man, as in *you old dog*, it has positive connotations. There are exceptions. The word *foxy* has positive connotations when used of women and the word *rat* negative ones when used of men.

One area where connotations and social attitudes can be clearly seen is in the case of euphemism. When people have to talk about something **euphemism** unpleasant or embarrassing, some of the words dealing with this area come to have negative connotations. Many of the classical English 'four-letter words' are like this. Words like *piss* were once just simple one-syllable words to describe a perfectly normal activity. However, when English society became squeamish about certain bodily functions the word *piss* came to have negative connotations and was replaced in polite speech by a variety of euphemisms such as the clinical word *urinate*, the baby word *pee*, or the phrase *going to the toilet*. The word *sweat* had a similar fate. The polite synonymous word *perspire* came to rescue speakers who did not wish to be associated with the negative connotations of *sweat*. As you might imagine, euphemisms have a way of taking on the same opprobrium as their less polite synonyms. English has gone through quite a few words to designate the room in the house where the toilet is, including *toilet*, *bathroom*, *powder room*, *WC*, *loo*. Terms used for handicapped people have gone through the same process, giving us *idiot*, *mentally retarded*, *educationally subnormal*, *learning disabled*, and currently *special needs*.

taboo

When the senses of words have very negative connotations they sometimes become taboo, that is their use is socially forbidden.

> Think of as many euphemisms as you can for the death of people. How many of these words are taboo?

You will find that because they are social, taboos are context-determined. One would not expect a priest at funeral to say that the person being buried had snuffed it, while this might be acceptable in another context.

Taboo words are usually involved in the act of swearing. People swear to express their negative emotions and so when people swear they use words with strong negative connotations, often taboo words. In English these words often deal with religion, sex, or excretion since these are major topic areas in which words have developed strong negative connotations (and, consequently, euphemisms). To swear, one utters one of the words with powerful connotations to express one's negative feelings about something such as hitting one's thumb with a hammer. The stronger the negative feelings, the closer to a taboo word speakers tend to get. So it does not do to use a euphemism instead. Swearing at something by saying 'Oh, excrement.' is funny just because *excrement* is a clinical term and therefore a way to escape saying the word *shit* which is taboo in a formal situation, but therefore suitable as a swearword.

Again, swearing is a contextual matter and so part of pragmatics.

6.2 Vocabularies

So far we have looked at words as individual units but they can also be looked at in sets.

> Do you know how many words there are in the English language?
>
> How many words do you think you know?

It is impossible to know exactly how many words there are in the English language. New words are being added to the language all the time, while others are being lost. For example, the word *dryhten* used to be part of the English vocabulary. It meant 'lord'. Not even the most recent and comprehensive dictionary will list all the words in the language. The average educated adult speaker of English may know as many as 25,000 or more words. That is a lot of words. This is even more of a feat when we consider that, for each word, we know how to pronounce it, what it means, what part of speech it is, and what other words may appear with it.

Any well-defined group of words, such as all the words of the language, can be called a vocabulary. A language has a total vocabulary of all the words that there are in the language. No person knows all these words. Individual people have their own total vocabulary consisting of all the words they know.

vocabulary

Take a small pocket dictionary, and taking five pages at random, see how many words on each page you know. You can calculate roughly what proportion of the words in the dictionary you know by taking the proportion of words you know in these five pages and multiplying that proportion by the total number of pages in the whole dictionary and an approximation of how many words there are on each page.

You should also take into account that most dictionaries contain only a small sample of the total number of words in English. Of course these words are usually the more common ones, so that the chances are you will know an even smaller proportion of the total vocabulary of English.

The total vocabulary of an individual person can be subdivided into active and passive. Most of the words we know, we do not use ourselves, but we recognise them when other people use them. Think of weather forecasters and the technical vocabulary they use to talk about the weather. For them words like *precipitation* and *isobar* are active vocabulary, but they are passive vocabulary for the rest of us. We may know what they are talking about when they talk about precipitation but ordinary folks talk about rain. One of the things that tends to happen to people as they pass through the education system is that the size of their total vocabulary increases. Usually this happens when words first pass into people's passive vocabulary and then move from there into their active vocabulary. In this book, the words in bold in the margins are in many cases moving from being not part of your vocabulary at all, to being part of your passive vocabulary. But when you sit a test on the material, these words must become part of your active vocabulary when you actually use them and write about them.

active, passive

6.2.1 *Adding to vocabularies*

The total vocabulary of a language is never static. Nor is that of a speaker. Words pass into and out of both. The normal way this happens in the case of a language is through a process that can be called lexical borrowing (usually just termed borrowing). Lexical borrowing involves a word being copied from the vocabulary of one language into that of another. Many of the words of current English came originally from other languages and were borrowed into English. For example, the word

lexical borrowing

wienerschnitzel does not look like a native English word and isn't. It came originally from German and arrived quite recently.

Borrowing takes place when two speech communities are in contact. If we look at the speech communities with which English speakers have been in contact then most of these contacts have left a record of themselves in the form of borrowed words. In the early Middle Ages Vikings raided and then settled northern England. Words from the Norse dialects which the Vikings spoke and which were borrowed into English include: *egg*, *husband*, and *window*. Later in the Middle Ages the Normans invaded and settled in England. Norman French was spoken by William the Conqueror and those who came with him from Normandy in 1066. Borrowed vocabulary which dates from this period includes the following words: *warden* and *castle*. If one traces the colonial period of settlement, when, unlike the previous situation where foreign speakers settled in England, English speakers settled in places like North America and India, then we find that most of these language contacts lead to some degree of borrowing. *Tomahawk* came from North America and *curry* from India.

One of the consequences of borrowing words is that occasionally some of their internal structure remains marginally in evidence in the English form of the word, particularly when a number of words with the same structure are copied. This has happened with both Latin and French borrowings in English. Look, for example, at the following words: *incline*, *recline*, *decline*. They look as though they are formed with a prefix added to a bound stem. They were. But not in English. That is why we feel a bit uneasy about placing a morpheme boundary here while a speaker of Latin would have been in no doubt. A borrowing like *blitzkrieg*, which clearly still shows evidence of its German origins, is a compound in German. Is it still a compound in English where a speaker may not know that its two constituents are both words? Well, neither constituent is an English word and so the internal structure is not available to us unless someone tells us about the German origins of the word.

Exercise 6.10

Finding source languages

From which languages did the following words come and when did they transfer into English?

yacht, curry, transfer, pyjama

* * * * * * * * * *

You could now try to find some interesting source languages for words of your own choice in a good dictionary and see if your friends can guess where the words come from. In many cases you will be able to trace why the words came to be borrowed from the languages they did, which makes for its own interesting stories.

Application

Considered stylistically, native words, words which were not borrowed, often belong to basic central vocabulary whereas borrowed words belong to more peripheral areas. As a result a piece of writing largely made up of native vocabulary often has a very simple style.

Look, for example, at the following two texts. Find out which are the native and which the borrowed words and then see what impact the word choice (or diction) has on the style of the writing.

(a)   CONVERSATION

Said my daughter, It rained
cats and dragons, and the wind —
you know — lay down
in our house, licking
its wounds and panting
and wagging its tail;
it had eyes as large
as mine, you know.

Asked her mother, What
happened next?

Said Sina, Oh nothing.
It just died.

(Albert Wendt)

(b)   ... discrimination against women violates the principles of equality of rights and respect for human dignity, is an obstacle to the participation of women, on equal terms with men, in the political, social, economic and cultural life of their countries, hampers the growth of the prosperity of society and the family and makes more difficult the full development of the potentialities of women in the service of their countries and of humanity, ...

(from the UN Convention on the Elimination of All Forms of Discrimination against Women)

* * * * * * * * *

Lexical borrowing is usually a two-way traffic, but the majority of the traffic is from the vocabulary of people who are seen as being more powerful or more advanced in a particular area. So, for example, words having to do with computing are currently transferring from English into many of the world's other languages. Words to do with cooking and wine have transferred to English from French. For example, in the Middle Ages the French word for sheep, *mouton*, became the English word for sheep meat, *mutton*. In more recent times words like *casserole*, *sauté* and *soufflé* have been borrowed from French. When one wants to go out to a particular kind of fast-food chain in Japan, which we call, *MacDonald's*, one asks one's friends to *Makudonaru*. Lexical borrowing in the early days of colonisation in New Zealand saw many Maori words transfer into New Zealand English and many English words transfer into Maori. Early colonists saw Maori as being knowledgeable about the land and its flora and fauna and borrowed Maori words for these. The colonists also brought with them the Christian religion and many early borrowings from English into Maori were of biblical origin.

Vocabularies can also be added to by tools that each language has for making new words. We have already looked at the major tools in the case of compounding, derivation and conversion. However, there are some interesting minor tools for creating new words. They are not rule-governed in the way that derivation and compounding are, but are the result of people being lexically creative.

blend

New words are occasionally made by putting the first part of one word together with the second part of another as a blend. The word *smog* is a blend of *smoke* and *fog*. A cross between a tiger and a lion is called a *liger*. *Avionics* is aviation electronics. Again you can make up such blends yourself although it takes some ingenuity to make them stick. For example, you might want to call blithering idiots *blithiots*.

acronym

A relatively new way of creating new words is through the use of acronyms. An acronym is a word made up from the first letters or syllables of a phrase. For example, one United Nations agency is the United Nations Education and Cultural Organisation. This has given rise to the acronym *Unesco*. Acronyms are of two kinds. Some sets of initial letters actually make up possible words, such as *Unesco*. Others do not, for example, the United States Central Intelligence Agency is usually called the CIA. It is pronounced with each of its letters being pronounced separately rather than being pronounced 'keeya' or 'seeya'. Only acronyms which are pronounced as words really constitute new words. Other acronyms are just sets of initials which are stored in memory.

Like all lexical items, acronyms do not carry their history about with them. So if you want to know what that is, you normally have to look it up.

Exercise 6.11

Find the sources of the following acronyms;

radar, laser, IATA, NATO, quango, AIDS

* * * * * * * * *

Acronym formation has become very productive in some areas of society, particularly in high-tech development. For example, the United States defence agencies such as the navy have created thousands of acronyms to the point where they employ specialists whose task it is to write dictionaries of all the acronyms they currently use, ICBM, 'intercontinental ballistic missile', being one example. You can imagine how important it might be in areas where military hardware is concerned not to get your acronyms mixed up.

Sometimes acronyms incorporate a syllable as well as just the first letter of a word. Two examples from the US navy are the ranks of cincpac and cinclant: Commander in Chief Pacific Forces and Commander in Chief Atlantic Forces.

Very occasionally words are created from scratch. Someone puts some sounds together and gives them a grammatical function and new meaning. For example, the brand names *Kodak* and *Exxon* are reputed to have come into existence that way. This might be termed root creation.   **root creation**

Very occasionally also, something gets named after the sound it makes. For example, the English bird the peewit, and the New Zealand native owl, the morepork, are reputed to make birdcalls a bit like their names. These can be termed echo words. However, both these last,   **echo word** rather obvious ways of creating new words are nowhere near as productive as compounding, derivation, and, in modern English-speaking society, acronym creation.

6.2.2 Coining new words

When a new word is first created one talks of it being coined. This is an   **coining** apt metaphor because after a word has been coined one of two things can happen to it. It may be used once, for the purpose for which it was coined by whoever coined it. Most such words, termed nonce words, are   **nonce word** used just the once and then are not used again. However, if the coinage gains currency, that is other people use it as a medium of linguistic exchange, then it has become lexicalised, that is, it has been copied   **lexicalisation** into the lexicons of a number of speakers who all know it and perhaps use it. What causes a word to be lexicalised has nothing to do with the language but a great deal to do with social factors. A word is lexicalised when it meets a lexical need, usually because there isn't already a word to fill the particular conceptual niche it comes to occupy. For example, in computer technology, new items of technology are invented frequently. They have to be called something. Usually someone comes up with a word by accident. The word catches on and then gains currency. Someone must have coined the term *floppy disk*. It has certainly gained currency. Coiners of words are normally unsung heroes and heroines. Occasionally the coiner is known. For example, the scientist who gave the sub-atomic particles called quarks their name is Murray Gell-Mann. (But he actually borrowed it from the Irish writer James Joyce, for whom it certainly didn't name a class of sub-atomic particles.)

6.2.3 *Change through time*

After a word has been coined and then lexicalised it normally under-goes sometimes subtle but often wide-ranging changes. Most common are changes in meaning. While a morphologically complex word is often compositional when it is coined, it is coined for specific purposes and those purposes end up affecting it in the lexicon. For example, a black-board is, in many cases, a black board. But there is more to it than that. It is actually a board of any kind which is made so that one can write on it with chalk. As a result, blackboards can be green without this being a logical contradiction. Virtually every compound noun which is lexica-lised has some such idiosyncrasy built into its lexical entry as the result of its lexicalisation.

drift

The meanings of complex words also change over time. Meanings drift. The word *revolver*, for example, might mean 'something which revolves', but is now normally used to refer to a kind of pistol with a revol-ving firing chamber. The word *communism* originally had to do with living in communes, but has now only a non-compositional meaning to do with a political ideology.

widening

There are some general directions in which word meanings change over time. They may widen so that their denotation covers more than it did. For example, the word *barn* used to denote a storage place for barley but its denotation generalised to cover any kind of farm-based storage shed. Similarly the word *mill* used to denote a place where grain was ground. Now it denotes a much larger set of places where things are made, for example a woollen mill.

narrowing

The opposite effect is narrowing, where the denotation of a word shrinks. The word *starve* used to denote dying in general but now denotes dying of hunger. (It is probably also currently expanding again to denote the state of being very hungry.) The word *disease* used to be compositional in its semantics, i.e. it meant not being at ease. It has now narrowed the source of the lack of ease, specifically – some kind of medical source.

pejoration, amelioration

The connotations of words can also change. They can worsen (which is termed pejoration) or they can get better (which is termed ameliora-tion). *Lewd* started out denoting those who were lay people as opposed to clergy. Since the clergy were educated and the lay people, by and large, were not, it then narrowed to denote those who were ignorant, and from there narrowed to obscene, clearly with worse connotations. *Knight*, by contrast, used to denote a servant, and then a special kind of servant of the sovereign who had been knighted. Along with the new denotation came better connotations.

One of the mechanisms for changing meaning is metaphor, which we looked at earlier. Look, for example, at these phrases: *a tall story, a blind alley, a strong smell.* In each case the adjective is use metaphori-cally rather than literally. In time, such metaphorical usages can become institutionalised as a further sense of the word. For example, the word *grasp* has a metaphorical sense of 'understand'. (You cannot literally grasp an idea.)

While meanings may drift, all aspects of a word's representation can change over time. For example, its phonological form can change. One notable change is clipping. If a word's form seems rather long and cumbersome it is sometimes shortened. When motorised public vehicles first came to be used, a Latin name was used for them. They were called omnibuses, which meant, in Latin, 'for everyone'. But it was a long word and so has been clipped to *bus*, so that now almost no one remembers the old form. The same has happened to *influenza*, and numerous other words are routinely clipped when they are used in speech. Usually the clipped form exists alongside the unclipped form as in the case of the Australian clipping *beaut*, which is a common clipped form of *beautiful*.

clipping

Can you think of any vocabulary items which you might clip in informal speech?

The internal structure of a word can drift to the point where it is no longer recognisable. The word *window* was once a compound noun and its first constituent word is still the same one, *wind*. The second constituent was, a thousand or so years ago, the word *eye*. So a window was a wind *eye*. Before the advent of glass, one can see how this would be so. However, the word has now drifted to the point where its internal structure has dissolved and it is just a single morpheme.

A word's syntactic functions can also change. The word *freight* was able to be used as an adjective once, as in *a truck freight with apples*. That possibility is now gone.

Another way in which the syntactic representation may change is if a proper noun becomes a common noun. For example, one of the pioneers of automotive engineering was a European engineer named Diesel. His name has now become a common noun denoting a type of engine with which he was associated. This kind of change is sometimes termed proper noun conversion.

proper noun conversion

The best source for studying the individual history of words is the *Oxford English Dictionary*, which contains the history of a very great number of English words. This dictionary is an essential aid when reading texts from earlier periods of English because one can never be sure what words meant in the past or even whether a particular spelling represents the same word that it does now.

Exercise 6.12

Drift and reading early texts in English

The following poem by John Donne was written in about 1600 in England. Using the *Oxford English Dictionary*, find the contemporary meanings of the underlined words and see what they add to your understanding of the poem.

AIRE AND ANGELS

Twice or thrice had I loved thee,
Before I knew thy face or name;
So in a voice, so in a shapelesse flame,
Angells affect us oft, and worship'd be.
    Still when, to where thou <u>wert</u>, I came
Some lovely glorious nothing I did see,
    But since, my soule, whose child love is,
Takes limmes of flesh, and else could nothing doe,
    More <u>subtile</u> than the parent is,
Love must not be, <u>but</u> take a body too,
    And therefore what thou <u>wert</u>, and who
        I did Love aske, and now
That it assume thy body, I <u>allow</u>,
And fixe it selfe in thy lip, eye, and brow.

Whilst thus to <u>ballast</u> love, I thought,
And so more steddily to have gone,
With wares which would sinke admiration,
I saw, I had love's <u>pinnace</u> <u>overfraught</u>,
    Ev'ry thy haire for love to worke upon
Is much too much, some fitter must be sought;
    For, nor in nothing, nor in things
Extreme, and scattring bright, can love <u>inhere</u>;
    Then as an *Angell*, face, and wings
Of aire, not pure as it, yet pure doth weare,
    So thy love may be my loves <u>spheare</u>;
        Just such disparitie
As is <u>twixt</u> Aire and Angells puritie,
T'wixt womens love, and mens will ever bee.

(John Donne)

* * * * * * * * *

6.2.4 *Reduced usage, archaism and loss*

The ultimate drift is for a word to drift right out of the language. In a pre-literate society this happens when no-one can remember the word. At that point it has disappeared. In a written language things are not as clear cut. So long as a word is written down somewhere, it is at least accessible even if it is not part of anyone's passive vocabulary except the editor of the *Oxford English Dictionary*, about which we will have more to say later in this chapter. We can therefore talk of various degrees of archaism. Look at the following passage on nineteenth-century horse drawn carriages: **archaism**

> Of the various types of carriages now in vogue, the Victoria, in its many varieties of form, is the most popular, accompanied, as of necessity by the Double Victoria, Sociable, Brougham, Landaulet and Landau.
>
> (from the entry for *Carriage*, in the 10th edition of the *Encyclopedia Britannica*)

None of these will be familiar words to most English speakers. For anyone except an antiquarian or specialist, these words are now archaisms. They were in quite common use but have now dropped out of common use.

Medieval armour similarly consisted of many different pieces with a term for each. In a short passage describing the arming of Sir Gawain in the medieval poem *Sir Gawayne and the Green Knight*, a prose translation provides the following italicised terms:

> He stayed there all that day, and dressed the next morning, asked early for his armour, and it was all brought. First a red carpet was laid on the floor and heaped with much gleaming gilded clothing. The sturdy man stepped onto the carpet and picked up the steel equipment dressed in a doublet of expensive Turkistan cloth and skilfully cut cape, fur lined and fastened at the neck. Then they put the *sabbatouns* on his powerful feet, bound his legs in steel with lovely *greaves* and cleanly polished *polaynes* which were fastened round his knees with golden knots. Then came the goodly *cuisses* which skilfully encased his thick thighs and were tied on with thongs. Then the *hauberk* of bright steel rings resting on bright fabric was wrapped about the warrior and well burnished *braces* placed on both his arms along with bright, goodly *cowters* and gloves of plate armour.

We can guess what most of these terms mean. Gawayne is being dressed from foot to head, with steel shoes (sabbatouns) and greaves on his lower legs, polaynes at the knees, and cuisses on the upper leg, a chainmail corslet over the torso, braces on the lower and upper arm, and cowters at the elbow. All these terms have become archaisms and are now known only to those with a specialist interest in armour.

Word loss is particularly common in slang, the everyday colloquial in-talk vocabulary used particularly by teenagers. Words go into and out of use with great rapidity in teen vocabularies. Some years ago there were groups of young people in Great Britain called teddyboys. There were also mods and rockers. With the teddyboys having grown up, the word *teddyboy* has begun a journey out of the active vocabulary of most speakers of British English, as have *mods* and *rockers*, although no doubt in the passive vocabulary of nostalgia they live on. In one hundred years these words are likely to be known only to social historians. In other words, they will have become specialist vocabulary items like those of medieval armour and Victoria horse-drawn carriages. In a thousand years they will probably have gone the way of *dryhten*.

6.2.5 *Word histories*

etymology

The historical development of a word is its etymology. Some words have an etymology which is entirely native. This means the words have been in the language for as far back as one can tell. Other words are non-native in that they were borrowed at some point during the history of the language and since then have evolved within it.

folk etymology

Coming to the wrong conclusion about the origins and particularly the meaning of words is termed folk etymology. It is very entertaining for others when people make such mistakes. Folk etymologies also make good puns and jokes; for example, the definition of the word *briefcase* given in a cartoon strip was 'a trial where the jury goes out to form a lynching party'. Another splendid folk etymology is the word *wealthfair*, constructed by a North American student on a folk etymology of the word *welfare*. Welfare is something which gives people some wealth and it makes things more fair. However, in modern English *welfare* is not a compound word and the student who made up the etymology clearly thought that it was.

Exercise 6.13

Create your own folk etymologies

Find five compound words and say what they mean. Then make up two other meanings that they could have, for example *treetrunk* means 'the trunk of a tree'. It could mean 'a trunk of an elephant shaped like a tree' or 'a wooden suitcase'. Then try and construct one joke using one of the folk etymologies you have made.

* * * * * * * * * *

6.2.6 *Dialect vocabularies*

So far we have been looking at total vocabularies, both those of individuals and of languages. But there are also partial vocabularies of various kinds. Like the sounds of a language, the words of a language can often belong to particular dialects. For example the word *croft* is a word used in parts of Scotland for the houses of tenants on an estate. So this

regional dialect word

is a regional dialect word. In the southern provinces of Otago and Southland in New Zealand, locals may call a holiday cottage a *crib*, while northerners call it a *bach*. Speakers of English elsewhere might call such places *holiday homes*.

Application

When authors convey the regional dialect speech of their characters they can do so by using dialect words or words which have dialect senses, that is, meanings which the words have only in a particular regional dialect. If an author chooses a word which is spoken only in the area in which his story is set, then what the character says may be opaque to the reader, whereas if the words are common in other dialects then the regional flavour of the speaker may not be clear. Look at the following two passages of Scots and North Country English dialect respectively and see what kind of balance has been struck.

> 'Bide a wee – bide a wee; you southrons are aye in sic a hurry, and this is something concerns yoursell, an ye wad tak patience to hear't – Yill? – deil a drap o' yill did Pate offer me; but Mattie gae us baith a drap o' skimmed milk, and ane o' her thick ait jannocks, that was as wat and raw as a divot. – O, for the bonnie girdle-cakes o' the North! – and sae we sat doun and took out our clavers.'

> (Sir Walter Scott, *Rob Roy*)

> Just as I was going back up the yard to get my tea at home, hoping the others had come back from the pictures so's I wouldn't have anything to keep on being black about, a copper passed me and headed for the bloke's door. He was striding quickly with his head bent forward, and I knew that somebody had narked. They must have seen him buy the rope and then tipped-off the cop. Or happen the old hen at the yard-end had finally caught on.

> (Alan Sillitoe, 'On Saturday Afternoon')

* * * * * * * * *

dialect vocabulary

In the passage from Rob Roy the regional dialect vocabulary is almost impenetrable without the aid of a dialect dictionary. Words such as *jannocks* and *clavers* cannot be understood by people from outside the dialect area. The Sillitoe extract, on the other hand, allows us to guess what the dialect words might mean. We can guess that the *yard* must be something like a street. *Being black* presumably means being in a bad humour. *Narked* must mean something like 'informed'. A *hen* must be a woman. You find many more works of fiction which make similar interesting contrasts, particularly in the literatures of countries where the English which is spoken there is richly influenced in its vocabulary by words borrowed from indigenous languages. Such literatures are to be found, for example, in Africa and the West Indies.

COTTAGE CHEESE

△ DUTCH CHEESE
● POT CHEESE
○ SMEAR CASE

0   25   50
SCALE IN MILES

Figure 6.4   Dialect map of *Dutch cheese, pot cheese* and *smear case*.

If regional dialect vocabulary items are spoken in geographically distinct areas then it should be possible to survey an area to find out where particular words are spoken. Such a regional dialect survey is, as you can imagine, a delicate operation. There is no point in surveying the local doctor who comes from another region. But, with all their difficulties, regional dialect surveys of a number of areas in the English-speaking world have been conducted. There are notable dialect surveys of England and the United States, for example: Orton and Halliday's *Survey of English Dialects* (Orton, Harald, and Wilfred J. Halliday, *Survey of English Dialects*, vols I and II, Leeds, 1962–3); and Kurath's *A Word Geography of the Eastern United States* (Kurath, Hans, *A Word Geography of the Eastern United States*, Ann Arbor, MI, 1949). As a result of doing such surveys, maps can be drawn which contain isoglosses, lines which mark the **isogloss** approximate boundaries for the use of a particular linguistic feature of a dialect, such as the use of a particular dialect word.

Figure 6.4 is a dialect map marking the division in the United States between the areas where people call a particular kind of fresh cheese either *Dutch cheese*, *pot cheese*, or *smear case*.

Authors who wish to represent the social status of speakers will often include social dialect words. Social dialect vocabularies are determined **social dialect vocabulary** on the basis of the social class or status of the speaker. For example, what you call the *toilet* tends to be part of your social dialect. Some people might call it the *loo*. There are a variety of words for the last course of a meal: *pudding*, *dessert*, *afters*. There are a variety of words for the most important room in a house. It can be called the *sitting room*, the *parlour*, the *living room*, the *lounge*. What you call it is often a matter of social dialect.

It has been found that linguistic clues such as social dialect vocabulary are often very powerful indicators of a speaker's social status and therefore of how they will be regarded by others. Many linguists see the responses which the speech of lower socio-economic speakers evoke in middle-class people as being the result of prejudice. By analysing the actual linguistic form that gives rise to these responses linguists have been able to explain that, contrary to the prejudice, there is nothing in the speech forms themselves that is inferior. That only leaves the prejudices of the hearer, about which, as a linguist, it is hard to do much.

Application

Which words in the following passage tell you about the speakers' probable social status, and what is that status likely to be?

'Mrs Barrows has worked hard, Martin, very hard. It grieves me to report that she has suffered a severe breakdown. It has taken the form of a persecution complex accompanied by distressing hallucinations.'

'I am very sorry, sir,' said Mr Martin.

'Mrs Barrows is under the delusion,' continued Mr Fitweiler, 'that you visited her last evening and behaved yourself in an – uh – unseemly manner.'

(James Thurber, 'The Catbird Seat')

* * * * * * * * * *

Clearly Mr Martin is a subordinate because he addresses Mr Fitweiler as *Sir*. Mr Fitweiler is in a socially superior position and probably polite upper middle-class, to judge by vocabulary such as: *grieves*, *report*, *distressing*, *delusion*, and *unseemly*.

ethnic dialect vocabulary

Ethnic dialect vocabulary are the words used by people who belong to particular ethnic groups and characteristic of these groups. These are usually words which have been borrowed from the language or languages which members of the ethnic group spoke when they emigrated. For example, there are quite a number of Yiddish borrowings in the English spoken by people of Jewish origin in New York City. The word *lox*, which denotes thinly sliced kosher smoked salmon, often eaten with cream cheese on bagels, is a borrowing from Yiddish and originally an ethnic dialect word. The words *chutzpah*, *mensch*, *schlemiel*, are also of Yiddish origin. In Black English in the USA there are words of African origin such as *goober*, 'peanut', and *juju*, 'amulet'. In New Zealand English there are words which were previously ethnic dialect words for Maori speakers of English such as *whakapapa*, 'genealogy' and *kaumatua*, 'tribal elder'.

Such ethnic dialect words and expressions can be and often are in turn borrowed into the more general vocabulary.

6.2.7 *Specialist vocabularies*

A speaker has a regional, social and ethnic dialect vocabulary because of where he or she comes from, either regionally or socially or ethnically. But every speaker is also in command of a number of specialist vocabularies that are related to particular interests and occupations. Doctors, when they are speaking as doctors to other doctors or to their patients, use some vocabulary items that are peculiar to their occupation. So do surfies and drug addicts. Rock music has its own vocabulary, which is different from that of jazz music.

specialist vocabulary

Here is a piece of scientific writing. Notice how difficult it is to understand because of its specialist technical vocabulary.

Assuming conversions of gluons into sea quark–antiquark pairs, any gluon contribution is implicitly taken into account in the sea quark distribution.

(Gensch and Kriegel, 'Discussions of Vector Meson Production in Kp Interactions in Terms of a Simple Quark Fusion Model')

How big are specialist vocabularies? They can be very big indeed. The maintenance manuals for the European airbus airliner are reputed to weigh more than the airbus itself. Imagine how many specialist vocabulary items there will be in such manuals. And imagine the task of translating them into other languages.

Application

Below is a piece of dialogue containing a number of specialist vocabulary items. Which words seem to have developed specialist senses? Can you guess what they might mean?

'Ah well, Toby's come up in the world since your day, Mr Smiley,' Tarr explained. 'They tell me even his pavement artists ride around in Cadillacs. Steal the scalphunters' bread out of their mouths too, if they get the chance, right, Mr Guillam?'

'They've become the general footpads for London Station,' Guillam said shortly. 'Part of lateralism.'

(John le Carré, *Tinker, Tailor, Soldier, Spy*)

Pavement artists, *scalphunters*, *footpads*, and *lateralism* all seem to be specialist terms. Since John Le Carré's novels are usually about spying, the first three must be occupations, and lateralism some kind of policy concerned with spying. Without reading the rest of the novel, it is difficult to get much further.

Exercise 6.14

Find an area in which you have a specialist vocabulary and note down ten words from it that you think at least some of your friends will not know. Try to write good definitions of the meaning of these words and look at their etymologies to see how they have come to have the meaning and structure that they do. Frequently, you will not be able to find specialist words or specialist meanings in a dictionary. For example, the word *tube*, used in the vocabulary of surfing, is a metaphor because waves that are tubes are similar to literal tubes.

* * * * * * * * * *

6.2.8   *Formality and vocabulary*

Many vocabulary items can only be appropriately used in certain environments. For example, slang or colloquial vocabulary is out of place at a formal church service or on being presented to royalty. Conversely, formal vocabulary is out of place in a school playground unless it is used for humorous or ironic effect.

Many speakers are uncomfortable with very formal situations, do not quite know which words to choose and therefore remain tongue-tied. However, this is a matter of how familiar one is with the situation. Ambassadors are not tongue-tied at embassy parties because they have been to many of such parties and thus know what to say. Students entering tertiary education are, by contrast, often not sure how formal their writing must be. In such a situation people often hypercorrect, that is they use what they consider more prestigious linguistic forms than are the norm for the situation. However, once one is familiar with a situation, the language, including vocabulary choice, usually looks after itself.

hypercorrect

Application

Here is Joe Gargery, the blacksmith in Charles Dickens' novel *Great Expectations*, hypercorrecting when he is in London visiting his nephew and step-son Pip, now a gentleman.

> 'Us two being now alone, Sir', resumed Joe, 'and me having the intentions and abilities to stay not many minutes more, I will now conclude – leastways begin – to mention that which have led to my having the present honour. For if it was not,' said Joe, with his old air of lucid exposition, 'that my only wish were to be useful to you, I should not have had the honour of breaking wittles in the company and abode of gentlemen.'

Joe and Pip are together in private, which is not a context in which two relatives need to be formal with one another. However, Joe feels so out of his social depth that he is more formal in his choice of vocabulary than is required. So he uses words which are morphologically more complex than one would normally expect a blacksmith to use in any context, for example *intentions, abilities*. Also he uses formulae in an interesting way. *Having the present honour* is formal, whereas *breaking wittles* is not. In other words the hypercorrection is not consistent.

This brings us to the question of what constitutes the right form to use in any situation. We can say that one might be a native speaker of a language but still not have nativelike competence in it in every situation. To gain that, one must become a native speaker in each situation in turn. That takes time. So hypercorrecting is only hypercorrecting by reference to some norm of nativelike performance in a particular situation or range of situations.

6.2.9 *Dictionaries*

Whole vocabularies, as we have seen, exist in languages, and in people's heads. In a society where there was no writing, dictionaries would not exist but then neither would they be needed. Speakers would learn all the words they needed from others' use of them. However, writing makes it possible to look up in dictionaries words which one might not come across in the normal course of events. Indeed the first dictionaries of English were published with this in mind. As the speakers of English became more socially stratified and as literacy became more common among middle-class people, there were words in writing that were not in people's own vocabularies. Clearly they needed a dictionary, and that market niche was filled first by rather simple lists of 'hard' words but later and most notably by Samuel Johnson's dictionary, in which he attempted to list all of the words in the eighteenth-century English of his time.

Currently many kinds of dictionaries exist for particular purposes. There are bilingual dictionaries, dictionaries of idioms, technical dictionaries, large dictionaries and small dictionaries. To understand what all these different dictionaries can do for those who consult them we need to understand two things: the way dictionaries come into existence and how they compare with the internalised vocabularies of actual speakers, with which we have dealt earlier.

Dictionaries are books compiled by lexicographers and published by publishers. Since they are published by publishers, they are, for the most part, written for particular markets and in the hope that they will make a profit. This means that dictionaries are always a compromise. In a reasonably sized, and therefore reasonably priced, dictionary of English it isn't possible to list all the words a reader might conceivably want to look up. So lexicographers make a choice of the words which they think more people will want to look up and leave out the more marginal and arcane words, which are less likely to be useful. This choice can now be made easier by searching large computer-based corpora of text looking for each word, its context, and how frequently it appears in the corpora.

In order to make things easier and therefore cheaper, publishers who publish dictionaries will publish various versions of the same dictionary materials by selecting entries and what is said about each entry. Small pocket dictionaries will be cheap and will contain a smaller number of entries than desk dictionaries.

Knowing all this it is obvious that dictionaries cannot be authoritative in all respects. They attempt, as best they can, to list as many words as possible within the bounds of the particular dictionary format. They attempt to give as many senses of the words as they can. They provide a few examples and hints of how the word might be used but they cannot be authoritative in the sense that they provide unimpeachable information on all the aspects of all the words of the language that the totality of its native speakers might want to know. That is why, when playing Scrabble, one must nominate a dictionary as an authority even though it cannot be an authority. There is no other option.

So how can you tell a good dictionary from a bad one? That depends on the purpose you have for referring to a dictionary. Most native speakers use dictionaries to check the spellings of words. Dictionaries don't normally get spelling wrong. People also look up dictionaries for unfamiliar words. Here, the bigger the dictionary the more likely it is to contain an unfamiliar word. But not necessarily. A very large number of technical words will not appear in a standard dictionary. For them you must turn to a technical dictionary in the area.

If a word is unfamiliar then one usually looks it up for its meaning. Here one is again at the mercy of the lexicographer who wrote the entry. There is an art to writing good glosses for the meaning of words and for getting all the ones that a reader might need. For example, in Section 6.1 we saw that the word *imposter* is glossed as 'swindler'. This is clearly not a full synonym and thus can lead a reader astray. Many words have multiple meanings and so a reader wants as many of the meanings represented as is possible within the limits set by the dictionary. Again, if you do not find what seems like the right meaning, it may well be a shortcoming of the dictionary.

Figure 6.5 and 6.6 give two sample entries for the same word to illustrate some of the things we have been saying.

freight /freɪt/ *n. & v.* —*n.* **1** the transport of goods in containers or by water or air or *US* by land. **2** goods transported; cargo. **3** a charge for transportation of goods. **4** the hire of a ship or aircraft for transporting goods. **5** a load or burden. —*v.tr.* **1** transport (goods) as freight. **2** load with freight. **3** hire or let out (a ship) for the carriage of goods and passengers. □freight ton see TON[1]. [MDu., MLG *vrecht* var. of *vracht*: cf. FRAUGHT]

Figure 6.5 Entry for *freight* from *Concise Oxford English Dictionary*

The first entry for the word *freight* is from the *Concise Oxford English Dictionary*. It begins with the spelling of the word and this is followed by its pronunciation in brackets, in the IPA characters of Chapter 2. Other dictionaries may use systems devised by the dictionary editors. To understand what they mean you must look up the section on the pronunciation guides at the beginning of the dictionary. Next are its two syntactic categories, in italics and abbreviated. Again, if you are not sure what these abbreviations mean you must look them up at the front of the dictionary. In the case of *freight*, it has two categories: noun, and verb gap noun, i.e. transitive verb. Then come the senses of the word, each numbered and related to the syntactic category of the word. Only the main senses are given, each introduced by a number, the second set being the senses the word has when it is a transitive verb. The last piece of the entry, given in square brackets, is its etymology. Again the abbreviations must be looked up if you don't know what MDu happens to be. In this case the etymology section indicates that the word *freight* was borrowed

freight (freit), *sb.* Also 5 freyte, freyght, 6-7 fraight, 6 frate. [prob. a. MDu. or MLG. *vrecht*, var. of *vracht*: see FRAUGHT *sb.* The word has passed from Du. or LG. into some of the Rom. langs.; F. *fret* hire of a ship (from 13th c.), Sp. *flete*, Pg. *frete*.]

1. a. Hire of a vessel for the transport of goods; the service of transporting goods (originally, by water; now extended, esp. in *U.S.*, to land-transit); the sum of money paid for this. In early use also: Passage-money.

1463 Mann. *& Househ. Exp.* 194 My mastyr toke hym ffor his ffreyte to Caleys..vj. *li.* *1483* CAXTON *Gold. Leg.* 283/2 Whome they receyued in to theyr Shippe gladly and sayd they wold brynge hym thyder without ony freyght or huyr. *1538* STARKEY *England* II. i. 172 Specyally yf to that were joynyd a nother ordynance..wych ys, concernyng the frate of marchandyse. *1580* HOLLYBAND *Treas. Fr. Tong*, *Naulage*, the fraight or fare payed for passage ouer the water. *a 1687* PETTY *Pol. Arith.* (1690) 19 Those who have the command of the Sea Trade may Work at easier Freight with more profit. *1712* E. COOKE *Voy. S. Sea* 353 Having agreed to pay no Freight there. *1764* BURN *Poor Laws* 180 Let a small deduction be made from the freights of ships, and from seamens wages. *1765* T. HUTCHINSON *Hist. Mass.* I. ii. 257 They purchased a ship-load of masts, the freight whereof cost them sixteen hundred pounds. *1854* HAWTHORNE *Eng. Note-bks.* (1883) II. 123 The captains talk together about..how freights are in America. *1861* GOSCHEN *For. Exch.* 18 The charge for freight acts with the same force as a charge for a commodity actually produced and exported. *1868* ROGERS *Pol. Econ.* ix. (1876) 83 The passage from the East to Europe has been so shortened, that a freight from thence to England is reduced to one-fourth.

† b. *to take freight*: to take passage for oneself and goods. *Obs.*

1719 DE FOE *Crusoe* II. xvi, We all took freight with him.

2. a. The cargo or lading (of a ship); a ship-load. Hence, anything carried by sea or land; 'goods' in transit or being transported by rail, road, or sea. Chiefly *N. Amer.* with reference to the carriage of goods by railway. *fast freight* (U.S.): see FAST *a.* 11.

1502 ARNOLDE *Chron.* (1811) 229 We..charge you precisely that the forsayd [merchants] wyth their shyp's freight..ye suffer and let go passe. *1540* *Act 32 Hen. VIII*, c. 14 Beyng mynded..to take any freight or ladynge..into any of the saide shyppes. *1694* *Acc. Sev. Late Voy.* II. (1711) 3 When they have their full Fraight of Whales, they put up their great Flag. *1789* BRAND *Hist. Newcastle* II. 255 [A vessel] trading to Newcastle upon Tyne with corn, and returning with a freight of sea coals. *1832* HT. MARTINEAU *Ireland* 131 Do you know that Vessel? You cannot be aware what freight it bears? *1856* KANE *Arct. Expl.* II. xix. 196 They offered to exclude both clothes and food in favor of a full freight of these treasures.

b. *transf.* A load, burden,

1618 CHAPMAN *Hesiod* I. 574 At thy purse's height, And when it fights low, give thy use his freight. *1697* DRYDEN *Virg. Georg.* II. 599 With the ruddy Freight the bending Branches groan. *1805* WORDSW. *Prelude* v. 84, I..looked self-questioned what this freight Which the new comer carried..Could mean. *1878* HUXLEY *Physiogr.* 73 These warm moist winds..deposit their freight of moisture in showers of rain.

c. *fig.*

a 1631 DONNE in *Select.* (1840) 43 Keep up that holy cheerfulness, which Christ makes the ballast of a Christian, and his freight too. *1755* YOUNG *Centaur* v. Wks. 1757 IV. 223 Every moment shall return, and lay its whole freight.. before the Throne. *1812* J. WILSON *Isle of Palms* I. 127 An earthly freight she bears Of joys and sorrows. *1872* HOLLAND *Marb. Proph.* 97 A man who lifted On ready words his freight of gratitude.

† 3. A journey of a laden vessel. *Obs.*

1716 CHURCH *Philip's War* (1865) I. 157 He made use of Canoo's: But by that time they had made two fraights..the Wind sprung up.

4. orig. *U.S.* Short for *freight-train*: a goods-train. *by freight*: by the usual means of transportation, as opposed to *by express*.

1861 *Remin. Life Railroad Engineer* 123 He was running the Night Express,..while I was running the through freight. *1881* *Chicago Times* 18 June, A freight of thirty loaded cars..collided with the other train. *1922* M. B. HOUSTON *Witch Man* i. 14 There were four trains a day in Innessburg, not counting the freights. *1955* E. HILLARY *High Adventure* ix. 158 Feeling a little like an express train overhauling a slow freight.

5. *attrib.* and *Comb.*, as *freight agent, car* (= goods truck or van), *carriage, container, depot, elevator, engine, forwarder, house, locomotive, -man, rate, route, shed, steamer, terminal, traffic, train* (= goods train), *wagon, yard*; also *freight-handler, -handling*. Also '*freightliner*, a train carrying goods in containers; † *freight-money*, payment for conveyance of freight.

1843 *Rep. Western R.R.* 17 **Freight-agent.* *1875* *N. Amer. Rev.* CXX. 403 He has been promoted to the office of freight-agent. *1944* Sears, Roebuck Catal. 900 If there is a freight agent at your station, you pay freight charges when shipment is received. *1833* *Amer. Railroad Jrnl.* II. 325/2, 10 **freight cars.* *1856* OLMSTED *Slave States* 55 There were, in the train, two first-class passenger cars, and two freight cars. *1947* *Chicago Daily News* 17 Jan. 4/2 A freight car and caboose were destroyed by fire. *1967* Freight car [see CAR *sb.*[1] 2 a]. *1884* *Pall Mall G.* 25 Sept. 5/2 They will put up their rates on the *freight carriage eastward. *1969* *Jane's Freight Containers* 1968-69 12/1 A *freight container is an article of transport equipment. *1841* *Spirit of Times* 25 Sept. 354/1 *Freight depot. *1904* W. N. HARBEN *Georgians* I The long, brick freight depot. *1906* *Springfield Weekly Republ.* 4 Oct. 7 What the English call a 'railway goods station', and what we call a freight depot. *1903* ADE *In Babel* 18 He had patented certain devices which were used by all makers of passenger and *freight elevators. *1911* *Daily Colonist* (Victoria, B.C.) 21 Apr. 16/3 Expedition combined with safety, can only be secured by means of a freight elevator. *1968* *Globe & Mail* (Toronto) 3 Feb. B5/2 'Do you know that only three apartment buildings in Toronto have freight elevators?' he asked. 'We sometimes have to get furniture on top of elevators to get it into buildings.' *1922* G. T. STUFFLEBEAM *Traffic Dict.* 64 *Freight forwarder, one who is located at a port, attends to documentation, booking space, securing marine insurance and other detail in connection with export shipments. *1968* *Economist* 14 Sept. p. xxv/1 There is more pressure on the British freight forwarders than there is on their continental counterparts. *1969* *Jane's Freight Containers* 1968-69 28/1 The members of the Canadian International Freight Forwarders Association Inc. *1970* *Times* 2 June (Container Suppl.) p. iv/3 The increasing range of forwarding work, the changing conditions under which it is carried out, and the new physical equipment—containers, in particular—have called for the new and wider description as freight forwarders. *1882* *Pall Mall G.* 12 July 8/2 A riot has occurred [at Jersey city] between the *freight-handlers on strike and the Italian labourers. *1887* *Bureau Statist. Labour* (N.Y.) 327 There was also a great interruption of *freight-handling. *1848* *Hunt's Merch. Mag.* XVIII. 383 The Worcester Railroad.. has a *freight-house in Boston. *1918* *Essex Inst. Hist. Coll.* LIV. 218 They should be run as one road, thus doing away with the expensive separate staffs, repair shops, freight houses, etc. *1948* *Daily Ardmoreite* (Ardmore, Okla.) 28 July 13/2 The car was shunted to a siding near the freight house yesterday afternoon. *1965* *Times* 12 July 14 (caption) A typical *Freightliner..will be loaded..by the latest equipment... The container is lifted off the road transport ..and immediately transferred on to the rail wagon. *1966* *Daily Tel.* 11 Aug. 22/7 British Rail is to build 60 refrigerated glass fibre containers to carry meat and perishable goods in its freightliner trains. *1969* *Lebende Sprachen* XIV. 65/2 A grain terminal and a British Railways freightliner terminal are to be built at Tilbury. *1934* WEBSTER, **Freight locomotive.* *1935* *Discovery* Nov. 326/1 The freight locomotives were designed to haul considerably heavier trains than the passenger locomotives. *1855* *Gen. Term Rep., Goods*..should be sent forward by a carrier, or *freightman. *1755* MAGENS *Insurances* II. 189 All Insurances on expected Gain..future *Freight-Monies. Seamens Wages and Mens Lives are universally forbid. *1848* *Hunt's Merch. Mag.* XVIII. 101 *Freight-rates—Iron, 25 cents per 100 pounds. *1881* *Chicago Times* 12 Mar., A freight-rate war between the eastern lines of railroads is regarded..as unavoidable. *1907* *Westm. Gaz.* 20 Nov. 10/2 Startling freight-rate experiments of the German railways. *1943* J. S. HUXLEY *TVA* xii. 114 The inter-territorial

Figure 6.6 Part of entry for *freight* from *Oxford English Dictionary*

from the Middle Dutch word *vrecht*, which was a variant spelling of the word *vracht*, and it is related to the English word *fraught*, which comes from the same historical source.

This entry is an edited down version of the entry in the *Oxford English Dictionary*, often called the big Oxford. The big Oxford started to be compiled in the mid-nineteenth century and took three editors to finish. It was based on the idea that entries should show the development of the word over the whole of its recorded history, and that the entries should illustrate this history through quotations. Part of the entry for *freight* from the big Oxford is shown in Figure 6.6.

You can see from the size of this one entry that the big Oxford is going to be a big dictionary. It is in fact twenty volumes in its second edition. The most convenient and lightweight way to gain access to it is through a CD ROM reader, since the OED is now available in a form which looks like a CD but which you read with a computer rather than listening to it by means of a stereo. This new technology allows you to search for the word you want very rapidly.

You may ask what place a huge dictionary like this has in the study of English. In the first place it can be used just for its own sake, to look up the historical development of a word. But it is also an essential tool when reading English written in earlier periods when English words did not mean what they do now. When you do that and are not sure about the meaning of a word, when it sounds as though it can't mean what it does now, or perhaps the word is so archaic that you don't know it at all, then by searching for the word in the CD ROM and checking the dates of the illustrative quotations so as to find a quotation near the period in which the book was written you can understand what the writer at the time actually meant. Many Shakespeare editors do some of this work for you in the notes to editions of Shakespeare's plays. But in many other cases the big Oxford must be accessed by you, the reader. Doing that with the paper version of the dictionary is a long business. Doing it with a CD ROM version is easy.

Dictionaries, by convention, arrange their entries according to alphabetical order of the written version of the word. Clearly that is a useful way to look words up. However, there are other ways that have their uses. A **rhyming dictionary** often lists words in reverse alphabetical order, and that way all the words which rhyme with each other are listed together.

Another means of listing words is to list them according to their meaning. Essentially this is what a **thesaurus** does. If you want a word with the same meaning as a given word you look it up in the thesaurus. Again, computer technology is able to help here. In many modern computers a thesaurus is available as a piece of software, and thus if you are writing and would like to use a different word, but one which has the same meaning as the one you have just thought of, you can get a range of options from the thesaurus.

Further exercises

Exercise 6.15

Are the italicised words synonyms?

- (a) I want to *buy/purchase* some tomatoes.
- (b) My *mother/mum* doesn't like you.
- (c) These tomatoes are *red/ripe*.
- (d) I nearly fell into the *river/stream*.
- (e) Your tie is too *broad/wide*.
- (f) I *almost/nearly* fell in.
- (g) Denis has bought a *house/home*.
- (h) He's not a bad *bloke/fellow*.
- (i) That car needs a new *muffler/silencer*.
- (j) My *arm/elbow* still hurts.
- (k) Our host was *drunk/intoxicated*.
- (l) His father is even *slimmer/skinnier*.
- (m) This model is *expensive/valuable*.

Exercise 6.16

Put the following set of words into pairs with opposite senses. Then work out whether the words are an antonym pair, a complementary pair, or a converse pair:

- (a) high
- (b) cold
- (c) tender
- (d) uncle
- (e) accept
- (f) whisper
- (g) aunt
- (h) shout
- (i) hot
- (j) low

Exercise 6.17

How have synonyms and antonyms been put to use in this poem:

> love is more thicker than forget
> more thinner than recall
> more seldom than a wave is wet
> more frequent than to fail
>
> it is most mad and moonly
> and less it shall unbe
> than all the sea which only
> is deeper than the sea
>
> love is less always than to win
> less never than alive
> less bigger than the least begin
> less littler than forgive
>
> it is most sane and sunly
> and more it cannot die
> than all the sky which only
> is higher than the sky

(e. e. cummings)

Exercise 6.18

Examine the following list of words and then answer the questions given below, taking your examples from the list. (Note: some words can be used more than once.)

deep, villain, buy, animal, illegal, by, profound, legal, deer, shallow, sell.

(a) Identify a pair of gradable antonyms.

(b) Comment on the polysemy of the pair of gradable antonyms.

(c) Identify a pair of converses.

(d) Identify a pair of complementaries (ungradable opposites).

(e) Identify a pair of words related by hyponymy. Identify which is the hyponym and which the superordinate.

(f) Identify a pair of partial synonyms.

(g) Explain briefly why the two words are not perfectly synonymous.

(h) Identify a pair of homophones.

Glossary

Acronym   Word made up from the first sounds or syllables of words in a phrase.

Active vocabulary   The words that a speaker uses in speaking or writing.

Adjective   Head word of an adjective phrase. *See* Chapter 7. Some adjectives inflect for the morphosyntactic category of comparison.

Adverb   Head word of an adverb phrase. *See* Chapter 7.

Affix   General name for prefixes and suffixes.

Allomorphy   The various forms of the same morpheme.

Amelioration   The historical change which improves a word's connotations.

Antonym   A word that has the opposite sense to another where the oppositeness comes about from the senses being at the ends of a scale, for example, *young* and *old*.

Archaism   The historical process whereby a word comes no longer to be in use, or a word which is no longer in use.

Associations   The associations of words come about because of the attitudes people have to the word and its sense.

Auxiliary verb   Verb which modifies a lexical verb in a verb phrase. Auxiliary verbs appear to the left of, or before, lexical verbs. *See* Chapter 7.

Base   The lexeme (or set of lexemes) which a word formation rule takes and turns into a constituent (or constituents) of the new lexeme(s) created by the rule.

Blend   A word whose phonological form is formed from the first half of the phonological form of one word and the second half of another, for example *smog* is a blend of *smoke* and *fog*.

Bound morpheme   A morpheme that cannot function as an independent word, that is, a morpheme which must attach to a stem to form a word.

Clipping   Shortening the phonological representation of a word.

Closed class   Classes of words where no new members of the class can be created by regular word formation rules.

Co-hyponym   Two or more words whose senses are hyponyms of the same superordinate, *chair* and *table* are co-hyponyms of *furniture*.

Coining   Making up a new word.

Collocation   Conventional associations of words within a linear sequence in sentences.

Common noun   A noun that will go with *the*.

Comparative   A morphosyntactic property of an adjective or adverb. Its form may be the inflectional suffix *–er* or alternatively the word *more* used immediately before the adjective or adverb. The comparative form is usually used in the context where the referents of two noun phrases are being compared in respect of some property, as in *the Atlantic Ocean is smaller than the Pacific Ocean*.

Comparison   A morphosyntactic category of adjectives and adverbs having three morphosyntactic properties: **positive**, the unmarked form of the word, **comparative** and **superlative**.

Complementary senses   Words have complementary senses if they belong to a semantic field with only their senses in it.

Componential analysis   Finding the sense components of the meanings of words.

Compositional   If the meaning of a linguistic unit which is itself made up of constituents is made up in a predictable way out of the meanings of its constituent parts then it is semantically compositional.

Compound   A word made up from two other words.

Conjunction   Word that links two grammatical structures. *See* Chapter 7.

Connotation   The connotations of words are conventional social associations that words have developed. They tend to be negative or positive depending on people's attitudes to what the words denote.

Converse senses   Two words have converse senses if they are essentially synonyms but the 'actors' or relationship which they denote are differently allocated by the two senses. For example: *buy* and *sell*, *husband* and *wife*.

Conversion   The word formation process whereby a lexeme having one syntactic category acquires a further syntactic category and thus creates a new lexeme.

Count noun   Noun that takes plural inflection and can occur with the determiner *a*.

Denotation   The set of things, actions, properties etc. that a word's sense gives it the potential to refer to.

Derivation   The formation of lexemes by means of adding a derivational affix.

Derivational affix   *See* **Derivation**.

Derivational morpheme   An affix which is part of the word-building system. Derivational affixes take as input one lexeme and through the addition of the affix create a new lexeme.

Determiner   One of: *a, the, this, that, these, those. See* Chapter 7.

Dialect vocabulary   Vocabulary that is (recognisably) used by a sub-group of speakers of the language.

Distribution   A grammatical constituent's characteristic place(s) in sequence with other grammatical constituents.

Drift   The changes which take place in the representation of a word in the lexicon after it has been lexicalised.

Echo words   Words made up by attempting to imitate the sound of the thing the word denotes.

Entailment   When what one sentence means follows logically from what another sentence means, the meaning of the second sentence entails the meaning of the first.

Ethnic dialect vocabulary   Words that are distinctive of the speech of members of an ethnic sub-group of society.

Etymology   The origin and history of words.

Euphemism   A word or expression which tries to evade drawing attention to the socially uncomfortable nature of what it denotes.

Folk etymology   An incorrect guess about the origin of a word.

Free morpheme   A morpheme that can function as a word.

Gradable adjective   An adjective that will take comparison.

Grammatical category   The syntactic function of a word, for example noun.

Grammatical word   The form a lexeme takes when it includes one of its possible morphosyntactic properties, for example, the plural form of a noun, such as *women.*

Head   The head of a lexeme is that constituent which determines the syntactic properties of the whole lexeme.

Homonym   A word that has the same form as another but is otherwise unrelated to it.

Hypercorrecting   The use of linguistic forms which are more formal than is considered appropriate by the speakers who are familiar with the situation.

Hypernym   Synonym for **Superordinate**.

Hyponym   A word whose sense is a more particular instance of that of its superordinate, for example, *chair* is a hyponym of *furniture.*

Infinitive   Form of a verb having no inflection.

Inflection   An affix that is part of the grammatical system of a language.

Isogloss   Line on a map representing the boundary between geographic areas where two alternative regional dialect features are used.

Labelled bracketed notation   A way of showing hierarchical organisation by surrounding each unit in a structure with two brackets and enclosing within them a label to show to which category the unit inside the brackets belongs.

Lexeme   A word as an abstract entity, distinct from the inflected forms which it may assume in different syntactic contexts, for example, *write*, *writes*, *wrote*, *writing*, *written* are forms of the lexeme WRITE.

Lexical borrowing   The adoption of a word from the vocabulary of one language by that of another.

Lexical item   An entry in the lexicon of a speaker or language.

Lexical verb   Head of a verb phrase. *See* Chapter 7. Verbs inflect for the morphosyntactic category of tense.

Lexicalisation   The process whereby a coinage becomes an established lexical item.

Lexicon   Used in three senses:

1.   the dictionary which a speaker of a language has in his or her head;

2.   the set of lexemes of a language, and the processes which relate them;

3.   the set of lexical items of a language.

Metaphor   Using a word while breaking some of its selectional restrictions.

Morpheme   An element of word structure.

Morpho-phonemic   Having to do with the phonemic form of morphemes.

Morphology   Word form or the study of word form.

Morphosyntactic category   Grammatical categories which have to do with both morphology and syntax, such as tense, case, number. *See also* **Morphosyntactic property**.

Morphosyntactic property   One of the grammatically relevant properties within a morphosyntactic category. For example, in English, the category *Number* in nouns contains the properties *Singular* and *Plural*, and the category *Tense* contains the properties *Present* and *Past*.

Narrowing   The historical process whereby the denotation of a word covers less than it did.

Non-count noun   Noun that does not take plural inflection and cannot occur with the determiner *a*.

Non-gradable adjective   An adjective that will not take comparison.

Nonce word   A word coined and used once but not lexicalised.

Noun   Head word of a noun phrase. *See* Chapter 7.

Open class   Classes of words that can be added to by the word formation processes of a language.

Part of speech   A traditional name for **grammatical category**.

Participle   Verb form with some adjectival properties. In English, most participles end in *–ing*, *–en*, or *–ed*.

Passive vocabulary   The words a speaker knows but does not use in speech or writing.

Pejoration   The historical process whereby a word comes to have worse connotations than it previously had.

Perfect participle   A form of the verb regularly ending in the inflection *–en* or *–ed* (provided the *–ed* is not the past tense), or irregularly by such means as a change in the vowel, for example *sung*. (Traditionally termed the past participle.)

Personification   A particular kind of metaphor where something that is not human is given human attributes.

Phonological form   The way the sound of a word is represented in the lexicon.

Polysemy   The property of having different but semantically related senses.

Positive   A morphosyntactic property of adjectives or adverbs. Its form is the standard form, i.e. without inflection.

Pragmatics   That part of the meaning of an utterance that comes from things other than the senses of its words and the grammar of its sentence(s).

Prefix   An affix that attaches to the left of the stem.

Preposition   Head of a prepositional phrase, for example *in*. *See* Chapter 7.

Productivity   The extent to which a word formation process, such as affixation, is able to apply to lexemes of the appropriate kind so as to create new words.

Progressive participle   A form of verb regularly ending in the inflection –*ing*. (Traditionally termed the present participle.)

Proper noun   A noun that will not go with the determiner *the*. The name of a person, or thing, e.g. *Sally*, or of a place.

Proper noun conversion   A change in a proper noun's syntactic representation whereby it becomes a common noun, for example *Bowler*, the man, to *bowler*, the hat.

Pun   The use of a word that has two senses for humorous effect.

Reference   Words, through their denotation, can be used by speakers to refer to things, actions, properties, relationships etc., that is, to pick them out for the hearer from other things, actions etc. This activity is called reference.

Referring expression   A word or phrase which can be used to refer.

Regional dialect word   Word characteristically used by speakers from a particular geographic region.

Rhyming dictionary   A dictionary which lists words by their reverse spelling.

Root creation   Words made up from scratch by putting together a new phonological, syntactic, and semantic representation.

Selectional restrictions   Restrictions created by the way senses fit with each other in phrases and sentences.

Semantic field   An area of meaning covered by words with related senses.

Semantic redundancy   Semantic redundancy occurs when the sense of, say, an adjective has a semantic component (or components) which is already present in the sense of, say, a noun of which it is a modifier.

Semantic representation   The representation of a word's meaning.

Sense   The meaning of a word excluding its connotations or associations. Meanings of words as seen from within the language.

Simile   A comparison in which one thing is said to be *like* or *as* another, for example, 'Britten motorcycles ride like the wind'.

Social dialect vocabulary   Words characteristically used by members of a particular social class.

Specialist vocabulary   Technical vocabulary of a group of specialists.

Standard form   Form of the adjective not inflected for either the comparative or the superlative.

Stem   The form of a word to which affixes are attached.

Suffix   An affix that attaches to the right of its stem.

Superlative   A morphosyntactic property of adjectives or adverbs. Its form is usually an inflection *−est*, or alternatively the word *most*, placed immediately before the adjective or adverb.

Superordinate   A word has a superordinate sense to another word (or words) if its sense is that of the whole set where the sense of the other word(s) denote sub-categories of the set, for example *furniture* has the superordinate sense where *table*, *chair*, *stool*, etc. have hyponymous senses.

Suppletive form   An unpredictable and unrelated form of a word for a particular morphosyntactic realisation, for example *better* as the comparative form of *good*.

Syncretism   This occurs when a morphosyntactic contrast systematically shows no difference in form even though elsewhere the morphosyntactic properties concerned are distinguished inflectionally. For example, both the perfect and past-tense forms of regular verbs in English are the same, e.g. *John called the office* and *John has called the office*.

Synonym   A word or expression that has the same sense as another.

Syntactic category   A word's part-of-speech label representing where a word will fit in a sentence. Synonymous with **grammatical category** and **part of speech**.

Taboo word   A word whose use is socially prohibited (at least in some contexts).

Tautology   Synonym for **semantic redundancy**.

Thesaurus   A dictionary which lists together words which have the same meaning.

Unmarked   In the case of pairs of antonymous senses and the lexical items which bear those senses, one of the pair of lexical items often has, as well as one of the antonymous senses, a neutral sense which subsumes both anonymous senses. This is the unmarked sense. It is the lexical item we use in questions such as 'How tall is she?', where we do not have any idea whether the person is tall or short.

Vocabulary   A set of words that have something other than their linguistic form, function, or meaning in common.

Widen   The historical process whereby a word's denotation comes to encompass more than it did.

Further reading

Aitchison, J., *Words in the Mind: An Introduction to the Mental Lexicon* (Oxford: Basil Blackwell, 1994).

Bauer, L., *Introducing Linguistic Morphology* (Edinburgh: Edinburgh University Press, 1988).

Blakemore, D., *Understanding Utterances: An Introduction to Pragmatics* (Oxford: Blackwell, 1992).

Chierchia, G., and McConnell-Ginet, S., *Meaning and Grammar: An Introduction to Semantics* (Cambridge, Mass.: MIT Press, 1990).

Green, G., *Pragmatics and Natural Language Understanding* (New York: Erlbaum, 1988).

Hurford, J. R., and Heasley, B., *Semantics: A Coursebook* (Cambridge: Cambridge University Press, 1983).

Katamba, F., *Morphology* (London: Macmillan, 1993).

Marchand, H., *The Categories and Types of Present-Day English Word-Formation*, 2nd edn (Munich: C. H. Beck'sche Verlagsbuchhandlung, 1969).

Matthews, P. H., *Morphology*, 2nd edn (Cambridge: Cambridge University Press, 1991).

Palmer, F. R., *Semantics*, 2nd edn (Cambridge: Cambridge University Press, 1981).

Szymanek, B., *Introduction to Morphological Analysis* (Warsaw: Panstwowe Wydawnictwo Naukowe, 1989).

Thomas, O., *Metaphor and Related Subjects* (New York: Random House, 1969).

PART III

Sentences

Introduction to Part III

Concepts

In this part of the book we will look at the formal properties of sentences, that is, their phrase structure and major internal functions. We will see that for each major lexical category there is a phrase of which it is the head. These phrases in turn perform functions within clauses, and clauses and phrases are constituents of sentences. We will also look at how constituents may be moved within the phrase structure of sentences and how this gives rise to the structural properties of questions, relative clauses, passive constructions, and imperatives.

Skills

By the end of this part of the book you should be able to recognise the noun phrase, adjective and adverb phrase, prepositional phrase, and verb phrase. You should be able to determine the internal structure of these phrases and be able to draw tree diagrams of their structure. You should also be able identify the constituents of complex phrases and sentences and how movements may have altered the underlying structure of sentences.

7 The structure of simple sentences

Introduction

We have seen earlier that morphemes are the building blocks that go to make up words. But English is not just a collection of words. Words are put together to form sentences. The way in which words are put together to form sentences is called the syntax of the language (literally the orderly arrangement of parts). To recall that there is such a thing as syntax, remember the following exercise from Chapter 1.

syntax

Make a sentence out of each of the following sets of words:

(a) sleeps, a, baby, newborn

(b) in, house, live, green, the, a, people

(c) the, kicked, boy, ball, a

If it were the case that English had no syntax, that is, no rules for creating sentences, then these words could be put together in any order. However, you will have noticed that there are only a very few orders that go to make English sentences. All the other possible orders (including the order the words are given in, above) do not make English sentences.

But what is it exactly that enables you to do this ordering? We saw in Chapter 1 that there is an infinite number of sentences in English and that we create new ones all the time. So out of the building blocks of words we are able to construct an infinite number of sentences. How exactly do the rules of syntax come into this? First, we have decided that there must be such rules because they are what enables us to structure sets of words into sentences. Secondly, there must be a finite set of them.

There are a number of reasons why this must be so. First, if English had an infinite set of syntactic rules no-one would be able ever to learn

214 ~ Part III: Sentences

them all. Yet we do learn them, and quite early in life. Secondly, if the set of rules was infinite then we would not be able to understand sentences spoken by someone who had learned a different set of English rules, just as we have difficulty in understanding people who use words which we do not know. However, this happens very infrequently and only with a small number of syntactic rules, which differ from one dialect to another. For the rest, our difficulties in understanding other speakers of English do not come about from their knowing and using different syntactic rules. Thirdly, the set of syntactic rules must be finite because they fit inside our heads, and heads, for all their capacity, are nevertheless finite.

So we have a finite set of syntactic rules and a finite set of words. But we can use these finite means for infinite ends, the creation of new, never before uttered sentences.

We will suppose that the syntax of English has phrase structure, that is the sentences are made up of phrases and the phrases are made up of words. In looking at the phrase structure of English we will begin by looking at simple phrases and seeing how they consist of heads and modifiers. We will then look at the major functions within clauses.

7.1 Simple phrases

7.1.1 *Three ways to identify phrases*

In this section we will be looking at simple phrases. To do that we must first have some idea of what a phrase is. The sentence *Mary swims*, whose structure we discussed in Chapter 1, contained only two words, that must come in that order if the sentence is to follow the rules of English syntax. In the box diagram we drew for it in Chapter 1, there is no unit between 'word' and 'sentence'. However, if we look again at the sentences you put together earlier we can identify an intermediate unit.

None of the following strings of words follows the rules of English syntax. Change the order of each so that it is a grammatical sentence.

(a) Has been eating the chocolate cake the old man.

(b) The old man the chocolate cake has been eating.

(c) Has been eating the old man the chocolate cake.

To make each of the above strings of words conform to the rules of English syntax you will have moved not single words, but groups of words, for example, *the old man*, or *the chocolate cake*. These groups which move as whole units are intermediate between words and sentences. They are called phrases.

phrase

There are three tests we can use to identify which groups of words in a sentence are phrases: movement, meaning, and substitution. To produce grammatical sentences in the above exercise you moved groups of words, and not individual words. If a phrase can be moved then it moves as a whole unit. This movement may be further illustrated by the following examples:

(a) *The old man* ate *the chocolate cake*.

(b) What *the old man* ate was *the chocolate cake*.

(c) It was *the chocolate cake* that *the old man* ate.

(d) *The chocolate cake* was eaten by *the old man*.

If we consider the italicised sequences of words in the first sentence above, we can see that when they are moved to give us the other sentences they always move as a whole. We do not find sentences like:

(a) *It was man the chocolate cake which the old ate.

(b) *The the cake was eaten by chocolate old man.

These two examples are ungrammatical because only part phrases have been moved, leaving other parts of the phrase behind. For example, the phrase *the old man* has been broken into two parts: *man* and *the old* in the first example, and *the* and *old man* in the second. It seems, therefore, that it is not possible to move anything but a whole phrase.

Phrases do not just form grammatical units, but also form units of meaning. The following sequences of words all have a coherent identifiable meaning:

(a) the old man, the chocolate cake,

(b) the large evil leathery alligator,

(c) in a bad mood,

(d) unbelievably boring,

(e) quite large,

(f) is reading a book.

Each one of these sequences is a phrase.

Consider the following groups:

(a) the the old,

(b) cake which the,

(c) the leathery,

(d) in the,

(e) cake ate,

(f) large evil.

Can you figure out the meaning of these sequences of words?

It is difficult (if not impossible in many cases) to identify a meaning for each of these groups. These groups do not form phrases.

Exercise 7.1

In each of the following sentences identify sequences of three or more words which are phrases.

(a) An ancient monument fell down during the bombing.

(b) Several young Latvian artists danced gracefully before the Empress.

* * * * * * * * * *

Finally any sequence that will substitute for another, that is, which can occupy the same location, is also a phrase.

Look at the following sentence:

Davina sold *petrol* yesterday *at the corner store*.

Substitute another phrase for each of the italicised phrases.

You might have got any of the following and innumerable other sentences:

(a) *My old friend Ahmed* sold *tulips* yesterday *in the market at Zurich*.

(b) *The angry tenants* sold *all of the furniture of the apartment block* yesterday *out of spite*.

Each of the italicised phrases which is substituting for the original phrase above is itself also a phrase.

7.1.2 *Heads and modifiers*

In section 5.1 we looked at five major lexical categories: noun, verb, adjective, adverb, and preposition. We said that each is the head of a **head** phrase. We now need to come to a better understanding of what makes the head of a phrase significant. The major grammatical property which gives heads their distinctive role in phrases is that they determine the major grammatical properties of the whole phrase. Recall that grammatical properties have to do, basically, with where in a sequence particular phrases will fit. When we talk about the order in which syntactic constituents come we are talking of their 'distribution' or 'distributional **distribution** properties'.

Look at the following arrangements of the phrases we used as examples earlier.

(a)   *The old man in a bad mood.

(b)   *In a bad mood is reading a book unbelievably boring.

(c)   *Is reading a book the large evil leathery alligator.

None of these arrangements of phrases make grammatical sentences of English although the phrases themselves are internally grammatical. The reason for these arrangements being ungrammatical must therefore be that the phrases are in an ungrammatical sequence, that is, they are ungrammatically distributed.

What is it that determines how a phrase may be distributed? Every phrase has one constituent which is responsible for determining this, and it is its head.

Look at the phrase *in a train*. It can fit in a variety of 'slots' in a sentence. For example, it can fit into the following places in sentences:

(a)   Granville met his beloved in a train.

(b)   You always get an odd range of smells in a train.

(c)   The emergency cord in a train should not be touched without good reason.

If we take a phrase like *a train* it cannot fit in these places:

(a)   *Granville met his beloved a train.

(b)   *You always get an odd range of smells a train.

(c)   *The emergency cord a train should not be touched without good reason.

This shows that it is the preposition and not the following words which is responsible for the fact that the phrase *in a train* will fit where it does, i.e. that it has its particular distribution.

noun phrase

Where a phrase consists only of its head it often has the same distributional properties as a phrase with the same head and other content. For example, a noun phrase like *gorgeous looking Bentleys with walnut dashboards* can be located in the same places in sentences as its head noun, *Bentleys*. For example, they both fit in the slots in the following sentences:

_____ make Clive drool.

Clive loves _____ .

Some of the inflectional properties of the phrase are also determined by its head. For example, noun phrases have number, either singular for one or plural for more than one. This is shown by the fact that the head noun inflects for number, as we saw in section 5.1. It happens that when a head noun is singular or plural the whole noun phrase of which it is the head is also singular or plural. You can see this is so when the noun phrase is replaced by a pronoun, because then the pronoun has the number of the head noun and not of any other noun in the phrase. Take, for example, the noun phrase *the witches' discovery of the secrets of life*. This noun phrase is singular because *discovery*, which is its head noun, is singular. But the phrase also contains two plural nouns, *witches* and *secrets*, and another singular noun, *life*. The number of these nouns has nothing to do with the number of the phrase as a whole.

The heads of phrase we will deal with in this book are also obligatory. This is significant for the meaning of the phrase because the phrase is about the head in some very general sense. A red coat is a particular kind of coat. Here *coat* is the head of the phrase *a red coat*. Swimming in a pool is basically about swimming rather than about the pool. Again, *swimming* is the head of the phrase *swimming in a pool*. It is also significant because it means that there can be one-word phrases. In such cases only the head is present.

Exercise 7.2

Using the above properties of phrases, find the heads of the following phrases. Note that in some cases there are phrases within these phrases. You should find only the word which is the head of the whole phrase, and not the heads of any of the phrase's other constituents:

(a)   the great big elephant

(b)   several very old books

(c)   all the women in the moon

(d)   excellently presented material on Lady Havisham

(e)   rather thick in the head

(f)   most awfully pleasant

(g)   delighted by their arrival

(h)   sitting in the room

(i)   bored out of his skull

(j)   having delayed writing to you

(k)   syncopated rhythms of Africa

(l)   very lovely

(m) in trouble with the law

(n)   almost out of the woods

(o)   right above his neighbour's house

(p)   singularly unimpressed with Jeffrey

(q)   is eating a big dinner

* * * * * * * * * *

Exercise 7.3

Now, by way of revision, identify the grammatical category (part of speech) of the heads of the following phrases:

(a)   out of the stratosphere

(b)   given his intransigence

(c)   cycled to work

(d)   dreadfully slowly

(e)   quite inappropriately large

(f)   tawdry work by the amateur painters

(g)   right up in Scotland

(h)   so nearly correct

(i)   genuinely silly about his aunt's fortune

(j)   right beside a dirty factory

* * * * * * * * * *

Having looked in general at heads, we are now going to set objectives for the following account of English syntax. In doing so we are going to simplify things by supposing that there is only one other kind of functional

modifier

constituent of phrases other than the head, namely the modifier (although there are many structurally different kinds of modifier). In other words, once you have found the head we are generally going to say that all the other constituents are modifiers. In more advanced treatments of grammar you would find that this is not correct. Later we will also explore at least one way in which this is an oversimplification.

We are also going to suppose that the structure of phrases is rather flat, that is, that it has fewer intermediate levels of structure than an advanced treatment of grammar would suppose phrases to have. The reason for this is that our objective will be to help you identify where phrases begin and end, what the head of a phrase is, and thus what its modifiers are. More detailed treatment can wait.

7.1.3   *Noun phrase*

Look at the following phrases:

(a)   the dog

(b)   a moderately short programme

(c)   some very old cars

(d)   six bags of wholemeal flour

(e)   very dirty marks on the walls

Each of these phrases has a noun as head: *dog, programme, cars, bags,* and *marks* respectively. The other constituents are, by our definition, modifiers. Roughly speaking the modifiers tell us about the head while the head does not tell us about the modifiers.

But what are these other modifier constituents? To decide this question we have to look whether they are themselves phrases. There is clear evidence that some of the constituents of these phrases are themselves phrases. *Moderately short* is a phrase, since it has a head, *short*, which has its own modifier, *moderately*. *Moderately* tells us how short but not how programme. So it must be modifying *short*. *Short* is an adjective, so *moderately short* must be an adjective phrase.

Find the clear cases of other phrases in the above examples.

You will probably have figured out at least some of the following: *very old, of wholemeal flour, wholemeal flour, very dirty, on the walls, the walls.*

Figure 7.1

We can see an important grammatical process at work within these phrases, namely that a phrase can function within another phrase. This process is termed embedding; one phrase is said to be embedded within another.   **embedding**

We can represent embeddedness by containing one phrase within another in a Chinese box arrangement, as in Figure 7.1. Such an arrangement will be familiar from the previous chapters where we used it to represent the structure of morphologically complex words.

Tree diagrams can also be used in Figures 7.2 and 7.3. (We have left out the labels of constituents we have not yet dealt with).

The tree diagram in Figure 7.2 is a way of representing the fact that the phrase *the dog* consists of the word *the* and the noun *dog* and that the whole phrase is a noun phrase.

The tree diagram in Figure 7.3 represents the fact that the phrase *a moderately short programme* consists of the word *a* followed by the

Figure 7.2

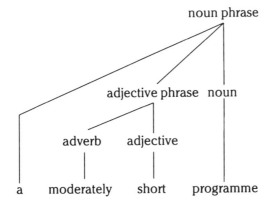

Figure 7.3

adjective phrase *moderately short*, which in turn consists of an adverb, *moderately*, and the head adjective, *short*. The final constituent of *a moderately short programme* is the head of the phrase, the noun *programme*, and since this is a noun, the whole phrase is a noun phrase.

Exercise 7.4

Provide similar paraphrases for the two tree diagrams in Figures 7.4 and 7.5

* * * * * * * * * *

From the above examples it would appear that two kinds of phrase can appear as modifiers within noun phrases: adjective phrases to the left of the head and prepositional phrases to the right.

Figure 7.4

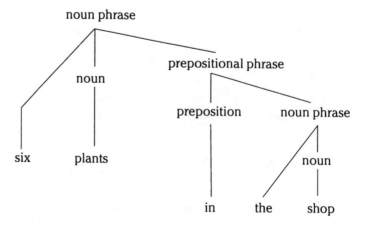

Figure 7.5

We have so far not put a category label on every constituent in some of the noun phrases in the above examples. The first such category we need to deal with is exemplified by *a* and *the*. Words like these are generally called determiners. English has a small closed class of determiners. (Closed classes are closed because they cannot be added to.) There are the two articles: *a* and *the*. *A* is often called the indefinite article because the noun phrase it introduces is not one that the speaker and hearer have mentioned recently or that is clearly defined in the context. For example, if someone says, *I have a new car*, then we can take it that this is the first time it has been mentioned, at least in the current conversation. *The* is termed the definite article and is normally used when what its noun phrase denotes has been mentioned before or is clearly known about in the context. For example, if someone says *I saw the teacher yesterday*, then we take it that there is only one teacher being referred to and both speaker and hearer(s) know which one. (These characterisations of the uses of articles are just to give an idea of their use. Their actual conditions of use are more complex.)

determiner

articles, indefinite article

definite article

The set of demonstratives: *this*, *that*, *these*, and *those* are a further sub-class of determiners. Determiners come before adjectives in the noun phrase. You can tell that this is their distributional pattern by trying them out of position: **old the car*, **very a long truck*. Numerals like *six* and *sixth*, and quantifiers like *some* and *many*, appear between a determiner and adjective phrases within a noun phrase. *The six tall trees* but not **the tall six trees*. To make things easy we will just suppose that numerals are heads of adjective phrases.

demonstrative

Quantifiers, words like *many*, *most*, *some*, *all*, *few*, *several*, and *both*, are not so easy to assign to a syntactic category. Two of them, *all* and *both*, can come before the determiner slot, as in *all the cars* and *both the tandems*. Others seem to fit in the determiner slot, for example *some*, as in *some red boats*, but **the some red boats*. Still others come following the determiner, for example *many* in *the many soldiers*. Because of this complexity we will leave quantifiers for more advanced treatments than this.

quantifier

Now look at the noun phrase *Joan's car*. The head noun of this phrase is *car*. But what of *Joan's*? It is clearly a modifier since it tells us more about the car. But it is a noun and therefore that noun must be the head of its own noun phrase. So we have two noun phrases, one a modifier of the head of the other. We can see the same thing with a more complex example. In the phrase *an old building's fences* the head noun of this phrase is *fences*. That is because the whole phrase is about these fences. If we look carefully at *an old building's*, then it consists of a noun phrase, *an old building*, with an apostrophe *s* added to it. This phrase has the identical distribution to that of determiners in that it comes in the same position in noun phrases, for example *a park's six tall trees*. Notice that the definite article *a* in the above phrases is a modifier of *park* and not of *fences*. We can tell this is the case because *a* only goes with head nouns which are singular. In *an old building's rather green fences* there is one building but a number of fences. What is happening here is that a noun

Figure 7.6

possessive noun phrase

phrase is itself a modifier of a head noun within a noun phrase. These noun phrases are termed possessive noun phrases. They must take the possessive marker of apostrophe *s* if the noun phrase to which they are attached is singular, or *s* apostrophe where they are attached to a plural noun phrase. This possessive marker is distinct from the plural inflection as you can see in the case of irregular plural inflection. For example, in the *oxen's yoke*, *oxen* is already plural but takes the possessive marker when it is functioning in the same slot as determiners.

A further fact to note about the possessive marker is that it is not an inflection since it does not attach to a word but comes at the end of the whole noun phrase. It is not attached to the head noun. In the phrase the *old mill by the stream's green fences*, the head noun of the whole phrase is *fences*. The possessive noun phrase is *the old mill by the stream*. Its head is *mill* and not *stream*. So the possessive marker attaches to the whole possessive noun phrase and not its head. (Of course if the head happens to be the last word in the phrase then it will look as if it is attached to the head.)

So how does one draw a tree diagram for such possessives? The easiest way is probably the one shown in Figure 7.6.

Exercise 7.5

Pick out the heads and modifiers in the following noun phrases. (Pick out the head first and ignore phrases embedded in the example phrases.)

(a)   The old grey mare down in the paddock.

(b)   My uncle with the fish and chip shop.

(c)   These three intelligent bus drivers I met yesterday.

(d)   An other person whom I don't know.

(e)   Six goblins in green.

* * * * * * * * *

Application

Compare the two small poems below for their use of modifiers in noun phrases.

GIPSY

I, the man with the red scarf,
Will give thee what I have, this last week's earnings.
Take them and buy thee a silver ring
And wed me, to ease my yearnings.

For the rest, when thou art wedded
I'll wet my brow for thee
With sweat, I'll enter a house for thy sake,
Thou shalt shut doors on me.

(D. H. Lawrence)

A WHITE BLOSSOM

A tiny moon as small and white as a single jasmine flower
Leans all alone above my window, on night's wintry bower,
Liquid as lime-tree blossoms, soft as brilliant water or rain
She shines, the first white love of my youth, passionless and in vain.

(D. H. Lawrence)

* * * * * * * * * *

Discussion

The noun phrases in both poems tend to have modifiers to the left of the head, sometimes quite a few. The noun phrases in the first poem do not often have modifiers to the right whereas some of the noun phrases in the second poem have modifiers to the right of the head as well.

The first poem is more active than the second in that the speaker is making a proposal of marriage and making promises to the person he is addressing of what he will do for her after they are married. So there is relatively little modification of nouns since the emphasis is on the verbs. In the second poem the emphasis is on description of the blossom and so it is perhaps appropriate that there is rather more modification of nouns within noun phrases.

7.1.3.1 *Pronouns*   **pronoun**
In dealing with words in Chapter 5 we did not discuss a further grammatical category that is relevant to noun phrases, namely pronouns. Having looked at noun phrases we are now able to work out more exactly what pronouns are. Pronouns are traditionally thought of as standing for nouns. For example, in the sentence *Most teachers work very hard and they earn all the money they get*, we know that *they* 'stands for' *most teachers*, or to put it more technically, *most teachers* is the antecedent of the   **antecedent**
pronoun *they*. If we change this so that the sentence reads *All the older teachers at Bridgewood High work very hard and they earn all the money*

they get, we can see that the pronoun *they* has the noun phrase *all the older teachers at Bridgewood High* as its antecedent. In these two examples the pronouns do not have nouns but noun phrases as their antecedents. Sometimes it is true that a pronoun has only a single noun as antecedent but that is an accident. It comes about when the antecedent noun phrase happens to contain only one word, its head.

English pronouns take various forms according to the morphosyntactic categories of number and person, and according to the gender and grammatical role of the noun phrases which are their antecedents. Number, as we saw in Chapter 5, takes account of whether the antecedent is singular or plural. Person takes account of whether the antecedent is the speaker (the first person), the addressee (the second person), or is being spoken about (the third person). Gender takes account of whether the antecedent is male, female, or neither. The grammatical functions of noun phrases for which pronouns vary in form will be dealt with in the next section.

Pronouns show a specific form for the possessive function. The fact that there are possessive pronouns such as *your*, *their*, and *her*, as in *her brother*, shows that possessive noun phrases really are noun phrases, because pronouns (which have noun phrases as antecedents) can substitute for them. For example, in the sentence *The old steam train travelled to its nearest destination*, *its* is in possessive form within the noun phrase *its nearest destination*. The antecedent of *its* is the noun phrase *the old steam train*. You can tell this is so because you can substitute the antecedent for the possessive pronoun as follows: *The old steam train travelled to the old steam train's nearest destination*.

We said earlier that these various forms of pronouns are in evidence if the antecedent is neither the speaker, i.e. first person (*I*, *we*), nor the addressee, i.e. second person (*you*), that is, if it is third person. If such an antecedent is plural, then the pronoun will be either *they*, *their* or *them*.

See if you can work out which position the pronoun occupies for each of the three forms: *they*, *their* and *them*.

Their is clearly the possessive form, as you can tell from such noun phrases as *their old car* and *their many friends*. *They* is the form the pronoun characteristically takes when it comes in front of a verb like *saw*, and *them* is the form the pronoun takes after *see*, for example *they saw them*. We will look in greater detail at these roles which noun phrases play in Section 7.2.

If the third person pronoun is singular then it is sensitive to the gender of the antecedent, and its forms are: *he*, *she*, *it*, or *his*, *hers*, *its*, and so forth. The various forms of personal pronouns are given in Table 7.1.

Table 7.1   The pronoun categories

Person	Case	Gender	Number	
			Singular	Plural
First person	Subject		I	we
First person	Complement		me	us
First person	Possessive		my	our
Second person	Subject		you	you
Second person	Complement		you	you
Second person	Possessive		your	your
Third person	Subject	Feminine	she	they
Third person	Subject	Masculine	he	they
Third person	Subject	Neuter	it	they
Third person	Complement	Feminine	her	them
Third person	Complement	Masculine	him	them
Third person	Complement	Neuter	it	them
Third person	Possessive	Feminine	her	their
Third person	Possessive	Masculine	his	their
Third person	Possessive	Neuter	its	their

Exercise 7.6

Find the pronouns in the following passage and for each pronoun indicate its number, person, and gender. Remember that gender only appears in the third person singular.

> Marie and her brother had worked together for a long time in the family business while it was developing. I had known them since school and you must have known them too. He was a short fellow while she was much taller.

*   *   *   *   *   *   *   *   *   *

7.1.4   *Adjective phrase*

Just as noun phrases have nouns as heads so adjective phrases have adjectives as heads. Look, for example, at the following phrases:

(a)   *quite old,*

(b)   *moderately expensive,*

(c)   *quite moderately long in the arms.*

The heads of these three phrases are *old*, *expensive*, and *long*. The other constituents are modifiers. The modifiers can be single-word degree adverbs like *very* and *quite*, which we will suppose to be the heads of adverb phrases. (Degree adverbs are adverbs which cannot themselves take modifiers.) They can be adverb phrases containing modifiers, as we saw earlier. They can also be prepositional phrases, as in the case of *quite moderately long in the arms*, where the head is *long* and *in the arms* modifies *long*.

Draw labelled tree diagrams of the three example phrases above.

Your answers should be as shown in Figures 7.7, 7.8, and 7.9.

Adjective phrases characteristically appear in two places, as illustrated by the following contrasting positions:

(a) *the very old goat,   the goat was very old*;

(b) *the rather dreadful holiday,   the holiday which was rather dreadful*.

Figure 7.7

Figure 7.8

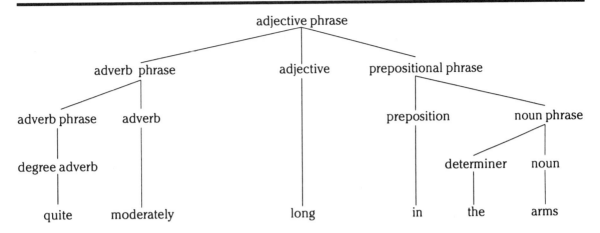

Figure 7.9

The first position is termed 'attributive' position and adjectives which are located in this position are called attributive adjectives. Here the adjective phrases come after determiners and before the head noun in noun phrases, for example, *the very old blanket* and *a moderately expensive shirt*. The other position is termed predicate position and the adjectives which are located in this position are called predicate adjectives. It is the position an adjective phrase takes when it comes after verbs, for example, *John was very long in the arms*. (We briefly made mention of these two positions in section 5.1.)

attributive adjective

predicate
predicate adjective

There are some interesting differences between the attributive and predicate positions for adjectives. First, attributive adjectives have a preferred sequence. For example, *a friendly former conductor* sounds better than *a former friendly conductor*, *a small blue car* is better than *a blue small car*. This ordering appears not to be grammatical, in that alternative orders are not totally prohibited. (There is some dispute not only about the facts of the matter but also concerning what to do about them and so we will say no more about it.) Adjective phrases in predicate position do not have this ordering property because it is not possible to put adjective phrases one next to the other in predicate position, for example *a car is small, blue*. Adjective phrases in predicate position can be co-ordinated, in which case they will not have a preferred order, for example *the car is small and blue*, *the car is blue and small*. (We shall have more to say about co-ordination in section 8.1.2.)

Secondly, attributive adjective phrases cannot have constituents after their heads, so that *the long in the arms young man* is ungrammatical, whereas in predicate position modifiers after the head are permitted, for example *the young man is long in the arms* is grammatical.

Exercise 7.7

Identify the adjective phrases in the following passage and italicise their heads.

In other ways he was a very hard man. He was big and rather clumsy-looking, with big heavy bones and long flat muscles, and he had a big, expressionless, broken-nosed face. Yet he moved with surprising ease and silence as well as having a gift for stillness.

(M. K. Joseph, *A Soldier's Tale*)

* * * * * * * * * *

Application

The choice between attributive and predicative adjectives can have an impact on descriptive writing. Look, for example, at the following description of an Icelandic warrior.

> ... he was <u>tall</u>, <u>strong</u>, and **<u>skilled in arms</u>**, <u>even-tempered</u> and <u>very shrewd</u>, **<u>ruthless with his enemies</u>** and **<u>always reliable in matters of importance</u>**.

(From *Njal's Saga*, translated by Magnus Magnusson and Hermann Pálsson)

* * * * * * * * * *

Discussion

All of the underlined adjective phrases are in predicate position. The author had no choice but to choose predicate position for the adjective phrases in bold type because they contain constituents after the head adjective. Not only that, adjectives phrases in predicate position can come in any order and so by placing adjective phrases in predicate position the writer of a description has a choice about the order in which the adjective phrases appear. The sequence here begins with the warrior's physical size, then moves on to his physical abilities, then mental attributes, and lastly his social attributes. You can see that this is a logical sequence if you want to introduce someone into a story for the first time. It is a sequence that is not available in attributive position since the sequencing of adjective phrases in attributive position is more fixed than in predicate position and also adjective phrases in attributive position cannot take modifiers after their heads.

7.1.4.1 *Adverb phrase*
Adverb phrases have a structure similar to that of adjective phrases. They have adverbs as their heads and the modifiers which they take on their left include degree adverbs as in the following examples: *very quickly, quite slowly*; or adverb phrases, for example *quite moderately slowly*. Also, quite a number of words such as *fast* function as both adverbs and adjectives, as in *a fast boat* and *the boat sailed fast*. Given these similarities it is often supposed that adjective and adverb phrases can be termed 'A phrases' or AP for short.

7.1.5 *Prepositional phrase*

We can now revisit another of the word classes from section 5.1, the preposition. Look at the following verb phrases:

(a) play *in the moonlight*,

(b) sat *by the gate*,

(c) has come home *in a couple of hours*,
               on a motorbike,
               through a tunnel.

Each of the italicised phrases is a prepositional phrase. This is because **prepositional phrase** the preposition is its head. Prepositional phrases can have just a head, as in the verb phrase *take the book out*, where *out* is a prepositional phrase consisting only of a preposition. Prepositions often have noun phrases immediately following them within the phrase, as is the case in all the above examples. They can also take adverb phrases to their left as modifiers, for example, *rather in trouble, very directly in the way*.

In the above examples the prepositional phrases are clearly functioning as modifiers in the verb phrase, telling us more about the action denoted by the verb. Some pages earlier, prepositional phrases also appeared as modifiers in noun phrases and adjective phrases. In a more general sense their function is descriptive and you will notice a preponderance of them in descriptive writing.

Exercise 7.8

Find the prepositional phrases in the following extract.

> At first it seemed there was no one about. Then he saw a single figure, a girl, far down the beach, close to where the surf was breaking, sitting under a beach umbrella. He went towards her. When he was close enough to see her clearly he sat down on the white sand.
>
> He could not see her face. She sat with her back to the land, staring out to sea. The umbrella above her was dark blue, with white frills and tassels that swayed in the breeze. Her hair was long and blonde and it too was dragged at by the breeze from the sea. She was slender, her shoulders broad only in proportion to her long tapering back and narrow waist. She sat cross-legged, her knees appearing to Smith projecting on either side, like outriggers. She was pale-skinned, lightly tanned. She sat perfectly still. From where Smith watched the highest waves appeared to lift above her. He saw her framed in green. Then as the wave broke and shot forward up the sand he saw her against the white froth and the blue of the sky. Sometimes in the relative quiet

between breakers he heard faintly the sound of music and guessed
that somewhere among her things, scattered about the beach towel on
which she sat, was a battery radio.

(C. K. Stead, *Smith's Dream*)

* * * * * * * * * *

Summary

To judge from the phrases we have looked at so far, it would seem that all
phrases have heads, and modifiers either before the head or after it. The
head of a phrase is the word that has the same category as the phrase as a
whole. Nouns are the heads of noun phrases, adjectives are the heads of
adjective phrases, and prepositions are the heads of prepositional
phrases.

7.1.6   *Verb phrase*

verb phrase

Phrases with verbs as heads have a complicated structure. That is why we
have left them until last. Look at the following verb phrases:

(a)   gave Jill a book,

(b)   has given Jill a book,

(c)   will be giving Jill a book.

We would all agree that in all three verb phrases an act of giving is
being referred to. In both *Fred has been putting money into the bank* and
April could have been putting candles on the table an act of putting is
being referred to. But, in each example, as well as the head verb *give*
and *put* there are other verbs present: *have, be, will,* and *could*. So we
can draw a distinction between the head of the verb phrase, often
lexical verb   called the lexical verb, and verbs which precede it such as *will, have,*
auxiliary verb   and *is*, which are called auxiliary verbs. They can be considered verbs
because, for instance, they can change their form according to tense: *is*
vs *was, has* vs *had*. Tense inflection, as we saw in section 5.1, is characteristic of verbs.

modal auxiliary verb   Auxiliary verbs are of three major kinds: modal auxiliary verbs: *can,
could, shall, should, will, would, may, might,* and *must*, which, if the
aspect auxiliaries   verb phrase has one, always come first; the aspect auxiliaries, *have* and
be, which, if they are present, come in that order and after any modal
passive auxiliary   auxiliary verb; and the passive auxiliary which is also *be* and which, if it
is present, comes last. That means we should be able to find verb phrases
such as *could have been being taken*. This is a complex verb phrase but it
is certainly grammatically possible.

There are other constituents which can precede lexical verbs. Look again at some examples:

(a)   does give Jill a book,

(b)   did give Jill a book,

(c)   doesn't give Jill a book,

(d)   hasn't given Jill a book.

Under certain circumstances the auxiliary verb *do* appears before the lexical verb. It only appears when there are no other auxiliary verbs and then only under two circumstances: if the verb phrase is emphasised strongly with a heavy stress on the *do*, or if there is a negative like *not* or *n't* in the verb phrase. The distribution of *do* is therefore very restricted. The negative *not* (or *n't*) is an optional constituent which, if it occurs, always comes just after the first auxiliary verb whatever that is. So, for example, we can get any of the following sequences:

(a)   hasn't given Jill the book,

(b)   isn't giving Jill the book,

(c)   will not give Jill the book.

Given the above restrictions, why are the following verb phrases ungrammatical?

(a)   *does be giving Jill the book,

(b)   *has beenn't giving Jill the book.

Answer:

They are ungrammatical because in (a) a form of *do* appears when there is another auxiliary present, and in (b) the negative is attached to the second auxiliary when it can only be attached to the first.

Now look at the following verb phrases:

(a)   has very suddenly given Jill the book,

(b)   is almost certainly giving Jill the book,

(c)   could not very easily be giving Jill the book.

What constituents other than auxiliary verbs and negatives appear in front of the lexical verb?

These examples show that one further constituent can precede the lexical verb and that is an adverb phrase, specifically, in the above examples: *very suddenly*, *almost certainly*, and *very easily*. Such adverb phrases tend to occupy the same position as the negative, i.e. to come immediately after the first auxiliary verb if there is one or, if there is also a negative, immediately following the negative. So much, for the meantime, for the distribution of auxiliary verbs.

So what do all these various auxiliary possibilities indicate? Modal auxiliaries deal with many different possible ways for seeing the action of the lexical verb. Recall from section 5.1 that there is no future tense inflection in English. But that does not mean English speakers cannot refer to times in the future. Future time for the action is often expressed by the modal *will*. If Jill *will* give John a book, then the giving is in the future. Possible action is often indicated by *could*. For example, if Jill *could* give John a book, then she hasn't yet given it to him. It is just a possibility for the future. The perfective aspect auxiliary *have*, which we looked at in section 5.1 indicates that the action is completed relative to a given point in time. For example, if we say, Jill *has given* John the book, then the action is over relative to now, when we are speaking. The progressive aspect auxiliary *be* indicates that the action is on-going at a particular point in time, so that if Jill *is giving* John a book, then it is happening now while we are talking.

perfective aspect

progressive aspect

The passive auxiliary *be* and its involvement with syntax is more complex. To understand the full import of that we must look at the grammatical units which follow the verb (which we do in section 7.2) and the way phrases may be moved (which we do in section 8.2).

We saw earlier that, in total, it is possible for four auxiliaries to precede the lexical verb, for example *The stone might have been being lifted by Brünhilde*. There are interesting relationships to do with inflections in such verb phrases between each auxiliary verb and the verb which follows it. Let us look at some verb phrases which contain the perfective auxiliary *have*:

(a)   have eaten their breakfasts,

(b)   have taken the train to Blackpool,

(c)   have been opening many windows.

You will notice that the verb immediately following *have* takes the ending *–en*. This inflected form of the verb is the perfect participle, whose morphology we looked at in section 5.1. The perfect auxiliary verb always selects the perfect participle form of the following verb, typically the affix *–en*, but also irregular forms such as *has sung*. The progressive auxiliary selects the progressive participle form of the following verb: *is eating*, *was walking*, *were riding*. The passive auxiliary selects the perfect participle form of the following verb: *was eaten*, *were tickled*, *have been cut*. A number of explanations have been offered for

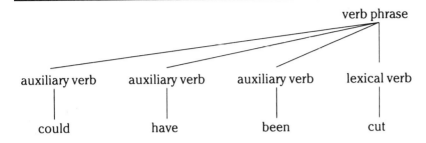

Figure 7.10

this selection process but for our purposes it is sufficient to point out that this is again a matter of distribution, that is, where syntactic constituents come relative to others, and it is rule-governed.

We will suppose that all auxiliaries are immediately dominated by a verb phrase in the tree diagrams as illustrated in Figure 7.10.

Application

Look carefully at tense inflection (past and present) and aspect (*have* and *be*) in the following narrative.

> The European Guest House stood two hundred feet above the water, on the crest of a rocky and wooded spur that jutted from the jungle. By the time Aziz arrived the water had paled to a film of mauve-grey, and the boat vanished entirely. A sentry slept in the Guest House porch, lamps burned in the cruciform of the deserted rooms. He went from one room to another, inquisitive, and malicious. Two letters lying on the piano rewarded him, and he pounced and read them promptly. He was not ashamed to do this. The sanctity of private correspondence has never been ratified in the East.
>
> (E. M. Forster, *A Passage to India*)

* * * * * * * * * *

Discussion

Tenses and their relationship to modal and aspect auxiliary verbs as indicators of time relationships are a rich source of interest in narratives because there are so many ways of telling a story. If we look at the passage, we will see that it is, except for the last sentence, in the past tense. The first sentence has a plain past tense verb, *stood*. But after a second plain past tense verb, *arrived*, there is one verb phrase with perfective aspect, *had paled*. (This is perfective because of the presence of the perfective auxiliary *have*. But notice that *have* is itself inflected for past tense.) Since perfective aspects always require reference to a particular point in time, by which time the action of the verb was completed, in this case by which time the water had paled, the perfective arranges events around the arrival of Aziz. This pivotal event then leads on to the other events which happen after the arrival of Aziz and which are all again indicated by plain past tense forms of the verbs. The paragraph finishes with a present perfective passive verb with a negative after the first auxiliary, *has never been ratified*. This, a more complex form than all the preceding ones, does not deal with the actual events of the paragraph, but is a general comment on those events and is not in the past tense.

Narratives can be examined in this way to see how the narrator uses tense and aspect to give focus to certain events and present other events as relating to these focal events.

Up until this point our examination of the verb phrase has looked only at what is on the head verb's left. We will return to look at what is to the verb's right in the verb phrase in the next section, since the constituents on the verb's right need to be looked at in the context of another unit, the clause.

Some hints for drawing tree diagrams of simple phrases

1. Find the head of the phrase. Remember that every noun, adjective, verb, adverb and preposition is the head of a phrase.

2. Find the modifiers which go with a head. Modifiers always tell you more about the head. For example, in the phrase *the red mill by the river*, *red* tells you more about the mill, and the fact that it is by the river tells you more about the mill. Even the determiner *the* tells you that there is a particular mill being mentioned. In the verb phrase *has swum the lake three times*, the head is *swum* and the *has* tells you that the swimming is completed. The lake is what was swum and *three times* is how often the lake was swum. So all the modifiers add detail to the swimming. In the prepositional phrase *down the sink*, *the sink* indicates the location or direction of the *down*.

Exercise 7.9

You should now be able to pick out what kinds of words and phrases function as modifiers. This exercise gives you some examples of three kinds of phrase. You should draw tree diagrams of all of them to get a feel for the structural properties of simple phrases. To make life easier you can use the following abbreviations, which we will use from now on:

> N for noun
> A for adjective and adverb
> P for preposition
> V for verb
> DET for determiner
> DEG for degree adverb
> A also for numerals and quantifiers

PRON for pronoun
NP for noun phrase
POSS for possessive noun phrase
AP for adjective and adverb phrases
PP for prepositional phrase
VP for verb phrase
LexV for lexical verb
AuxV for auxiliary verb

Noun phrases

	modifiers	head	modifiers
(a)		Angus	
(b)	the	man	
(c)	the old	man	
(d)	a moderately old	man	
(e)	the seven very silly	people	
(f)	many	undertakers	
(g)	too many	undertakers	
(h)	the	cottage	in the woods
(i)	a very grim	beast	on the moors
(j)	the animals'	captivity	in dirty cages

Prepositional phrases

	modifiers	head	modifiers
(a)		in	
(b)		down	the hatch
(c)		across	the street
(d)		from	behind the house
(e)		down	into the mud
(f)	completely	down	the drain
(g)	right	after	the meeting

Adjective phrases

	modifiers	head	modifiers
(a)		silly	
(b)		fearful	of the consequences
(c)		yellow	with age
(d)	thoroughly	disreputable	
(e)	quite ecstatically	moved	by Englebert's music
(f)	so	boring	
(g)	too	involved	in Fred's affairs

* * * * * * * * * *

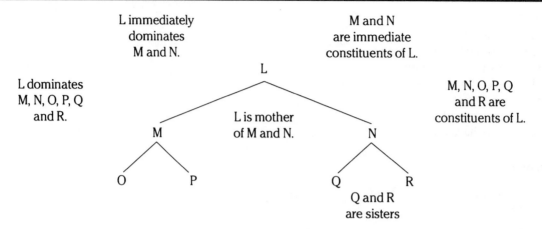

Figure 7.11

Having now had some practice at drawing tree diagrams and seen how they represent syntactic structure, we are in a position to learn some basic terms to describe the relationships which units in a sentence have one to another. As we saw in Chapter 1, a tree diagram shows the units of which a sentence is constructed in two dimensions. The horizontal dimension represents the sequence of units in the order they come, i.e. **precedence** the precedence of syntactic units (that is how one word precedes the next). When we speak, this precedence order is the order in which words come out of our mouths over time. In writing, the precedence order is given spatially from left to right on the page. The vertical dimension represents the way in which words are linked together into phrases, **dominance** i.e. the dominance of syntactic units.

Some basic relationships in tree diagrams can be seen in the tree diagram in Figure 7.11, which indicates the relationships in tree diagrams and the terminology used to refer to those relationships. Some of this terminology we have already used. Some will be new.

Exercise 7.10

Examine the tree diagram in Figure 7.12 and then find the constituents and nodes listed below:

(a) the sisters of D

(b) the daughters of C

(c) the immediate constituents of A

(d) the constituents of A

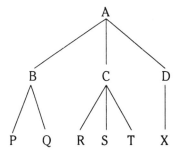

Figure 7.12

(e) the node which immediately dominates T

(f) the daughters of A

* * * * * * * * * *

Recall that what a tree diagram represents can also be represented by placing labelled brackets round each constituent. For example, the tree in the above exercise can be represented as follows:

[A [B PQ][C RST][D X]]

The A brackets surround the whole structure. The B brackets surround the constituents PQ, and so on. Labelled bracketed notation can be useful as a shorthand way of drawing trees, although it is also more difficult to 'read' than a tree representation of syntactic structure.

Exercise 7.11

Convert (a) and (b) to tree diagrams, and (c) and (d) in Figures 7.13 and 7.14 to labelled bracketings.

(a) [A[BCD]]

(b) [A[B[CD][EFG]]H]

(c)

Figure 7.13

(d)

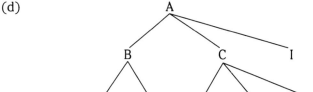

Figure 7.14

7.2 Simple clauses and their functional constituents

7.2.1 *Subject*

Having looked at the structure of simple phrases we can return now to the simple two-word sentence – *Mary swims* – which we looked at in Chapter 1, and look at it in more detail. Sentences clearly consist of phrases and we now need to look at how those phrases function in sentences. We decided earlier that the simplest complete sentence has two constituents and each constituent, at its simplest, is a single word.

Let us look at some further examples:

(a) The dogs played in the park.

(b) Some elephants were chewing the acacia trees.

(c) The film crew left the location for lunch.

(d) Sandra didn't like the neighbours.

(e) The building looked unstable.

(f) A journey up the Nile might take three months.

subject

In each case someone or something does something, or has a property. For example, in (a) the dogs are doing something, namely playing in the park; in (e) the building has the property of looking unstable. The unit which does something or has a property is called the subject. So the way to pick the subject is to ask who or what is doing things or who or what has the particular property mentioned. The answer to that question is given by the subject. On that basis the subjects of the above simple sentences are:

(a) the dogs

(b) some elephants

(c) the film crew

(d) Sandra

(e) the building

(f) a journey up the Nile

If the verb has to do with an activity then the subject is often the person or thing that is performing the action. For example, in the sentence *Chopin composes many polkas*, the subject is *Chopin* since he is composing the polkas. Unfortunately this semantic relatedness is not a hard and fast test. For example, in the sentence *Many polkas are composed by Chopin*, *Chopin* is not the subject but *many polkas* is (although Chopin is still doing the composing).

The who or what approach needs to be used carefully. It tells us what the subject is only if we use both the auxiliary verbs and the lexical verb. For example, Chopin is (as we saw) the one doing the composing in both versions of the sentence. But if we ask 'who or what are composed by Chopin' then we get the answer 'many polkas' and not 'Chopin' in the second case.

A second relationship to check is one involving inflectional morphology. If the subject of an English sentence can be substituted for by the pronouns *he*, *she* or *it*, and the tense of the sentence is the present tense, then the inflection *–s* must appear on the first verb in the sentence. Look, for instance, at the example sentences above. If we substituted *Polish composers* for *Chopin* we would get *Polish composers compose many polkas*. Notice that the *–s* on the end of the verb *compose* has disappeared. This is because the subject is no longer replaceable by *he*, *she*, or *it*, that is it is plural and not singular in number. This relationship between the subject and the presence or absence of *–s* inflection is a reliable indicator of what is the subject of the sentence. Of course if the subject is plural there is no *–s* and if the sentence has past tense there will be no *–s*, but you can always change both to check out your hunch about the subject. Look at the following example sentence: *In the twilight six dragoons gathered the prisoners together*. The sentence has past tense indicated by the *–ed* ending on *gathered*. So it needs to be changed to present tense if we are to have any chance of using the *–s* test. That would change the sentence to *In the twilight six dragoons gather the prisoners together*. We can now look for an *–s*. There is none. That means *the twilight* cannot be the subject because it is singular, but *the six dragoons* could be substituted for by *they* and could be the subject, since it is plural. If we change them to singular then an *–s* should be required. *In the twilight one dragoon gathers the prisoners together*. And there it is. So *six dragoons* must be the subject of the sentence. Notice that we are again using a substitution test here for checking syntactic properties of phrases.

7.2.2 *Predicate*

Let us turn now to the thing the subject is doing or the property it has; this is called the predicate. So the predicates of the above sentences are: **predicate**

(a) played in the park

(b) were chewing the acacia tree

(c) left the location for lunch

(d) didn't like the neighbours

(e) looked unstable

(f) might take three months

Exercise 7.12

Find the subjects of the following sentences:

    (a)   Peter joins the Navy tomorrow.

    (b)   The greatest magician of all time performs here next week.

    (c)   On Saturday morning three monkeys escaped from the zoo.

    (d)   They hate performing.

    (e)   That Lionel saw the escape interests the police.

* * * * * * * * * *

Predicates can themselves contain a number of important functional units. At this point we will be looking at those units to the right of the head of a VP (i.e. to the right of the lexical verb), which we left out of the discussion when we looked at the VP. This is because VPs are the phrases that perform the predicate function.

7.2.3 *Objects*

Look at the following three-word sentences:

    (a)   Martha kissed Jim.

    (b)   Elephants enjoy soccer.

    (c)   Sopranos sing arias.

The first unit in these sentences is clearly the subject and therefore the rest is the predicate. (*Who or what kissed Jim? Martha.*) But within the predicate there are now two further units. We can see that these two units belong together in some ways. They can, for example, be in a different location as a single unit (recall the movement test for phrases):

    (a)   What Martha did was *kiss Jim*.

    (b)   What elephants do is *enjoy soccer*.

    (c)   What sopranos do is *sing arias*.

And we can also say that:

    (a)   The person Martha kissed was Jim.

    (b)   What elephants enjoy is soccer.

    (c)   What sopranos sing is arias.

The second two elements together are the predicate and, as such, a single functional unit, but you can see that the verb phrase which is functioning as the predicate has within it a separate phrase. This third element in these examples is called the object. Object and verb are closely related **object** because verbs frequently require particular kinds of objects to complete their meaning. Laughing does not require anything to be laughed, but patting, kissing, or enjoying requires that there be something to be patted, kissed, or enjoyed. The object of the verb is usually that something. So the reason that the verb and its object form a functional unit is not only that they may be moved as a single unit but also that they form a unit of meaning.

To find whether a verb has an object we can say *who?* or *what?* after the verb. The answer to that question is given by the object. *Martha kissed who?*, *Elephants enjoy what?*, *Sopranos sing what?* The answer in each case is the object of the verb.

Each of the following sentences either has or has not got an object. (Remember, complete sentences must have both a subject and a predicate.) Sort out those sentences that have an object from those that do not.

   (a)   John was eating.

   (b)   Henry drank a milkshake.

   (c)   Martha fainted.

   (d)   She needed a milkshake.

   (e)   Henry fed his dog.

   (f)   The dog fainted suddenly.

Your answers should be:

   (a)   has not got an object.

   (b)   has

   (c)   has not

   (d)   has

   (e)   has

   (f)   has not

Sometimes a simple sentence will contain two objects.

Each of the following sentences has either no, one, or two objects. In each case, sort out how many objects there are.

(a) John gave his mother a present.

(b) Henry told me a story.

(c) Henry told a story.

(d) I took the dog.

(e) I asked my aunt a question.

(f) Geoffrey walked.

(g) Geoffrey walked his dog.

(h) She called.

(i) She called the general.

Your answers should be: (a) 2, (b) 2, (c) 1, (d) 1, (e) 2, (f) 0, (g) 1, (h). 0, (i) 1.

7.2.3.1 *Kinds of objects*

Look at the verb *tell* and its possible objects. *Tell* can have either one, or two objects. If there is one object, that object is either what was told or who it was told to. *Samantha told a story, Samantha told Jim.* However, in each case we know that telling involves both these items. The thing that is told or given is called the direct object and the person or thing it is told or given to or for is called the indirect object. Again it is because the meaning of some verbs requires it that some verbs have both direct and indirect objects. Giving requires someone to do the giving, something to be given and someone to whom it is given.

When a verb takes two objects, the objects can often come in two different grammatical orders. We can say *Mary gave Freda a boat* or *Mary gave a boat to Freda*.

direct object
indirect object

For each of the objects in the following sentences, say whether it is the direct object or the indirect object:

(a) Karl dropped his bike.

(b) Nathan gave Sarah her breakfast.

(c) The postmaster sent a parcel to Henry.

(d) Freda owed Marcia a dollar.

(e) Eve saw the serpent.

(f) Mary gave her aunt breakfast.

Answers:

(a) *His bike* is the direct object. (b) *Sarah* is the indirect object while *her breakfast* is the direct object. (c) *A parcel* is the direct object and *to Henry* is the indirect object. (d) *Marcia* is the indirect object while *a dollar* is the direct object. (e) *The serpent* is the direct object. (f) *Her aunt* is the indirect object and *breakfast* is the direct object.

We found when we looked at the structure of words and that of simple phrases that it was possible to represent their structure by tree diagrams. The same is true of sentence structure. If the subject and predicate are two units in the structure of a sentence then they form a simple binary tree as in Figure 7.15 and, looking at both the form of the constituents and their function, a Chinese box arrangement as in Figure 7.16.

If the predicate in turn consists of a verb plus an object then the tree looks like this Figure 7.17. Notice that we have one new abbreviation, namely S standing for sentence and that tree diagrams give only structural information.

Figure 7.15

Figure 7.16

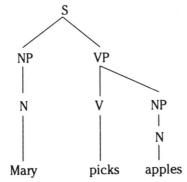

Figure 17.17

You will probably have realised that predicates are VPs and, up to now, that both subjects and objects can be NPs. This again illustrates the difference between form and function. The form of a phrase may be that of a noun phrase while its function might be that of subject or object depending on its relationship to other constituents in the sentence.

Exercise 7.13

Draw tree diagrams for the following sentences:

(a)   Dougal breeds rabbits.

(b)   Hans sent Arthur oranges.

(c)   Chieko told stories.

(d)   Alexander smiles.

(e)   Norah fed her dog his dinner.

* * * * * * * * * *

complement

As we said above, objects are required to complete the meaning of some verbs. Because of this property they are often termed complements, since they complement the meaning of the verb. Both types of object are clear cases of a complement but they are not the only kinds of complements. There are, for example, some verbs which require an adverb phrase to complete their meaning, an instance being the verb *behave*. You can behave *very badly*, or *well*, or *perfectly*. (If we use the verb *behave* without a complement then it is assumed that this means behave well.) The verb *put* requires both a direct object and a location. You cannot just put the car. You have to put it somewhere.

This allows us to distinguish genuine indirect objects, where the lexical verb requires there to be an object, from cases which have the same structure but where the constituent in question is not an object. Compare, for example, *Joanna fastened the picture for her mother* and *Joanna bought the picture for her mother*. The latter can take the form *Joanna bought her mother a picture* but the former cannot take the form *Joanna fastened her mother the picture*. It seems that in buying someone something there is a closer relationship between the buying and the one for whom something is bought than there is between the act of fastening something and the one for whom one might do that.

intensive complement

7.2.4   *Intensive complements*

Objects of both sorts are always different things from the subject. If Lisa welds axles, then Lisa and the axles are different things. If Liza gives Henry an axle then Henry and the axle are different things. But if she says that Fred seems an idiot, then Fred and the idiot are one and the same person. So *the idiot* is not an object. We may call it an intensive complement. Intensive complements appear after only a few verbs; typically after any form of the verb *be* (such as *is, was, were*) when it is used as a lexical verb (but not when it is used as an auxiliary verb), or verbs such as *seem, appear*, and *become*.

Look at the following examples:

(a) The car appeared a wreck.

(b) The jury seemed a disgruntled group.

(c) A whole town became a disturbed community.

Do the subject and complement refer to the same entity or group?

Answer:

The complements clearly refer to the same thing or things as the subject and they are thus not objects but intensive complements.

All the above examples have NPs acting as intensive complements but they are not the only type of phrase which can do so.

Look at the following examples:

(a) The car appeared in a mess.

(b) The jury seemed very nasty.

What phrase types are these complements and does the complement tell us more about the subject?

Answer:

In (a) the complement is a PP; in (b) an AP. But the complement still relates back to the subject just as it does if the structure is an NP. So these too are intensive complements. Adjective phrases in predicate position, which we looked at earlier, are therefore functioning as intensive complements.

There are also intensive complements that come after objects, and therefore look like a second object but are not. If we compare the sentence *Janet sold her brother a bike* with the sentence *Janet called her brother an idiot* you will see that in the first sentence there are two phrases after the verb, each one referring to someone or something different, whereas in the second sentence although there are also two noun phrases after the verb they refer to the same person. So the second complement in *Janet called her brother an idiot* is an intensive complement. It is telling you more about Janet's brother, just as the intensive complements which directly follow verbs tell you more about the subject. Complements of this sort come after a small class of verbs such as *call*, *name*, *elect*, and *appoint*. One more thing which these intensive complements have in common with those which follow directly after verbs is that, as well as being NPs, they too can be APs and PPs, as the following cases show:

(a) George thought Frederick [AP rather silly].

(b) Jemma found her dog [PP in great spirits].

Exercise 7.14

The following examples all contain complements. For each, determine whether it is a direct object, an indirect object, or an intensive complement.

(a) Jean sold Freda a bicycle.

(b) Tom owned a new camera.

(c) Sylvia likes her breakfast hot.

(d) Jonty appeared very shy.

(e) The captain judged Harriet the most valuable player.

* * * * * * * * * *

adverbial

7.2.5 *Adverbials*

We have now examined four main functional units in the sentence: the subject, and, within the predicate, the lexical verb and its possible complements. The last units that we still have to look at are the adverbials. Adverbials characteristically appear after the subject, verb, and object/ complement core of the sentence and indicate things like how, when, where, and why the things that are described by the sentence are going on. As you might guess, adverb phrases can and do function as adverbials, for example, the adverb phrase *rather clumsily* in *Derek dried the dishes rather clumsily*. But adverb phrases are not the only phrase types which can function as adverbials.

Look, for example, at the following sentences:

(a) John helped his father *in many situations.*

(b) Sally walked Jim home *at the film's conclusion.*

(c) The team played very badly *by their standards.*

The italicised units are all adverbials. What is their form?

Answer:

They are clearly prepositional phrases.

In the three example sentences above, where else might the adverbials be able to appear in the given sentences?

Your answers might include the following possibilities:

(a) In many situations John helped his father.

(b) John in many situations helped his father.

(c) At the film's conclusion Sally walked Jim home.

(d) By their standards the team played very badly.

We already saw when we looked at the verb phrase in the previous section that adverb phrases can come after the first auxiliary verb. This exercise shows that adverbials can appear in various other places in sentences than just at the end after the subject, verb, and any complements.

Adverbials are often sub-classified according to their content. If they deal with the time at which an event took place they are termed time adverbials. If they deal with the location of the event(s), they are place adverbials. If they deal with the way in which the events were performed or took place then they are manner adverbials and if they deal with the reason for the events taking place then they are termed reason adverbials: when, where, how, and why respectively.

time adverbial
place adverbial
manner adverbial
reason adverbial

Exercise 7.15

In each of the sentences below find the subject and any objects, intensive complements, and adverbials:

(a) Heather took the ferry across to Istanbul yesterday.

(b) Isabelle trimmed the lamp lightly.

(d) Cotton fabrics suit everyone this season.

(e) This season everyone is sending expensive presents to their friends for Christmas.

* * * * * * * * * *

We can now summarise some of what we have found by formulating a table that indicates what kinds of phrases perform the various functions in simple sentences.

Summary of simple sentence functions and the phrases that can perform them

Function   Structures

subject: noun phrase, e.g. *The boy* screamed.
predicate: verb phrase, e.g. John *had been eating his lunch.*

complements:

  direct object:
      noun phrase, e.g. He rode *a large horse.*
  indirect object:
    (a) noun phrase, e.g. I gave *Fred* a new bike.
    (b) prepositional phrase starting with *to* or *for*. (For such a prepositional phrase to be an indirect object it can be paraphrased with a simple noun phrase, e.g. *John gave a present to his mother* can be paraphrased by *John gave his mother a present.*)
  intensive complements:
    (a) noun phrase, e.g. She seemed *a nice person.*
    (b) adjective phrase, e.g. She appeared *very angry.*
    (c) prepositional phrase, e.g. She was *over the moon.*

adverbials:

    (a) adverb phrase, e.g. She ran *very quickly.*
    (b) prepositional phrase, e.g. She walked *by the river.*

Further exercises

Exercise 7.16

Draw tree diagrams of the following phrases:

(a) the red tulip

(b) is selling the silver

(c)   very deeply troubled

(d)   on the afternoon of the party

(e)   is cycling into town this afternoon

(f)   my auntie with the red hair

Exercise 7.17

Identify and label all the functional constituents: subjects, predicates, objects, intensive complements and adverbials, except heads and modifiers, in each of the following sentences:

(a)   We gave him a raise.

(b)   He donated his stamp collection to the gallery.

(c)   She put the wombat in the alligator's cage.

(d)   Xavier cried.

(e)   The key opened the door.

(f)   The alligator ate its prey.

Exercise 7.18

Study the following passage, identify all verbs and assign them to the categories lexical or auxiliary. For each lexical verb decide whether it denotes a state or an action.

Use a preserving jar which contains about 10cm of soil to which peat has been added in the proportion of two measures of soil to one of peat. Cover the top of the jar with muslin.

You must keep the atmosphere moist, but be careful that no mould is allowed to grow as this quickly kills the animals. Should the muslin feel dry sprinkle it lightly with water. Slugs will eat carrot discs, which may be supplemented occasionally with pieces of potato and green food. When the food begins to decay it must be removed from the jar.

(from *Form 5 Science: An Animal Study. Core Material*, Wellington, New Zealand: Department of Education)

8 Complex syntax

8.1 Complex phrases and clauses

In Chapter 7 we looked at phrases that have only a single level of embedding, that is they have only a single simple phrase as modifier, and at simple sentences containing only a single lexical verb. We can now put this knowledge to work by looking at more complex structures.

If we begin by looking at phrases, it is clear that the phrases embedded within phrases can, in turn, have phrases embedded within them. For example, in the phrase *the person on the seat inside the theatre*, the PP *inside the theatre* is telling us where the seat is and so must be embedded in the NP which has *seat* as head, as follows:

the person [pp on [np the seat [pp within [np the theatre]]]]

The tree diagram would look like Figure 8.1

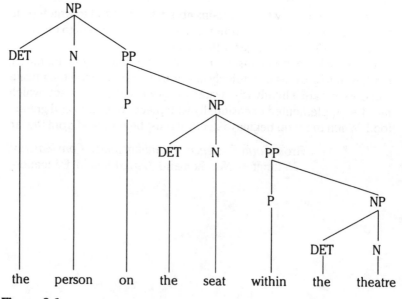

Figure 8.1

There is clearly no end to this process, as can be seen from the way one can embed possessive noun phrases within noun phrases, for example, *John's father's uncle's wife's mother's... dog*. Because of the capacity of phrasal embedding to go on ad infinitum, this process is technically referred to as recursive, that is, having the property of being able to **recursive** recur indefinitely many times.

Embedded phrases have the same structure regardless of whether or not they are embedded. For the purpose of drawing tree diagrams, therefore, the crucial question for any embedded phrase is to ask what head the phrase modifies. An embedded modifier phrase will always modify the head of another phrase. Whatever head that is, the modifier phrase and the head it modifies will be dominated by the same node of the tree. In this regard, more deeply embedded phrases are no different from other phrases.

Exercise 8.1

Draw tree diagrams for the following phrases:

(a)   the cottage by the edge of the lake

(b)   my aunt's dog's lead

(c)   Fred's family's old car in the city's museum

* * * * * * * * * *

Having looked at what happens within complex phrases, we can now see what happens with more complex sentences. So far we have looked only at sentences which have a single lexical verb in their predicate.

Look at the following sentences:

(a)   Sally hoped that Paul would meet her today.

(b)   Gerry understood why the jury found him guilty.

(c)   Horace cried after his dog died.

Find the lexical verbs in each sentence and their subjects.

You will notice that these sentences have two verbs each: (a) has *hoped* and *meet*; (b) has *understood* and *found*; (c) has *cried* and *died*. Each of these verbs has its own subject. Sally does the hoping, Paul does the meeting, Gerry understands, the jury finds, Horace cries, and the dog dies. So a sentence can have 'sentences' within it. Because of this, a

clause

distinction has traditionally been made between sentences and clauses. In a clause there is only one single lexical verb, while a sentence may consist of a number of clauses each with a lexical verb. In the previous section, in order to keep things simple, we dealt with the structure of sentences where each contained only a single clause. Now we will look at multi-clause sentences.

Such sentences show that clauses as well as phrases may be embedded. But, as we saw in the previous section, not all clauses are embedded. This allows for a distinction to be made between clauses which are not embedded, usually called main clauses, and embedded clauses.

main clause

Having just previously considered the relationship between heads which have phrases as modifiers, we can now look at the function of embedded clauses.

Look at the following two structures, which each contain the same embedded clause. What function does this clause perform in each case?

(a)   Joanna knew [that Henry would come].

(b)   the expectation [that Henry would come]

Answer:

In (a) the embedded clause is an object since it is what Joanna knew. In (b) it is a modifier of *expectation*, which is the head of a noun phrase. So embedded clauses can both be modifiers of heads within phrases and play other major functional roles such as object in clauses. We will look at both these situations.

First it has to be noted that, unlike embedded phrases, embedded clauses often change their grammatical structure in order to allow them to fit into a particular location in another clause or phrase. The simplest way is for them to be introduced by a subordinating conjunction or complementiser such as *that*. For example, in the sentence *She decided [that [her bicycle was defective]]*, the word *that* introduces the embedded clause.

subordinating conjunction
complementiser

There are a large number of subordinating conjunctions; many of them introduce adverbial clauses of one kind or another. For example, in the sentence *John was improving [because [the doctor had seen him]]*, there are two lexical verbs, *improve* and *see*, and therefore two clauses. The main clause is *John was improving*. A reason for John's getting better is given as part of the clause. That reason, *because the doctor had seen him*, is itself a clause, i.e. it is an embedded clause within the main clause. The complementiser *because* tells us that the clause it introduces is a particular kind of adverbial, namely one which gives a reason for something happening.

Embedded clauses can also be the complements of verbs. For example, verbs such as *ask*, *know*, and *say* often have whole clauses as their complements, as is shown in the following examples:

(a)   Bill knew [that [Freda was coming]].

(b)   Freda asked [whether [anyone knew the answer]].

(c)   Sophie asked [for [the teacher to explain the problem]].

Bill knew something, and what he knew is the object of the verb. So *that Freda was coming* is the object of *knew*.

Clauses can also be subjects. For example, consider the sentence [*That Bill leaves early*] *creates problems*. If you ask what it was that created problems then the answer is *that Bill leaves early*. You can also see that it is a subject from the fact that the verb *creates* has a third person singular present inflection. This shows that subject clauses must be third person and singular as far as the verb is concerned. So *that Bill leaves early* is an embedded clause with its own lexical verb and introduced by a complementiser.

Clauses can also modify heads of phrases, as we saw earlier. Look, for example, at the following noun phrases:

(a)   the goat [which was tied up at the back fence],

(b)   the ferry [which you take to Harwich],

(c)   the cleaner [who comes every evening],

(d)   the night [that you went to Monaco].

In each case the bracketed clause clearly modifies the head noun, telling us more about it. In the case of clauses which modify nouns, these clauses are termed relative clauses. However, clauses can also modify **relative clause** prepositions in prepositional phrases, and adjectives in adjective phrases, as the following examples show:

(a)   The cat was sleeping *in* [*what Freda had knitted*].

(b)   She seemed *quite astounded* [*that Fred played bridge*].

Sentences which contain embedded clauses are often called complex **complex sentence** sentences.

Now that we have looked at single and multi-clause sentences we need to ask how to draw tree diagrams of them. It is clear, if we look at many embedded clauses that the subordinating conjunction (or complementiser) is, in some sense, not part of the clause. For example, an embedded clause such as *that radios make a lot of noise* consists of a simple clause, *radios make a lot of noise*, introduced by the complementiser. For the purpose of this book we will label the clause itself S and the clause which includes the complementiser S', an abbreviation for S bar. All embedded clauses are thus S bars.

We can now set about drawing some tree diagrams of clauses and phrases which contain embedded clauses. Again, this is not difficult. Embedded clauses function just like embedded phrases. It is only their structure which is sometimes different from what it would be if they were main clauses. (We shall have more to say about these structural differences later in this chapter.) So if a clause modifies a head of a phrase, then it is telling you more about the head. For instance, in the phrase *the cat which lives with Nellie, which lives with Nellie* is telling you more about the cat and the embedded clause is therefore dominated by the same phrase category as its head, *cat*, namely NP. We can use a triangle for constituents whose internal structure we do not wish to analyse in the tree diagram, as shown in Figure 8.2.

If an embedded clause is functioning as a subject, then it is, just like a phrasal subject, the answer to the question who? or what? placed before the verb of the clause in which it is the subject. For example, in the sentence *What we did yesterday scared Tom*, if we ask 'What scared Tom?' then the answer is the embedded clause *what we did yesterday*. It is therefore the subject of the main clause, as shown in Figure 8.3. If you are still finding problems with the drawing of tree diagrams, here are:

Some rules of thumb for doing tree diagrams

1. *Find the lexical verbs*
For each lexical verb there will be one associated verb phrase and one associated clause. Therefore you know how many clauses there are in the sentence by counting the number of lexical verbs.

2. *Find the main clause*
To do this, ask yourself what the whole sentence would say at its most simple if it were to be put into a telegram or newspaper headline with one lexical verb. For example, the sentence *Three Spanish ballerinas murdered an impressive impresario in Morocco*, would be reduced to *Ballerinas murdered impresario*.

Figure 8.2

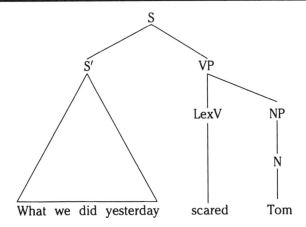

Figure 8.3

This telegram gives you the 'top' structure of the sentence by telling you who is doing what. That also gives you the head words of the main phrases. The phrase with *ballerinas* as head is the subject. The phrase with *murdered* as head will be the verb phrase and the phrase with *impresario* as head will be the object.

So you can now draw this much of the diagram, as shown in Figure 8.4. The pieces left over from your telegram (if you got it right), will either belong with the head words you have already found or will be adverbials.

Three and *Spanish* belong with *ballerinas*. *An impressive* goes with *impresario*, and *in Morocco* is an adverbial. We know this because *three* and *Spanish* tell us more about the ballerinas, so *ballerinas* must be the head of these two modifiers. *An* and *impressive* both tell us more about the impresario, so *impresario* must be their head; and *in Morocco* is the place where the murdering of the impresario took place, so it is an adverbial of place.

3. *Start at the top and work down*
Once you have worked out the main functions in the main clause you can fill in the 'top' of the structure as shown in Figure 8.5.

Figure 8.4

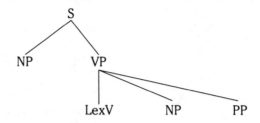

Figure 8.5

4. *Find embedded clauses*

All the rest of the clauses you have found that are not the main clause can be treated in the same way. Since they are embedded they must either be modifiers of a head of phrase, or functioning as the whole of a subject, object, intensive complement or adverbial.

   To find out if an embedded clause is functioning as part of a phrase, ask yourself if it goes with the head word of a phrase just as you would ask of a phrasal modifier.

   Now try to draw tree diagrams of a few simple examples for yourself.

Exercise 8.2

   (a) The red baroness crashed her plane into a haystack.

   (b) Anybody can see that.

   (c) The dog's kennel by the house looked untidy.

   (d) She gave her father a watch.

* * * * * * * * * *

8.1.1 *Subcategorisation of heads of phrase*

Now that we have seen something of the structure of single- and multiple-clause sentences we can revisit a topic we looked at in Chapter 5 and do some revision. In Chapter 5 we looked at grammatical sub-classes of words which are established on the basis of how they fit with other words. For example, we saw that proper nouns do not go with determiners. On that basis we established a sub-category of nouns, namely proper nouns. This analysis can be extended. Categories of words such as noun and verb can be broken down into sub-categories. One of the most important ways of doing this is in terms of the complements heads of phrase require. Because some verbs require complements to complete their meaning we can set up sub-categories of verbs on the basis of the complements they require. Some verbs, for example, take direct objects and some do not. For example:

(a)   Jill slept.

(b)   *Jill slept the bed/Bill/the child.

Verbs that require objects are called transitive. Verbs that cannot take objects are called intransitive.   **transitive**
    intransitive

   Other verbs have objects as an optional complement. For example:

(a)   The athlete jumped the hurdle.

(b)   The athlete jumped.

Some verbs take two objects: a direct and an indirect object. For example:

(a)   Jill gave her mother a treat.

(b)   *Jill gave her mother.

(c)   *Jill gave a treat.

A few verbs require the indirect object to be in the prepositional phrase form.

(a)   *The president donated Freda the trophy.

(b)   The president donated the trophy to Freda.

As we saw earlier, a verb like *put* must take both a direct object and a phrase or clause indicating location. Such a phrase would also be a complement in that it is a constituent required to complete the meaning of the verb. For example:

(a)   Jill put the book on the table.

(b)   *Jill put the book.

(c)   *Jill put on the table.

Put therefore belongs to another subcategory of verb.

   The verbs which take intensive complements form another subcategory. Those which take the intensive complement directly to their right include the lexical verbs *be, seem, appear*, and *become* as in:

(a)   Joanna became very ill.

(b)   Sean was quite bright.

(c)   Liz seemed terribly upset.

(Note that the verb *be* is a lexical verb here and not an auxiliary verb.) Those which require both an object and a following intensive complement form another sub-category. These include: *elect, appoint, nominate,* and *consider,* as in:

(a)   The voters elected Mr Bean president.

(b)   The Council appointed Mrs Bean national co-ordinator.

You can see that the verb has a central place in clause structure since the verb's sub-category determines what kinds of complement the clause will contain.

What sub-category a verb belongs to clearly depends on its meaning. It is in the nature of giving that there must be a giver, something given, and someone to whom it is given. It is in the nature of putting that something has to be put somewhere.

This property of sub-categorisation is not restricted to verbs. Take a noun like *sister.* For someone to be a sister there must be two people. You can only be a sister if there is someone else to be the sister of. So in a noun phrase such as *the sister of Bill, Bill* is in a very similar situation to the complement of a verb. In an adjective phrase such as *very wary of anteaters, anteaters* is a complement of *wary.* On the other hand, the adjective phrase *rather old* does not require the head, *old,* to have a complement. Someone can be old without any additional complementation. We might therefore want to say that all heads of phrase sub-categorise on the basis of the complements they take.

This is illustrated in the situation where a transitive verb has a derived form which is a noun. For example, *decide* requires a complement that can be either a noun phrase or a clause:

(a)   They decided the matter.

(b)   They decided that Freda should be president.

The noun derived from *decide* is *decision,* and it takes the same complements:

(a)   their decision of the question

(b)   their decision that Freda should be president

Previously we have suggested that the phrase *of the matter* and the clause *that Freda should be president* were modifiers of the head noun *decision.* You can see from the discussion above that some modifiers share important properties with complements.

Let us now look further at the ways verbs in one clause sub-categorise for their clausal complements. It appears that certain verbs sub-categorise for the complementiser of the clause which is their complement. Look, for example, at a complex sentence such as *Max understood* [*that* [*Joanna would drive his sportscar*]]. Here the lexical verb in the main clause is *understood*. It has as its complement a clause which has *that* as complementiser.

By way of contrast, *understand* cannot take as its complement a clause with *for* as complementiser, as the following case shows, **Max understood* [*for* [*Joanna to drive his sportscar*]].

In turn, complementisers themselves also belong to sub-categories. Their basis for sub-categorisation requires us to look at tense.

Main clauses in English are always tensed. Tensed clauses are often termed finite clauses and clauses without tense non-finite clauses. Embedded clauses may be with or without tense. Look, for example, at the following bracketed embedded clause: *Joanna asked* [s′*for* [s*Nick to come*]]. In the place where we would expect the tense to be we find the word *to*. This clause is therefore untensed. For the purpose of drawing tree diagrams we will regard this marker of the absence of tense as a modifier within the VP much as we would an auxiliary verb, but, as in the example in Figure 8.6, we will not give it a label itself.

finite clause
non-finite clause

So looking now at complementisers, *that* requires its following clause to have tense, so that it is grammatical in English to say *He knew that Freda had sat the exam*, but it is not grammatical to say **He knew that Freda to sit the exam*. By contrast, *for* requires the following clause not to have tense, so that *He asked for Freda to sit the exam* is grammatical, while **He asked for Freda had sat the exam* is ungrammatical.

All this suggests that there is a closer relationship between the head of a phrase and its complements than between a head and phrases and clauses which function as other kinds of modifier. But the way we have been drawing tree diagrams does not make this distinction manifest. For the purposes of this book, we merely point this out and leave it to more advanced treatments of syntax to deal with it in detail.

We can now update the table at the end of section 7.2 with some additional information. (You might like to look at it again to refresh your memory.) As well as the structural units mentioned there as functioning in various ways in clauses, we now know that clauses can function as subject, complement, and adverbial in other clauses. Clauses can also function as modifiers in phrases.

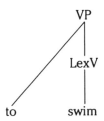

Figure 8.6

8.1.2 *Co-ordination*

co-ordinating conjunction

constituent

One further process that makes phrases and clauses more complicated is the process of co-ordination, which uses words called co-ordinating conjunctions. Co-ordination involves the joining of similar units by the conjunctions *and*, (*either*)... *or*, and (*neither*)... *nor*, and, for clauses, *but*. Any constituent in English can be joined to any other of the same kind by the first three conjunctions: *and*, *or*, and *nor*. In most cases the conjuncts joined by a co-ordinating conjunction must belong to the same structural category so that co-ordination joins noun phrases to noun phrases, VPs to VPs, APs to APs, PPs to PPs. But sometimes the conjuncts can have the same function. For example, co-ordinating conjunctions can join units both of which are intensive complements but which have different structures. For instance, in the sentence *He was [fabulously wealthy] and [a target for kidnappers]*, the two units joined by *and* are *fabulously wealthy* and *a target for kidnappers*. Although the first unit is an adjective phrase and the second is a noun phrase, i.e. of different structure, both are intensive complements of the verb *is*.

Exercise 8.3

In the following sentences bracket the structures that have been joined and say what kind of structures each is:

(a)   The man and the boy walked to town.

(b)   The singer sang at the concert and in the shower.

(c)   Gertrude whistled at boys and patted dogs.

(d)   Melissa ate chicken and Angela talked turkey.

(e)   Henry and Alfred walked, talked and fought in the park.

(f)   Neither Angela nor Melissa liked Brahms.

(g)   Gertrude either slurped or burped her soup.

(h)   Either the weather turned nasty or the opposition did.

(i)   The orchestra will play the Brahms or Angela's new concerto.

(f)   The orchestra neither played nor heard Angela's concerto.

* * * * * * * * * *

There are some interesting observations to be made about the meaning of co-ordination. Put simply, *and* has a kind of additive meaning in that the phrases or clauses co-ordinated by it give the total set of the conjuncts added together. In Noah's Ark, for example, the animals were the sum total of elephants and kangaroos and pigs and wombats, etc. *Or* is disjunctive in that a set of phrases or clauses linked with *or* allows for only one of the conjuncts to be selected. In a cage in the zoo there might be elephants or kangaroos or pigs or wombats, etc., i.e. only one of the set. Phrases or clauses co-ordinated with *neither . . . nor* mean you can have none of the set of conjuncts, neither elephants, nor kangaroos, nor pigs, nor wombats, etc. The cage is empty.

However, consider the following sentences:

(a) I crashed the car and drank too much.

(b) I drank too much and crashed the car.

Is there any difference in meaning between these two sentences? Which one would you use if you were being interviewed by a traffic officer and attempting to escape the charge of drink-driving?

In English we frequently tend to understand *and* as *and then*. Actions that are joined by *and* are thought to have happened in the order in which they appear in the sentence. Consequently, we would use the first sentence if we did not wish to incriminate ourselves. This point is made even more obvious by the following:

(a) She mounted the horse and rode off into the sunset.

(b) She rode off into the sunset and mounted the horse.

(c) He opened the can and poured out the contents.

(d) He poured out the contents and opened the can.

However, we do not always interpret *and* as *and then*. Sometimes the events or actions joined by *and* can occur in either order or at the same time:

(a) She read the newspaper and ate breakfast.

(b) She ate breakfast and read the newspaper.

(c) He plays the flute and she plays the violin.

(d) She plays the violin and he plays the flute.

What this shows is that there is a difference between the semantics of an expression, that is its meaning as contained in the words and in their structural configuration, and how that meaning is interpreted in context. *And* has a simple additive meaning but, in context, may be interpreted as having a chronological aspect. This again shows the distinction between semantics and pragmatics, which we mentioned in section 6.1.7 when we looked at word connotations. That distinction is therefore relevant not only for the meanings of words but also for the meaning of syntax.

Earlier we said that sentences containing embedded clauses are often called complex sentences. Sentences which consist of co-ordinated clauses are known as compound sentences.

compound sentence

Application

In the passage below, what impression do you get of the narrator who is telling the story, as a result of the author's frequent use of co-ordination?

> Curley's wife lay with a half-covering of yellow hay. And the meanness and the plannings and the discontent and the ache for attention were all gone from her face. She was very pretty and simple, and her face was sweet and young. Now her rouged cheeks and her reddened lips made her seem alive and sleeping very lightly.
>
> (John Steinbeck, *Of Mice and Men*)

* * * * * * * * *

Discussion

So much co-ordination makes the speaker seem very natural and simple, suggesting he or she is speaking, rather than writing. This is because when speaking people tend to use co-ordination in preference to embedding.

8.1.2.1 *Diagramming compound and complex sentence structure*
We can now update our procedures for drawing tree diagrams to include co-ordination. Tree diagrams indicate co-ordination by placing a co-ordinating conjunction between two or more structures which normally have the same syntactic category label, as shown in Figure 8.7. Their immediately dominating node, their mother, also has that label. In the few cases we mentioned where the conjuncts have different structural labels linguists are not too sure what the dominating node should be.

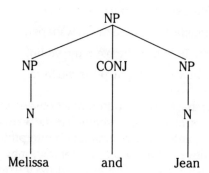

Figure 8.7

Exercise 8.4

Draw tree diagrams to show the structure of the following sentences, which contain co-ordinated and embedded clauses:

(a) Jean knew that Tom and Jerry would come.

(b) Sally asked for her father to sign the lease.

(c) Ibrahim had seen that the birds had left their perches and were flying away.

(d) The boy whom I admire has given the lady her present.

(e) The people in the old house decided to name their son Jim.

(f) James cooked tasty and cheap lasagne when Harry came to the flat.

(g) The plane which the test pilot had flown had suddenly been put in a hangar because it was wet.

* * * * * * * * * *

Having now completed our discussion of the structure of clauses and complex sentences we can briefly look at sentences in speech. From the way we have presented them it would appear that sentences are always syntactically well-formed but there are times when they are not spoken in their complete form.

First, we can distinguish between sentences that are complete and sentences that are incomplete. In formal written English, sentences must be complete, but when we speak, our sentences are often incomplete, interrupted or broken off. If you listen carefully to a tape-recorded casual conversation you will hear many incomplete sentences. Often it is impossible to work out exactly how the speaker would have completed them. Here is an example showing an italicised incomplete sentence. The speaker might have been going to say something like 'I never did get the hang of knitting,' but aborts this sentence in favour of another.

complete sentence
incomplete sentence

I never di I could never take to knitting . . .

(Crystal and Davy, *Investigating English Style*)

There is also another form of incompleteness where only part of the sentence is given but where we can be quite sure what the rest of it is. In such cases we make a distinction between major sentences, where everything is said, and minor sentences, where only a particular phrase is said but the rest can be filled in from context. Minor sentences are often given in answer to a question, for example, *Where did you go yesterday?* *To town.* The major sentence would be *I went to town.*

major sentence
minor sentence

Application

Writers occasionally use punctuation in ways which turn phrases into what look like minor sentences. If you were writing a formal essay, such punctuation would be marked as being ungrammatical, but in the example below it allows the writer to draw attention to a list of 'environmental hazards' by making each appear to be a sentence of its own rather than having them as phrases separated by commas.

> In the country of the old and sick there are environmental hazards. *Cautious days. Early nights. A silent, ageing life in which the anxiety of the invalid overrides the vitality of the untouched. A wariness, in case the untoward might go undetected. Sudden gratitude that turns bitterness into self-reproach.*
>
> (Anita Brookner, *A Start in Life*)

8.2 Syntactic relatedness

yes/no question

8.2.1 *Yes/no question formation*

So far it has seemed as if we have suggested that all that is needed to describe the syntax of English is to draw a tree diagram of each sentence and so show its syntactic structure. Sure enough this tells us what the syntactic constituents of the sentence are, and to what category each belongs, and how the constituents relate to each other. But one of the tests for phrases which we used in section 7.1 rested on the assumption that phrases can move. If that is so then the movement involves a tree which represents the syntax of the sentence before movement took place and another representing the results of making the movement. These two trees specify a location from which the phrase is moved and another location to which it is moved.

declarative
interrogative

Look, for example, at the following pairs of statements (declaratives) and questions (interrogatives):

(1a)		John is	eating.
(1b)	Is	John	eating?
(2a)		Geraldine has	dined.
(2b)	Has	Geraldine	dined?
(3a)		Pauline might	come.
(3b)	Might	Pauline	come?

You will see that there is a syntactic relationship between the question and its related statement. The relationship lies in the fact that an auxiliary verb appears before the subject in the question, whereas in the statement the same auxiliary appears after the subject.

How do we know that it is the same auxiliary?

Look at the following parallel cases:

(a)   *Is John has eaten?

(b)   *Has John is eating?

(c)   *Might John has been eating?

Remember that we discovered in section 7.1 that aspect auxiliaries select particular forms of the following verb. *Have* requires the following verb to be in its perfect participle form, and *be* requires the following verb to be in the progressive participle form. If we look at the sets of data above, it appears that the auxiliary at the left of a question must have that relationship not with the subject on its right but with the auxiliary that is on its right in the statement form of the sentence.

This suggests that we cannot put just any auxiliary at the left of a question but only an appropriate one, that is, one with the grammatical form required in the related statement. This in turn suggests that the first auxiliary is moved from the place it occupies in the statement form of the sentence to a position to the left of the subject in order to create the syntactic form of the question.

So let us suppose that, in general, it is possible that one tree diagram per sentence is not enough to represent all its syntactic properties. We may need two or more tree diagrams, where one tree diagram has a constituent moved from an original position, which we shall call its extraction site, into another in a position which we shall call its landing **extraction site, landing site** site.

We can now look in a little more detail at the movement which we have just begun to explore.

Here is a complication in the data relating to questions. See if you can sort out the source of the complication.

(1a)		Ethne	writes letters.
(1b)	Does	Ethne	write letters?
(2a)		Thomas	skates on thin ice.
(2b)	Does	Thomas	skate on thin ice?

Three things are notable about these data. First, there is no auxiliary verb in the (a) forms, that is, in the declarative form. Secondly, the third person singular present inflection *s* has moved in the (b) cases, that is, in the interrogative form, from the end of the lexical verb and into the left-of-subject position. Thirdly, in the interrogative form, the third person singular present inflection is attached to the auxiliary verb *do*, which was not present in the declarative form.

What sense can we make of this? The key is to recall that the tense inflection in English, if it is present, is attached to the first auxiliary verb if there are auxiliary verbs and to the lexical verb if there is not an auxiliary. Forming interrogatives must therefore be performed by moving the tense inflection and any auxiliary it may be attached to.

We can show that this is so by moving an auxiliary which does not have an attached tense, as in the following cases:

(a) *Been Joanna has walking the dog?

(b) *Have Joanna could walked the dog?

What makes these cases ungrammatical is that we have moved an untensed auxiliary. Remember that the tensed auxiliary is always the first auxiliary.

So what happens when there is no auxiliary and when the tense is attached to the lexical verb? It is not possible in contemporary English to move the lexical verb and an attached tense, as we shall see later, so the inflection moves on its own. Clearly it is not possible to have a verb inflection unattached to a verb stem, and so *do* comes along in a supporting role to allow the unattached tense to be attached to a verb stem. This should not surprise us when we recall the conditions under which *do* appears in statements – conditions which we explored in section 7.1.6. There too, *do* appeared only when there was no auxiliary present, and also carried the tense affix when the sentence contained a negative, as in:

(a) John didn't like mutton.

or a heavy emphasis as in:

(b) Joanna did like marmite.

On the basis of these facts we can think of the formation of yes/no questions as involving the movement of the tense affix.

We have also, and without setting out to do so, found a further test for the subject of a sentence. The tense which moves, moves over the subject from its right to its left, thus indicating the left- and right-hand ends of the subject by the tense's extraction and landing sites.

An interesting sidelight on this discussion is that we said that it was not possible to move the lexical verb and its attached tense to create yes/no questions in contemporary English. However, it was possible in earlier forms of English. In Shakespeare's time it was possible to ask the following questions:

(a) Come you to London tomorrow?

(b) Like not you the music?

By studying the grammar of a language in terms of rules such as the ones we have just looked at we can see how the grammar of a language has changed over time. We will look at some further examples of historical change in section 8.2.7.

8.2.2 *Wh questions and wh movement*

To support the theory that questions can be formed by moving constituents out of an extraction site and into a landing site we might look at other questions such as the following:

(a) When is Marcia coming?

(b) What has Marcel brought?

(c) Where will we eat tomorrow?

The answers to these questions might be:

(a) Marcia is coming tomorrow.

(b) Marcel has brought the champagne.

(c) We will eat in the bistro tomorrow.

or might be shortened to phrases such as:

(a) Tomorrow.

(b) The champagne.

(c) In the bistro.

These questions are called *wh* questions on account of their having a *wh* word or interrogative pronoun at their beginning.

wh question
interrogative pronoun

What is the form of *wh* questions? Those with an eagle eye will already have noticed that all the *wh* questions above also show the effects of tense movement. We can test this by trying a sentence without an auxiliary, for example *Harry eats when?* The *wh* question form of this sentence is *When does Harry eat?* Indeed *wh* questions seem to require tense movement, as shown by the presence of *do*, which has come to support the moved and therefore 'orphaned' tense affix.

But what of the interrogative pronoun?

Examine the data below and see what you can find out about the interrogative pronoun:

(1a)   The cat has caught a bird.
(1b)   *The cat has caught.

(2a)   The plumber fixed the pipe.
(2b)   *The plumber fixed.

(3a)   The storm damaged several boats.
(3b)   *The storm damaged.

(4a)   *The cat was purring a bird.
(4b)   The cat was purring.

(5a)   *The plumber laughed the pipe.
(5b)   The plumber laughed.

(6a)   *Several days elapsed the week.
(6b)   Several days elapsed.

(7a)   What has the cat caught?
(7b)   Which bird has the cat caught?
(7c)   How many birds has the cat caught?

(8a)   *What has the cat caught the bird?
(8b)   *Which pipe has the plumber fixed something?

(9a)   *What was the cat purring?
(9b)   *What has the plumber laughed?
(9c)   *What did several days elapse?

This data set brings together the discussion we held earlier on sub-categories of verbs, and the idea that constituents can move. The un-grammatical examples in (1), (2) and (3) are ungrammatical because the verbs in them are transitive, that is they require objects. The un-grammatical examples in (4), (5) and (6) are ungrammatical because the verbs in them require not to have objects. So much is familiar territory.

You might think that the cases in (7) should all be ungrammatical, because there is no object after the verb and the cases in (8) should both be grammatical, because there *is* an object after the verb. Also the cases in (9) should all be grammatical because the verbs are intransitive, since none has an object after the verb. But your intuitions are correct; the cases in (7) are grammatical and those in (8) and (9) are ungrammatical.

Let us suppose that the *wh* words are the objects of the verb, as they appear to be from the meaning of the sentences and the answers that one would give to these questions. If we ask who? or what? after the verb, then the answer is the *wh* word or phrase, for example, if we ask 'Who or what has the cat caught?', then the answer is *which bird*. That being the case, then the judgements as to whether or not the sentences are grammatical are as we would expect. The sentences in (7) all have objects, as they should. The sentences in (8) have two objects, the interrogative pronoun being one and the object after the verb being a second. Since the lexical verbs in these sentences require that they have one and only one object, then the sentences in (8) have an object too many and are thus ungrammatical. The questions in (9) have interrogative pronouns which are objects but the verbs are intransitive, that is, they should not have objects. The questions are therefore ungrammatical.

So this reasoning again suggests that a movement has taken place, namely that the interrogative pronouns have, in these cases, moved from object position after the lexical verb into a position on the far left of the clause. Let us suppose for the purposes of this book that the landing site for *wh* words is a similar slot to that occupied by complementisers, i.e. a position to the left and outside the S but within the S'. So is this the only possible landing site?

Look at the following two sentences and determine the extraction site and landing site of the interrogative noun phrase in bold type:

(a) [$_S$John knew **which hat** [$_S$Mary had hoped [$_{S'}$that [$_S$Arthur would wear.]]]]

(b) [$_{S'}$**Which hat** did [$_S$John know [$_{S'}$that [$_S$Mary hoped [$_{S'}$that [$_S$Arthur would wear?]]]]]]

In each of these two complex sentences *which hat* is the object of *wear* and has been extracted from the object location immediately to the right of *wear* and moved not just to the left of its own clause but to the left of a higher clause, that is, a clause in which the clause of which it is a constituent is embedded. This can be seen clearly from the bracketing in the examples.

Having looked at where *wh* phrases may be moved to, we can now look at where they may be moved from. The examples we have used up to now show that objects can be questioned by interrogative pronouns, which appear to have undergone movement from their underlying position on the immediate right of the lexical verb to a position on the extreme left, either of the clause in which they were originally contained, or of a clause in which that clause is embedded.

So is the object position the only extraction site from which *wh* words may be moved?

Which clause function has been questioned in each of the following *wh* questions?

(a)   When is Freda joining the party?
(b)   Where is the party being held?
(c)   How are you going there?
(d)   Why is Joanna holding a party?
(e)   What will Mary give Joanna for her birthday?
(f)   Who will drive the car?
(g)   What did Joanna become?

Answers:

As you will have worked out, (a), (b), (c), and (d) show that all the four kinds of adverbial (time, place, manner, and reason) which we looked at in section 7.2 can be questioned; (e) shows that indirect objects can be questioned; (f) shows that subjects can be questioned; (g) shows that intensive complements may be questioned.

In conclusion, we have now seen that two important constructions in English, yes/no questions and *wh* questions, appear to be the result of constituent movement. Such movements take constituents from extraction sites and relocate them in landing sites.

Application

Examine the passage below and sort out the yes/no questions from the *wh* questions, and then see if there is anything odd about the way these questions are answered. There are two speakers: Sherlock Holmes, who is answering the questions, and Dr Watson, who is asking them. Holmes is the great detective and Watson his well-intentioned but rather bumbling friend.

> 'When I say, therefore, that Mycroft has better powers of observation than I, you may take it that I am speaking the exact and literal truth.'
> 'Is he your junior?'
> 'Seven years my senior.'
> 'How comes it that he is unknown?'
> 'Oh, he is very well known in his own circle.'
> 'Where, then?'
> 'Well, in the Diogenes Club, for example.'
> I had never heard of this institution, and my face must have
> proclaimed as much, for Sherlock Holmes pulled out his watch.

(Sir Arthur Conan Doyle, 'The Greek Interpreter')

*   *   *   *   *   *   *   *   *   *

Discussion

Watson asks three questions. The first is a yes/no question and the other two are *wh* questions. Holmes plays with Watson in answering them. To the first question, where Watson would expect a yes or no answer, Holmes gives the answer to a *wh* question. (Notice that it is a minor sentence, the kind of sentence that is often given in response to a *wh* question.) To the next *wh* question Holmes gives what is close to a yes/no answer. He also suggests that Watson has made a mistaken assumption in asking the question. Finally Watson gets exasperated and asks a very short question, and is rewarded with a straight minor sentence answer to his *wh* question. Sherlock Holmes, being a great detective, is naturally a master in the art of asking questions. Here he appears to be showing up his friend's relative lack of skill in asking the appropriate kinds of questions.

8.2.3 *Relative clauses and wh movement*

We can now return to the relative clause, a construction which we looked at in the previous section. You will recall that relative clauses are typically introduced by relative pronouns, and you can now see as well that the *wh* words which introduce relative clauses are a kind of pronoun. Look at a noun phrase such as *the man whom I met*. *Whom* has an antecedent and that antecedent is *the man*. Because words like *whom* introduce relative clauses and are pronouns, they are termed relative pronouns. The following sentence, for example, contains two bracketed relative clauses and the two relative pronouns are in bold:

relative pronoun

The man [**whom** Bill liked] slipped on the ice [**which** the cold temperatures had created.

These relative pronouns look suspiciously like the interrogative pronouns we have just examined. They too are *wh* pronouns. They also are at the far left of their own clauses, as the bracketing shows. Are they also moved? It would seem so. In the first relative clause the lexical verb is *like*, which is a transitive verb, that is it requires an object. If we ask whom it was that Bill liked then the object of *like* is clearly *whom*. The pronoun *whom* has *the man* as antecedent and Bill liked the man. That *whom* has the form of the object (*whom* as opposed to *who*) supports the view that it is the object. Similarly the second relative clause contains the lexical verb *create*. In this clause it looks as though *which* (the pronoun with *the ice* as antecedent) is the object of *create*, since the low temperatures had created the ice.

This shows that *wh* movement is involved not only in forming *wh* questions but also in the formation of relative clauses. But in relative clauses it is not associated with tense movement since relative clauses do not move their tense to the left of the subject, as you can see from the following ungrammatical case:

*The man [**whom** did Bill like] slipped on the ice [**which** had the low temperatures created].

transformation

The rules we have been looking at which move constituents are often called transformations.

We will now look at some well-known constructions of English, many of which can be seen as being formed by movement of constituents.

8.2.4 *Commands*

Commands in English are structurally related to statements. For example:

(a) Henry eats his porridge.

becomes, as a command,

(b) Eat your porridge.

Commands are, as you can see, subjectless. They take a bare form of the verb, i.e. without inflection, and the lexical verb can take no auxiliary verbs before it. For example, it is ungrammatical to order someone to '*be driving the car tomorrow*'. However, there is some evidence that commands do have a subject. We might be tempted to think that the subject in (b), above, is *Henry*. But that cannot be the case because if it were, then the verb would be inflected for the third person singular present inflection.

However, if we add a tag question at the end of the command, as in *Eat the porridge, won't you?*, then the tag question on the end of the command suggests that the subject of the command is *you*, because other tag questions also contain a pronoun copy of the subject. For example, in the sentence *Martin ate his porridge, didn't he?*, *he* has *Martin* as its antecedent and *Martin* is the subject of the sentence.

imperative

The syntactic form of a command is termed the imperative form. Why the subjects of imperative sentences are missing is an interesting question. Some linguists have proposed that this is a result of their having been deleted. The important fact for our purposes is that statements and commands are syntactically related.

Application

Find the imperative sentences in the following advertisement. Why are they being used?

Come to life in Singapore and explore the fabulous 'Circle'. Take in the lyric isles of Tioman and Rawa. The virgin beaches and cool highlands across the causeway. Jewel-like Penang. Sensual Bali. Take home a million memories.

* * * * * * * * *

Discussion

All the sentences in the advertisement are imperatives. (Do not be fooled by the fullstops.) The imperatives are used to persuade you to do what the advertiser wants you to do. The persuasion is, however, not very binding since the advertiser has no right to order us to do anything.

8.2.5 *Passive*

In Chapter 1 and elsewhere we have spoken about language being rule-governed. We can see this again with another syntactic construction of English, the passive. **passive**

Let us start with familiar territory and look at the verb *occupy*. In the sense of 'to live in', *occupy* requires as object the kind of things that can be lived in and as subjects the kind of things that can live in such places. Abstract nouns cannot occupy anything literally and people can only occupy locations and not, for instance, psychological states, for example **Grizelda occupies anger*. Recall that passive sentences contain, as their last auxiliary verb, a form of the verb *be* or *get* followed by a perfect participle. If we look at a passive sentence, such as *The Whitehouse is occupied by the President*, it appears that the object of the verb has been moved into subject position since the basic situation is that someone is occupying somewhere. The logical subject, i.e., in this example, the person occupying the Whitehouse, may be expressed by means of a prepositional phrase introduced by the preposition *by*, or it may be unexpressed.

Passive sentences may be contrasted with the form they had before the movement of the object. That form is termed the active form of the sentence. The active form of the above sentence would be *The President occupies the Whitehouse*. In the following examples the (a) sentence is in the active form. The others are all in forms of the passive. **active**

(a)   Henry ate the porridge.

(b)   The porridge was eaten by Henry.

(c)   The porridge was eaten.

(d)   The porridge got eaten by Henry.

(e)   The porridge got eaten.

Whether you choose *be* or *get* in passives is a matter of social dialect or possibly of the degree of formality of your speech or writing. *Be* passives are often considered more correct or more formal than *get* passives.

In section 7.2, when we were discussing the function of subject, we saw that some sentences looked as though they had two subjects. One of these is the underlying or logical subject, the other is the surface subject, that is, the object which has been moved into subject position by movement.

logical subject

Passives, where the logical subject is unexpressed, i.e. where there is no prepositional phrase introduced by *by* containing the logical subject, are often used in political speech or writing when the speaker or writer does not wish to say who is responsible for something. For example, if an official says that the notes for a meeting have been mislaid, then that may be very convenient; and since the logical subject is unexpressed, no-one can be blamed. Politicians and government officials are a good source of such sentences. It can be an interesting, informative, if somewhat time-consuming exercise to record a set of questions to political figures and their answers, from the proceedings of a broadcast legislature, and try to find examples where unexpressed logical subjects are used as a tactic for evading responsibility or for not fully answering the question.

Exercise 8.5

Pick out the lexical and auxiliary verbs in the following sentences. What is distinctive about the way auxiliary verbs and particularly passives have been used in this extract?

> This system of training is best suited to vigorous growing vines. Weaker vines would be more suitable on strong rootstock. A mature vigorous vineyard can be readily converted to GDC training in one or two growing seasons.
>
> This trellising system is adaptable to mechanical harvesting by a new machine only recently developed. With this machine the wine grapes are shaken off the curtains by an impacting device and directed by shielding on to a conveyor which transfers them to a holding bin. The pivot bolt holding the T arms of the trellis permits the vine arms and suspended curtains of foliage to be vigorously shaken by the mechanical harvester.
>
> An alternative T-arm arrangement may also be used. With this, the arms are of angle steel bolted to the posts to remain in a fixed position. A stay wire is stapled on top of the post and connects the T arms. This wire connection is formed into a vertical holding guide permitting the enclosed trellis wire carrying the crop to be shaken up and down without movement of the trellis posts and T arms.
>
> (F. Berrysmith, *Viticulture*)

* * * * * * * * * *

8.2.6   *Main and subordinate clauses*

In the previous section we drew a distinction between main clauses and embedded (or subordinate) clauses. This was a rather arbitrary decision at the time. We can now look at some syntactic movements which show that there is a clear syntactic difference between main clauses and subordinate clauses.

Each of the following pairs of sentences shows a structural movement. In some environments this movement is permitted and in others it is not permitted. What are the allowing and prohibiting environments?

(1a)   He has eaten his porridge.
(1b)   He has eaten his porridge, hasn't he?

(2a)   They could be coming.
(2b)   They could be coming, couldn't they?

(3a)   The old man whom he saw can't come.
(3b)   *The old man whom he saw, didn't he, can't come.

(4a)   I haven't been to see Roger when he is late.
(4b)   *I haven't been to see Roger when he is late, isn't he?

(5a)   The cathedral by the river which flows through Paris is Notre Dame.
(5b)   *The cathedral by the river which flows through Paris, doesn't it, is Notre Dame.

The movement, which we have earlier called tag question, is permitted in main clauses but not in subordinate clauses. In (1) and (2) the tag is formed on the main clause. In (3) it is formed on a relative clause; in (4) on an adverbial clause, and in (5) again on a relative clause.

Just in case this might be an accident, look at the following movement data:

(1a)   John came in.
(1b)   In came John.

(2a)   The horse trotted down the road.
(2b)   Down the road trotted the horse.

(3a)   Henry strolled into the office.
(3b)   Into the office strolled Henry.

(4a)   The man left because John came in.
(4b)   *The man left because in came John.

(5a)   The man who was caught when the horse trotted down the road was Jim Anderson.
(5b)   *The man who was caught when down the road trotted the horse was Jim Anderson.

This inversion movement, like tag formation, appears to be sensitive to whether a clause is a main clause or an embedded clause because in (4) and (5) it has operated on embedded clauses and the results are ungrammatical.

We can now use these facts and the conclusions we have drawn from them to alter the definition of what constitutes a main clause.

Add the following data to your account of how movement is restricted within embedded clauses:

(a)   The boy shot a hare and Mary shot a partridge, didn't she?

(b)   John said, 'Mary shot a partridge, didn't she?'

(c)   *John said that Mary shot a partridge, didn't she?

(d)   The host clapped his hands and then in came Roger.

(e)   John said, 'Down the road trotted a horse.'

(f)   *John said that down the road trotted a horse.

(a) and (d) show that, as far as their behaviour with movement is concerned co-ordinated main clauses are each main clauses. (b) and (e) show that the main clause in direct speech (speech in quotation marks) is also a main clause; but (c) and (f) show that the highest clause in indirect or reported speech (speech with its own complementiser and without quotation marks) is not a main clause.

Note that the process we have just used is one we have mentioned earlier when we were looking at the phonology of English. We are proposing hypotheses and testing them to see what the facts actually are. So the distinction between main and embedded clauses is not just an arbitrary one but is supported by particular ranges of syntactic facts. Those facts in turn allow for the definition of main clauses to be refined.

8.2.7   *Empty constituents*

There are a number of situations in which syntactic constituents appear to be missing. For example, in the imperative and passive we have already seen that a subject may be absent; in the case of imperatives *you* is understood to be the missing subject, while often in the passive a logical subject may go unexpressed so that although the verb is one which requires someone to do something that someone is not present in the syntax. In these two cases the reasons for the subject not being expressed are different. In the passive it is the result of movement. That is not the case in the imperative.

Let us look at still another way in which constituents may be empty. In a sentence like *Geraldine promised [to help her grandfather]* we have two clauses, the embedded one being *to help her grandfather*. However, this clause has no subject, that is, the position where a subject ought to be is empty. Nevertheless we do know who will be helping. It is Geraldine. This means that although the subject position is empty, it can be interpreted. This kind of empty position is rather like a pronoun in that it has an antecedent. Such empty positions are often called PRO, partly on account of their similarity to pronouns.

It is particularly obvious that there is an empty position when a complement is missing. We know that complements are obligatory. In a sentence such as *John asked* we know that there must be a question or request that John put to someone. Someone would normally only utter such a sentence if they knew that their hearer knew what it was that got asked. For example, look at an exchange like this:

Speaker A: How was it you got permission to go on holiday?
Speaker B: John asked.

We know that John asked someone for permission for Speaker B to go on holiday. So again the empty position is interpretable in context. However, this time the empty position doesn't so much have an antecedent, but it is interpretable from the context. The process where constituents are missing but interpretable from context is termed ellipsis and the constituent is said to be 'ellipsed'. Minor sentences are therefore formed by ellipsis.

ellipsis

In the sentences below, find the antecedents for the empty positions, which are indicated by square brackets with nothing between them:

   (a)   Joanna wanted [ ] to come.
   (b)   Bill promised Joanna [ ] to come.
   (c)   The dog was put [ ] in a kennel.

Answers:

In (a) the antecedent of the empty position is Joanna, who is the one who will come, i.e. is the subject of *come*. In (b) Bill is the one who is coming, and in (c) *the dog* is the object of *put* but has been moved into subject position as a result of the passive construction.

The constructions we have looked at so far by no means exhaust all the cases of syntactic relatedness in English.

Look at the following sentence: *The waiter brought in the tea.* Then move its constituents into the same structural configurations as illustrated in the following examples:

(a) The climbers brought the body down.

(b) What the climbers brought down was the body.

(c) The body was what the climbers brought down.

The fact that you almost certainly got the following answers:

(a) The waiter brought the tea in.

(b) What the waiter brought in was the tea.

(c) The tea was what the waiter brought in.

means that these relationships are in the nature of rules which depend not on the words in a sentence but on its syntax. This again shows that syntax is a matter not just of phrase structure, i.e. the tree diagram of a sentence but also of relationships among tree diagrams.

8.2.8 *Grammatical change*

Just as vocabulary may vary in time and in geographic and social space so can syntax. Some syntactic constructions have become archaisms while others have evolved into different forms in different places. Translations of the Bible can provide interesting evidence for this. For example, in the fourteenth-century translation by John Wycliffe of one of the parables of Jesus is this passage (given here with modernised spelling and inflections):

> Therefore each man that hears these my words, and does them, shall be made like to a wise man, that has built his house on a stone. And rain fell down and floods came, and winds blew, and rushed into that house; and it fell not down, for it was founded on a stone.

You will see that some syntactic changes have taken place in the centuries between Wycliffe's English and ours. For us *these my words, like to a wise man* and *fell not down* are ungrammatical. However, these constructions are syntactically related to those of modern English and can be studied in much the same way as the relationships between active and passive. Let us take *fell not down* as an example. We saw earlier that when a lexical verb has no auxiliary before it and is preceded by a negative such as *not* then the 'dummy' verb *do* appears in order to carry the tense. Clearly this does not happen in Wycliffe's English. The question is, why not? One possible answer which uses some of the concepts we have just explored runs as follows.

Let us suppose that one of the facts of English syntax we need to explain is that, if a clause is tensed, then the tense is always attached to the first auxiliary verb whatever that auxiliary may be. We could explain this by supposing that tense starts out by itself and is attached to verbs. That way the verb phrase is free to select any of the available auxiliaries and a lexical verb, and the tense will always attach to the leftmost verb stem available. Let us also suppose that the attachment takes place by the verb moving to attach itself to the tense rather than the tense attaching itself to the verb. (There are good syntactic reasons to suppose this, which need not concern us here.)

However, we have seen that there is an exception to this verb attachment process and that is when, in the case of yes/no questions without auxiliary verbs, the tense moves on its own to the left of the subject and is then provided with the dummy stem *do*.

This account not only explains why the first auxiliary in tensed clauses receives the tense; it also explains why there can be tenseless clauses. This is because the choice of whether or not a clause is tensed is made independently of what verbs there are in the clause.

If we look at what happens when *not* comes between the verbs and the tense an interesting pattern is apparent in contemporary English.

Look at the following examples and see what you can discern about the attachment of the tense affix to verbs:

(a) Joanna was not coming.

(b) Joanna had not come.

(c) The ball was not found.

(d) Joanna did not find the ball.

It seems that the presence of *not* allows the auxiliary verbs to attach themselves to the tense affix, but it blocks the capacity of the lexical verb to attach itself. If there is only a lexical verb to the right of the tense and an intervening *not* then *do* must be inserted to provide a stem for the verb to attach to. This is the situation in contemporary English syntax.

But it seems that in Wycliffe's time the verb to the right of the tense and which moved leftward to attach itself to the tense affix could be either an auxiliary verb or a lexical verb. Hence the contrasting ways of saying the same thing: Wycliffe's *fell not down* and our *did not fall down*.

We might look at other related historical changes. Why can we say: *Didn't you come?* but not *Did not you come?*, whereas in Shakespeare's time *Did not you come?* was grammatical? In Shakespeare's time the *do* was not necessarily emphatic in sentences like *Why man he does bestride the world like a Colossus*, but in our grammar *does* in the same sentence must have emphatic stress. How has this change come about?

If you give this some thought you can see that explanations for how syntactic configurations change through history may require reference both to theories of phrase structure and to theories of movement.

8.3   Lexicalised phrases and clauses

In Chapter 6 we saw how words can be coined by the rules of word formation and then lexicalised, that is, at some historical point they become vocabulary items in the lexicons of speakers and languages. Phrases and clauses can also be lexicalised. They are initially constructed according to the rules of syntax; however, sometimes a particular expression comes to be used in much the same way by a community of people in a wholly or partly frozen form. This means that the expression has come to be stored in the memory of a speaker or speakers. In other words, it has been lexicalised. Lexicalised syntactic constructions are of many varieties.

idiom

The most commonly recognised variety is the idiom. An idiom is usually taken to be a syntactic constituent which has undergone semantic drift. In other words, it has acquired a new meaning in the way that words can also acquire new meanings over time. Many idioms can also be understood in a compositional way but that is not how they are normally interpreted. In the United States, if one says 'Give us a break' then one normally is talking of only oneself, i.e. *us* is semantically odd, and the word *break* is metaphorical. It is also not really a request or command but an expression of mild annoyance at someone taking you for a fool. But that does not mean that the expression cannot be taken literally although it might be hard to see the circumstances under which one would ask someone else to break, say, one of one's limbs.

It is interesting to look at a dictionary of idioms and compare the compositional meaning of some of the idioms given with their idiomatic meaning. In many cases the idiomatic meaning has come about through metaphorical extension of one of more of the words in the idiom. For example, the idiom *to hold the whip hand* has been metaphorically extended so that the whip hand is any kind of power, not just the power one gets from holding (and using) a whip. But for some idioms it is harder to imagine their source.

Clichés are another kind of lexicalised phrase. These frequently used, **cliché**
some might say overused, expressions have become the norm, the usual
way of saying, for example, *start the car*, rather than *turn the car on*; *catch
the bus*, rather than *fetch the bus*.

Proverbs are a third group of lexicalised syntactic constituents. They **proverb**
are usually a whole sentence in length and are used as a way of morally
evaluating human actions and giving advice on what to do. For example,
if one wishes to impress on a child the importance of having a clean
house, and one comes from a religious family, one might say *Cleanli-
ness is next to godliness*. If one wishes to get someone to do something
quickly one might say *A stitch in time saves nine*. Proverbs can be used
persuasively to attempt to get someone to do some cleaning or to act
quickly, or to express approval for performing these actions. There are
a great many English proverbs and looking at them gives a fair impression of the kinds of values which people might draw on to justify their
own or others' actions. They constitute a kind of folk morality. But the
morality is not consistent, in that the proverb which justifies one course
of action is often contradicted by another proverb which justifies the
opposite course of action. See if you can think of pairs, like *Sufficient
unto the day is the evil thereof* and *Never put off until tomorrow what you
can do today*.

Since they incorporate folk morality, proverbs can serve as templates
for subversive alternatives such as *Do it unto others before they do it unto
you*, *Never put off until tomorrow what can be put off until the day after*, or
James Thurber's *Early to rise and early to bed makes a man healthy and
wealthy and dead*. Such cases show that the people who make them up
must know the originals they are using as models, i.e. that the models are
lexical items in their personal lexicon.

A fourth kind of lexicalised syntactic phrase is often termed a formula **formula**
or 'speech formula'. Formulae are used in many situations to facilitate
social interaction, or just to facilitate speech itself. In English, if we wish
to apologise for doing something wrong we might say *I'm sorry* or *I'm very
sorry*, or *I apologise*, or *I do apologise*. None of these are original. We have
memorised them for the purpose for which we are using them. Greetings
are the same, as are leave-takings. We say *Hello. How are you? See you
later. Good-bye*. We take these formulae from the lexicon, where we
have them stored, and we store them along with the uses to which we
put them. We know that *Hello* is a greeting and that *I apologise* is used
when offering an apology.

Like lexicalised words, lexicalised syntactic constructions can drift not
just in their semantics but in other aspects of their linguistic form. *Good-
bye* was once *God be with you*. You can look at the Oxford English Dictionary for the history of some idioms. Most specialist dictionaries of
idioms, however, do not have an etymology for their entries.

Since we have now reached an end of the exposition in this book it is
appropriate for us, Scott Allan and Koenraad Kuiper, also to say good-
bye. We hope you have enjoyed reading and using this book.

Further exercises

Exercise 8.6

Draw tree diagrams of the following phrases and clauses:

(a) the man in the hut by the river,

(b) the coat which I bought in London,

(c) The policeman knew that the parson helped old soldiers.

(d) That Harold did not appear annoyed the police.

(e) They sang while the boat drifted down the river.

* * * * * * * * * *

Exercise 8.7

What complements can the following verbs take:

like, sob, clean, preserve, declare, drag, place, agree.

Exercise 8.8

Consider the following text:

Philip Swallow had been made and unmade by the system in precisely this way. He liked examinations, always did well in them. Finals had been, in many ways, the supreme moment of his life. He frequently dreamed that he was taking the examinations again, and these were happy dreams. Awake, he could without difficulty remember the questions he had elected to answer on every paper that hot, distant June. In the preceding months he had prepared himself with meticulous care, filling his mind with distilled knowledge, drop by drop, until, on the eve of the first paper (Old English Set Texts) it was almost brimming over.

(David Lodge, *Changing Places*)

In the above text, identify the following constructions:

(a) a passive sentence,

(b) a compound sentence where both conjuncts have the same subject,

(c) a sentence where the subject and direct object refer to the same entity,

(d)   a noun phrase which contains two adjective phrases,

(e)   a noun phrase which contains a single adjective phrase and a prepositional phrase,

(f)   a prepositional phrase which contains an abstract noun,

(g)   an example of a verb phrase which contains a progressive participle,

(h)   an example of a verb phrase which contains a perfect participle.

Exercise 8.9

In his novel *Bleak House*, Dickens tells the story through two voices: that of the narrator and that of one of the characters, Esther Summerson. These voices 'sound' quite different. Can you identify the speaker in the following extracts and demonstrate by what characteristics of their syntax Dickens establishes the different 'styles' or 'sound' of one voice which distinguish it from the other? Look particularly at the use of major and minor sentences.

(a)   LONDON.   Michaelmas term lately over, and the Lord Chancellor sitting in Lincoln's Inn Hall. Implacable November weather.

      . . .

      Smoke lowering down from chimney-pots, making a soft black drizzle with flakes of soot in it as big as full-grown snow-flakes – gone into mourning, one might imagine, for the death of the sun. Dogs undistinguishable in mire. Horses, scarcely better; splashed to their very blinkers. . . .

      Fog everywhere. Fog up the river, where it flows among green aits and meadows; fog down the river, where it rolls defiled among the tiers of shipping, and the waterside pollutions of a great (and dirty) city. Fog on the Essex marshes, fog on the Kentish heights.

(b)   I have a great deal of difficulty in beginning to write my portion of these pages, for I know I am not clever. I always knew that. I can remember, when I was a very little girl indeed, I used to say to my doll, when we were alone together, 'Now Dolly, I am not clever, you know very well, and you must be patient with me, like a dear!' And so she used to sit propped up in a great arm-chair, with her beautiful complexion and rosy lips, staring at me – or not so much at me, I think, as at nothing – while I busily stitched away, and told her every one of my secrets.

(c)   She was such a sharp little lady, and used to sit with her hands folded in each other, looking so very watchful while she talked to me, that perhaps I found that rather irksome. Or perhaps it was her being so upright and trim; though I don't think it was that, because I thought that quaintly pleasant.

(d) No. Words, sobs, and cries, are but air; and air is so shut in and shut out throughout the house in town, that sounds need be uttered trumpet-tongued indeed by my Lady in her chamber, to carry any faint vibration to Sir Leicester's ears; and yet this cry is in the house, going upward from a wild figure on its knees.

(e) It was in a state of dilapidation quite equal to our expectation. Two or three of the area railings were gone; the waterbutt was broken; the knocker was loose; the bell-handle had been pulled off a long time, to judge from the rusty state of the wire; and dirty footprints on the steps were the only signs of its being inhabited.

(f) DARKNESS rests upon Tom-all Alone's. Dilating and dilating since the sun went down last night, it has gradually swelled until it fills every void in the place.

Glossary

Active The form of a sentence where the object comes immediately after the verb, and without the passive auxiliary *be* followed by the perfect participle; contrasts with passive.

Adverbial Usually comes towards the end of a clause. It tells how, when, where, and why. Adverbials are normally grammatically optional constituents but there can be obligatory adverbials which function as complements of verbs such as *put*.

Antecedent The constituent which a pronoun 'stands for'.

Article Either *a* or *the*.

Aspect auxiliary verbs *Have*, which together with a perfect participle form of the following verb indicates perfective aspect, and *be*, which together with a progressive participle form of the following verb indicates progressive aspect.

Attributive adjective One which acts as a modifier before the head noun within the noun phrase.

Auxiliary verb Verbs which precede and modify a lexical verb.

Clause Unit with the basic structure of a sentence (e.g. having a lexical verb), but which may be part of a compound or complex sentence.

Cliché A (relatively) fixed way of saying something.

Complement A unit in the predicate which is required to be there by the lexical verb to complete the verb's meaning. Complements as a general class include objects and intensive complements.

Complementiser *See* **Subordinating conjunction**.

Complete sentence A sentence that has a subject and predicate.

Complex sentence A sentence containing embedded clauses.

Compound sentence A sentence consisting of two or more co-ordinated clauses.

Constituent A grammatically well-formed syntactic component.

Co-ordinating conjunction One of *and*, *(either)*...*or*, *(neither)*...*nor*. These conjunctions syntactically join constituents of the same syntactic category (or sometimes of the same function).

Declarative Form of a statement.

Definite article The word *the*.

Demonstratives The words: *this*, *that*, *these*, *those*.

Determiners Collectively the class of articles and demonstratives all function as determiners in noun phrases.

Direct object The answer to the question *Who or what did/does subject lexical verb*? For example, if you want to know the object of the sentence *Marsha loves Harold* you ask *Who or what does Marsha love*? Answer: *Harold*. So *Harold* is the direct object. If the sentence contains two objects, as in the case of *The committee sent Henry a letter*, then if we put the same question it becomes *Who or what did the committee send*? The answer is *a letter*. So *a letter* is the direct object.

Distribution Any syntactic constituent can fit in only a restricted range of syntactic environments. These are its distribution.

Dominance The property of having syntactic constituents as parts of other constituents.

Ellipsis The situation where a consituent is missing but interpretable from context.

Embedding The process where either a phrase or a clause appears as part of another phrase or clause.

Extraction site The syntactic location from which a moved constituent has been extracted.

Finite clause A clause with a tensed verb.

Formula A lexicalised phrase or clause used for a particular social purpose.

Head The obligatory word in a phrase which determines the distributional properties of the phrase of which it is the head.

Idiom   A lexicalised phrase which is semantically non-compositional.

Imperative   A form of a sentence that is characteristically used as a command. It does not generally have a subject or normally an auxiliary verb. The lexical verb is not inflected.

Incomplete sentence   A sentence that has been interrupted or is unfinished.

Indefinite article   The word *a*.

Indirect object   The answer to the question *To or for whom or what did/does subject verb object?* For example, if you want to know the indirect object of the sentence *Marsha gave Harold a book* you ask *To or for whom did Marsha give a book?* Answer: *Harold*. So *Harold* is the indirect object.

Intensive complement   A unit that follows a small group of verbs. It refers back to either the subject or object and introduces no new people or things into the clause.

Interrogative   Form of a question.

Interrogative pronoun   *Wh* pronoun which introduces a *wh* question.

Intransitive verb   A verb that does not take complements.

Landing site   The syntactic location which a moved constituent occupies after it has been moved.

Lexical verb   The head of a verb phrase.

Logical subject   The subject of the active form of a sentence.

Main clause   The 'top' clause in a sentence, i.e. highest in the tree diagram of the sentence, or a 'top' clause quoted in direct speech or any co-ordinated 'top' clause in the sentence.

Major sentence   A complete sentence with all its required phrases.

Manner adverbial   One which indicates how the action takes place.

Minor sentence   Part of a complete sentence, often given in answer to a *wh* question.

Modal auxiliary verb   One of *can*, *could*, *shall*, *should*, *will*, *would*, *may*, *might*, or *must*. If modal auxiliaries appear in a verb phrase they are the first unit in the phrase. Only one modal can appear in the verb phrase in most dialects of English.

Modifier   The function of a constituent of a phrase which is not the phrase's head.

Non-finite clause   One not bearing tense.

Noun phrase   Phrase that has a noun as its head.

Object   Units that immediately follow the verb and that are usually noun phrases. Two kinds: **Direct object** and **Indirect object**.

Passive   The passive form of a sentence has two crucial properties: the object has been extracted and placed in subject position, and a form of *be* or *get* is in final auxiliary position followed by the perfect participle form of the lexical verb.

Passive auxiliary verb   The auxiliary verb *be* followed by the perfect participle form of the lexical verb.

Perfective aspect   Indicated by the auxiliary verb *have* followed by a perfect participle. The perfective aspect indicates that the action of the lexical verb is completed relative to some point in time.

Phrase   The units intermediate between words and sentences in the structure of sentences. Phrases have heads, and all the constituents of a phrase belong together to make the phrase a syntactic unit.

Place adverbial   One which indicates where the action takes place.

Possessive noun phrase   These are noun phrase modifiers embedded in noun phrases, and occupy the same location as determiners. They have a possessive marker – *'s* or –*s'* attached.

Precedence   The syntactic property of having one constituent preceding another.

Predicate   A clause minus its subject.

Predicative adjective   An adjective or adjective phrase which is in the predicate functioning as an intensive complement.

Prepositional phrase   Phrase that has a preposition as head.

Progressive aspect   Indicated by the auxiliary verb *be* followed by a progressive participle. The progressive aspect indicates that the action of the lexical verb is on-going at a particular point in time.

Pronoun   Single-word noun phrase which has an antecedent.

Proverb   A lexicalised phrase, or more normally a whole sentence, which is used to provide moral advice or morally to justify a course of action.

Quantifier   A miscellaneous category of words indicating quantity, such as *many*, *some*, *both*, and *few*.

Reason adverbial   One which indicates why something took place.

Recursive   A process which has the capacity to go on infinitely many times has the property of being recursive, e.g. embedding of phrases within phrases.

Relative clause   An embedded clause which functions as a modifier in noun phrases. Often introduced by a relative pronoun.

Relative pronoun   A *wh* pronoun which introduces a relative clause.

Subject   The noun phrase attached directly to S and followed by VP in the tree diagram of the sentence. It can be found by asking *who* or *what* before the verb. In the sentence *Leisha breeds rabbits*, if we ask *who or what breeds rabbits?*, the answer is *Leisha* and that is the subject of the sentence.

Subordinating conjunction   A word which is used to signal that a unit with the structure of a clause is embedded within a phrase or other clause.

Syntax   The internal grammatical structure of phrases, clauses, and sentences.

Time adverbial   One which indicates when an event took place.

Transformation   A rule of syntactic movement.

Transitive verb   A verb that takes objects.

Verb phrase   A phrase containing a lexical verb as head.

Wh question   Question which starts with a *wh* word, such as *how*, *when*, *who*, *what*, *which*, etc.

Yes/no question   A question which takes *yes* or *no* for an answer.

Further reading

Baker, C. L., *English Syntax* (Cambridge, Mass.: MIT Press, 1989).

Burton Roberts, N., *Analysing Sentences* (London: Longman, 1986).

Fabb, N., *Sentence Structure* (London: Routledge, 1994).

Hurford, J. R., *Grammar: A Student's Guide* (Cambridge: Cambridge University Press, 1994).

Newby, M., *The Structure of English: A Handbook of English Grammar* (Cambridge: Cambridge University Press, 1987).

Wekker, H., and Haegeman, L., *A Modern Course in English Syntax* (London: Croom Helm, 1985).

Answers to exercises

Part I

Chapter 2

2.1

But the real horror among spiders was more likely to be encountered in the lavatory itself. This was the redback. The redback is
mainly black with a scarlet stripe where its spine would be if it
were a vertebrate.

2.2

wʌn əv ðə moust ɪntərestɪŋ θɪŋz əbaut ðə sɪks hedəd ɒmnɪkwɔ:gz əv
ðə plænət saigouswɒrəldɒŋ ɪn ðə sta: sɪstəm əv grʌdni:vougəækti:næks
ɪn ðə kɒnstəleɪʃən əv gouənʌpsetənʌðəskræbəlbɔ:d lez ɑi ni:d ə nju:
neim ɪz ðæt ðei hæv ounlɪ wʌn wɜ:d tə stænd fə ɔ:l fɔ: hʌndrɪd
mɪljən naunz ædʒəktɪvz prepəzɪʃənz vɜ:bz ənd ædvɜ:bz

Note: Not all dialects of English have exactly the same phoneme
inventory or use it in exactly the same way. The transcriptions are those
of the authors. We have aimed at a socially neutral form of British
English.

2.3

	Voiced	Voiceless		Voiced	Voiceless
bacon		√	cheese	√	
sa*l*ami	√	√	crea*m*	√	
rice		√	*sh*rimp		√
orange	√		*f*lour		√
*w*alnut	√		gra*p*e		√

2.4

*ca*bin, *c* is a stop and *b* is a stop
*ship*s, *sh* is a fricative and *p* is a stop
*th*an*k*s, *th* is a fricative and *k* is a stop
yach*t*, *y* is an approximant and *t* is a stop
*g*a*ther*, *g* is a stop and *th* is a fricative
*d*rop, *d* is a stop

2.5

[p] is a voiceless labial stop
[g] is a voiced velar stop
[z] is a voiced alveolar fricative
[j] is a voiced palatal approximant

2.6

(a)   busy, electricity, raising, pleasing
(b)   link, unit, youth, write
(c)   laugh, cuts, tough, bath
(d)   fly, flow, through

2.7

(a)   voiced palatal approximant   [j]
(b)   high back vowel   [u:]
(c)   voiceless post-alveolar fricative   [ʃ]
(d)   voiced alveolar nasal stop   [n]
(e)   voiced labio-dental fricative   [v]
(f)   high front vowel   [i:]
(g)   voiced velar stop   [g]
(h)   voiceless dental fricative   [θ]
(i)   low front vowel   [æ]
(j)   voiced alveolar lateral approximant   [l]

2.8

If a redback bit you on the behind you were left with the problem of
where to put the tourniquet and not long to think about it. Nor could
you ask anyone to suck out the poison unless you knew them very well
indeed.

He must have heard how boring they were since he never appeared.
But it was not for want of having his name invoked. The whole faculty
salivated *en masse* at the mere mention of him.

2.9

(a)   Vowels

/austreiljə/   /au/ should be /ɒ/ giving /ɒstreiljə/
/ʃælow/   /ow/ should be /ou/ giving /ʃælou/
/hu:ndrɪdz/   /u:/ should be /ʌ/ giving /hʌndrɪdz/

Consonants

/whait/   /wh/ should be /w/ giving /wait/
/ju:s/   /j/ should be /dʒ/ giving /dʒu:s/
/swɪmɪng/   /ng/ should be /ŋ/ giving /swɪmɪŋ/

(b)   /koust/, /ɒstreiljə/ or /hʌndrɪds/

2.10

/ai kɔːt θɪs mɔːnɪŋ mɔːnɪŋz mɪnjən kɪŋdəm əv deilaits dɔːfɪn dæpəl dɔːn drɔːn fɔːlkən ɪn hɪz raidɪŋ əv ðə roulɪŋ levəl ʌndəni:θ ɪm stedɪ eə ænd straidɪŋ hai ðeə hau i: rʌŋ ʌpɒn ðə rein əv ə wɪmplɪŋ wɪŋ/

/sou ai meid mai wei aut seiɪŋ guːdbai tə tɒd ænd ælɪsn ənd su: ənd ɔːl ðɪ ʌðə wʌndəfəl njuː frendz aid meid ənd stoul ə kæb nou nɒt lɪtrəli ɪts ən ould estæblɪʃt njuː jɔːk kʌstm wen jə si: ə lʌgɪdʒ leidn trævlə heilɪŋ ə kæb juː əbstrʌkt hɪz pæsɪdʒ wail i:z traiɪŋ tə hɔːl ɪz giə ənd dʒʌmp ɪntə ðə kæb əhed əv ɪm laːfɪŋ haːtɪli əz juː duː sou/

ðeə wɒz trʌbl ouvə ðɪ ɒrɪndʒəz ðə kʌstmz ɒfɪsəz staːtəd aːskɪŋ kwestʃnz ænd meikɪŋ dɪfɪkʌltɪz pɜːhæps ðə rait mæn wɒznt ɒn djuːtɪ ɔː hædnt bi:n peid i:nʌf ɪt si:md ə lɒt əv fʌs ouvə ə kreit əv fruːt wɜː ði: ɒrɪndʒəz stʌft wɪð drʌgz ɔː daimndz ɔː eksplouzɪvz fæntæstɪk ekspləneiʃnz prəpouzd ðemselvz mɔː redɪli ðən aːnsəz/

2.11

(a)	[d]	voiced alveolar stop	*d*eep
(b)	[m]	voiced labial nasal	*m*ud
(c)	[u:]	high back vowel	*oo*ze
(d)	[f]	voiceless labio-dental fricative	*f*ine
(e)	[dʒ]	voiced post-alveolar affricative	*g*in
(f)	[æ]	low front vowel	*a*sk
(g)	[w]	voiced labio-velar approximant	*w*ine
(h)	[k]	voiceless velar stop	*c*ake
(i)	[r]	voiceless alveolar approximant	*r*abbit
(j)	[e]	mid front vowel	*e*gg

Chapter 3

3.2

Both [k] and [g] always occur before consonants and back vowels, while [tʃ] and [dʒ] occur only before front vowels.

3.3

The fricatives occur between vowels and the stops elsewhere.

3.4

[s] occurs initially before vowels, and before voiceless consonants. [z] occurs before voiced consonants and between vowels.

3.5

[l] occurs word-initially, before vowels and the palatal approximant. [ɬ] occurs word-finally and before all consonants except the palatal approximant.

3.6

/k/ → [tʃ] / ____/i/   /g/ → [dʒ] / ____/i/

/k/ → [tʃ] / ____/e/   /g/ → [dʒ] / ____/e/

/b/ → [β] / V____V   /d/ → [ð]/V____V

/g/ → [ɣ] / V____V

/s/ → [z] / ____Voiced Consonant

/s/ → [z] / V____V

/l/ → [ɬ] / ____#   /l/ → [ɬ] / ____all C except /j/

3.7

[+back] → [−back, +del rel, +cor] / ____[V, −back]

[−cont] → [+cont] / V____V

[+cor, −cont] → [+voice] / V____V, ____[+cons, +voice]

[+lateral] → [+back] / ____#, ____[+cons, −back, +high]

3.8

There are three nasals in the data – [m n ŋ].

Only [m] and [n] are phonemic. Both occur in initial, intervocalic, and pre-consonantal positions. [ŋ] only occurs before the consonants [k] and [g]. The distribution of [m] and [n] suggests that they are phonemic, whereas the distribution of [ŋ] suggests that it is most probably an allophone of [n].

$$/n/ \rightarrow [\eta] / \underline{\quad} k \qquad /n/ \rightarrow [\eta] / \underline{\quad} g$$

or $\begin{bmatrix} +\text{nasal} \\ +\text{coronal} \end{bmatrix} \rightarrow \begin{bmatrix} -\text{coronal} \\ +\text{back} \end{bmatrix} / \underline{\quad} \begin{bmatrix} +\text{cons} \\ +\text{back} \end{bmatrix}$

3.9

The second member of each pair is the negative of the first.

The prefixes are: *im*, *in*, *il*, and *ir*.

The form of each prefix is phonologically conditioned. The consonant of the prefix assimilates to the initial sound of the stem to which it is attached. In selecting one prefix to represent the underlying form, we look for the prefix with the widest distribution. *in* has the widest distribution. It occurs with /t/, /d/, and vowels.

Chapter 4

(a)

(b)

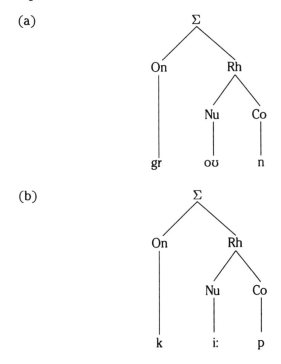

Figure 4.7

(c)

(d)

(e)

(f)

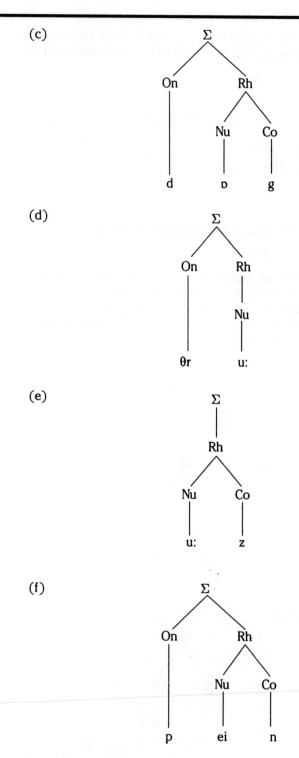

Figure 4.7 *Continued*

(g)

(h)

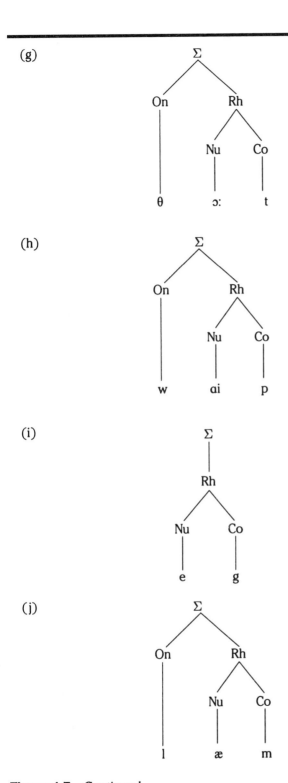

(i)

(j)

Figure 4.7 *Continued*

Part II

Chapter 5

5.1

rose, worm, night, storm, bed, joy, love, life.

5.2

modest, humble, threat'ning, white, bright.

5.3

are, heard, are, rise, turns, come, is, gone, arise, are, wasted.

5.4

witches, noun; *hopped*, verb; *in*, preposition; *red*, adjective; *drove*, verb; *gently*, adverb; *to*, preposition; *evening*, noun; *wines*, noun; *entertaining*, adjective.

5.5

LaserWriter, hard disk, built-in, read-only memory, download, random access memory.

5.6

Inflectional morphemes: singularitie*s*, neglectful, soil*s*, deliberation, sacrifice*s*, artificially.

Derivational morphemes: singul+*ar*+*iti*+es, neglect+*ful*, soils, delib-era*tion*, sacrifices, artific+*ial*+*ly*.

Note: In the last two words you might want to make a case for *sacri–*, and *arti–*, to be derivational morphemes. But notice how few words they come with. Perhaps they are just bound stems such as *cran–* in *cran-berry*. Perhaps they are not morphemes at all. The safest thing in many cases like this is to try and think of other words which have the same morpheme in them. If you cannot think of any other plausible cases, it is often clearer to follow your intuitions and say that these are not really morphemes.

5.7

Free	Bound	
	ation	
nation	pre	
post	post	Free if it is a thing you put in the ground; bound as in *postscript*.
angle	ible	
infra		
out		

5.8

Stems	Affixes
train	s
succeed	ed
light	er
determine	pre, ed
active	retro
confuse	ion, s
instruct	ion, al

5.9

(a) *clean*: free, *–ing*: bound, *lady*: free; *anti–*: bound, *skid*: free, *–ing*: bound, *device*: free; *mushroom*: free; *nation*: free, *–hood*: bound; *deputy*: free, *–ize*: bound; *de–*: bound, *rail*: free, *–ment*: bound, *–s*: bound; *pre–*: bound, *destin*: free, *–ation*: bound; *inter–*: bound, *nation*: free, *–al*: bound, *–ize*: bound, *–ation*: bound.

(b) *–ment*: affix, *involve*: stem; *–able*: affix, *support*: stem; *in–*: affix, *supportable*: stem; *sub–*: affix, *professorial*: stem; *–ial*: affix, *professor*: stem; *–or*: affix, *profess*: stem; *inter–*: affix, *subjectivity*: stem; *–ity*: affix, *subjective*: stem; *–ive*: affix, *subject*: stem; *sub–*: affix, *–ject*: stem.

(c) *–ful*: bound, derivational; *–ive*: bound, derivational; *–ary*: bound, derivational; *–ed*: bound, inflection; *thing*: free; *–es*: bound, inflection; *–al*: bound, derivational.

5.11

(a)

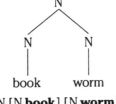

$$[N\ [N\ \textbf{book}]\ [N\ \textbf{worm}]]$$

Figure 5.9

(b)

[N[V **sing**] er]]

Figure 5.10

(c)

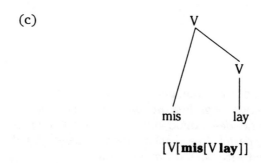

[V[**mis**[V **lay**]]]

Figure 5.11

(d)

[N[N **tax**][N[V **collect**] **or**]]

Figure 5.12

(e)

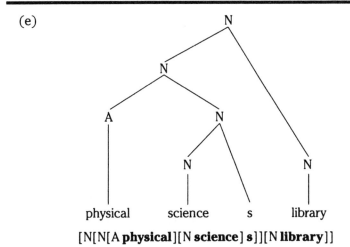

[N[N[A **physical**][N **science**] **s**]][N **library**]]

Figure 5.13

(f)

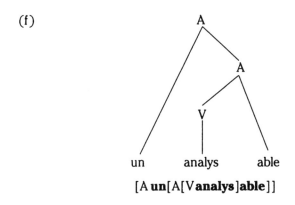

[A **un**[A[V **analys**]**able**]]

Figure 5.14

(g)

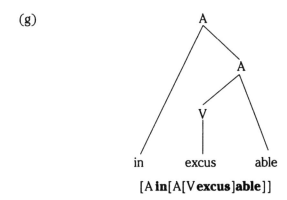

[A **in**[A[V **excus**]**able**]]

Figure 5.15

(h)

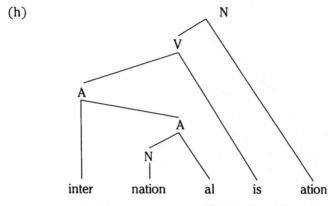

[N[V[A **inter**[A[N **nation**]**al**]]**ise**]**ation**]

Figure 5.16

5.12

old, adj; *by*, preposition; *of*, preposition; *seemed*, verb; *lost*, verb; *head-lights*, noun.

5.13

derive, stem, free; *–ation*, affix, bound; *–al*, affix, bound, derivational; *head*, free; *strong*, free; *un–*, affix, bound, derivational; *likely*, stem, free; *locate*, stem, free; *–er*, affix, bound, derivational; *beacon*, stem, free; *–s*, affix, bound, inflectional.

Figure 5.17

Figure 5.18

Figure 5.19

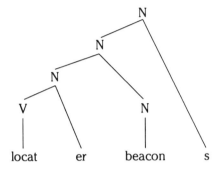

Figure 5.20

5.14

(a) [N [N peanut][N vendor]]
     [N [N [A new][N comer]]s]

(b) [N [V vend] *or*], i.e. *or* attaches to a verb stem and creates a noun.
     [N [V come] *er*], i.e. *er* attaches to a verb stem and creates a noun.
     [ADV [ADJ [N grace] ful] ly], i.e. *–ly* attaches to an adjective stem and creates an adverb while *–ful* attaches to a noun stem and creates an adjective.
     [ADV [ADJ [N/V marvell] ous] ly], i.e. *–ly* attaches to an adjective stem to create an adverb while *–ous* attaches to a verb (or maybe a noun) stem to create an adjective.
     Note that you need to look at more words that take the *–ous* suffix to see whether it attaches to noun or verb stems or both.
     [N [N rail] ing], i.e. *–ing* attaches to a noun stem to create a noun.
     [N [V hawk] er], i.e. *–er* attaches to a verb stem to create a noun.
     [ADJ [N sinew] y], i.e. *–y* attaches to a noun stem to create an adjective.

(c) new/come/er/s, marvell/ous/ly

(d) derivational suffixation

(e) All three are phonologically conditioned allomorphs of the regular plural morpheme. In *railings* the allophone is voiced because the preceding consonant of the stem is voiced. In *fruits* the *s* is voiceless because the preceding consonant of the stem is voiceless. In *fences* the plural is voiced and an epenthetic vowel /ə/ comes between the plural allomorph and the strident final consonant which is the conditioning environment for this process of epenthesis. In *trays* the plural allophone is voiced because it is preceded by a vowel in the stem. (See Chapter 3 for a discussion of this case of affixal allomorphy.)

(f) *–ed* on *pleased*, *started* and *lifted* is a past tense suffix.
–ing is a progressive participle suffix.

5.15

(a) *sunlight* is a noun made up of noun + noun, *downstream* is an adverb made up of preposition + noun, *inshore* is an adverb made up of preposition + noun, *newborn* is an adjective made up of adjective + adjective (perfect participle), *dragonfly* is a noun made up of a noun + noun.

(b) *un* D, *believ* F, *able* D, *dragon* F, *fli* F, *es* I.

(c) In these words *–ly* attaches to adjective stems and the derived words are manner adverbs.

(d) *important*: *–ant* attaches to a noun and the derived word is an adjective; *wildness*: *–ness* attaches to an adjective stem and the derived word is a noun; *ecstatic*: *–ic* attaches to a noun stem (*ecstasy*) and the derived word is an adjective; *lightning*: *–ing* attaches to a verb stem (*lighten*) and the derived form is a noun.

(e) *–s* is a plural inflection on noun stems, whereas the *–ed* suffix is a past tense affix on verb stems.

(f) These forms are irregular in that the regular past tense forms would be *swimmed* and *breaked*.

(g) The word appears in the dictionary as a modifier of a noun, no longer just as the name of a person but as having to do with something the person did. This is half way to a proper noun conversion, which we find with a noun like *diesel*.
  In the passage the word has been converted to a verb. This has also happened to the word *diesel* when it means 'to make the kind of sound typical of a diesel engine' as in *the car was dieseling*.

Chapter 6

6.1

(a) Each sentence entails the other but not because either contains a word or expression which is synonymous with one in the other.
(b) Here the two way entailments are the result of *hit* being synonymous with *struck*.
(c) If your socks are scarlet it follows that they must be red but if they are red it doesn't follow that they are scarlet.
(d) If you bought the tomatoes then you must have purchased them and if you purchased them then you must have bought them. This is because *buy* and *purchase* are synonyms.
(e) If your dog is bigger than my dog then my dog must be smaller than your dog, but this is not because any words or phrases in the two respective sentences are synonyms.
(f) If Roger owns the pencil then it must belong to him, and vice versa. This is not because *own* and *belong to* are synonyms.
(g) If Ken almost shot his foot then he must nearly have shot his foot and vice versa, because *nearly* and *almost* are synonyms.
(h) If your neighbour owns a pistol then he or she must own a firearm but if they own a firearm it need not be a pistol.

In summary:
   Reverse entailments: (a), (b), (d), (e), (f), (g).
   Reverse entailments resulting from synonymy: (b), (d), (g).

6.2

   Homonyms: (a), (d), (e).

6.4

(a) mammal, rodent, mouse
(b) structure, building, house, bungalow
(c) move, run, jog
(d) weapon, firearm, pistol, revolver
(e) person, relative, uncle
(f) beast, dog, hound, beagle
(g) take, steal, pilfer.

6.5

(a)

Figure 6.7

(b)

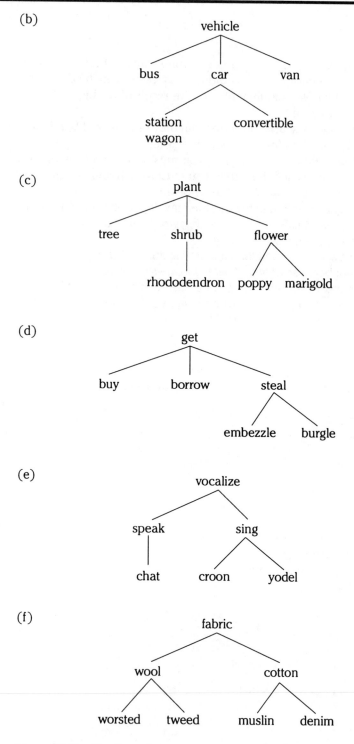

(c)

(d)

(e)

(f)

Figure 6.7 Continued

(g)

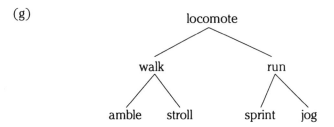

Figure 6.5 Continued

6.6

Entailments: (a), (b), (d), (f), (g), (i), (j), (k), (m).
Entailments resulting from hyponymy: (d), (i), (j), (k).

6.7

Some of the possible components are: metal vs fabric; twisted vs solid vs braided; relative cross-sectional diameter ranging from very thin through thin, medium, and fat.

6.8

Let us suppose that the significant semantic components of one's kin are whether they are male or female; whether they are the same generation as oneself or from one, two, or three generations older, or one, two, or three generations younger; and whether they are in a direct line of descent with oneself or at one or more removes from a direct line of descent. That gives the following semantic features:

(a)   male vs female;
(b)   same generation as self vs 1,2,3 generations older vs 1,2,3 generations younger;
(c)   direct line of descent vs 1,2,3 degrees of distance from direct line of descent.

Using these semantic features we can say that the senses of some of our kinship terms are:

Sister: female, same generation as self, same line of descent.
Aunt: female, 1 generation older than self, 1 degree of distance from direct line of descent.
Father: male, 1 generation older than self, direct line of descent.

6.10

yacht was borrowed from Dutch, *curry* from Tamil, a language of southern India; *transfer* from Latin; and *pyjama* from Persian via Hindi (the same route as pyjamas themselves took from Persia to India to England).

6.11

radar, radio detection and ranging; laser, light amplification by stimulated emission of radiation; IATA, International Air Transport Authority; NATO, North Atlantic Treaty Organisation; quango, quasi non-governmental organisation; AIDS, acquired immune deficiency syndrome.

6.15

(a) yes, (b) yes, (c) no, (d) no, (e) yes, (f) yes, (g) no, (h) yes, (i) yes, (j) no, (k) yes, (l) no, (m) no.

(*Note*: some of these pairs may differ in their senses in different dialects. For example, in North America a silencer is what one puts on a gun but not under a car, whereas it can be both in the UK.)

6.16

(a), (j) antonyms; (b), (i) antonyms; (c), (e) converses; (d), (g) complementaries; (f), (h) complementaries.

6.18

(a) deep, shallow
(b) Both are often used metaphorically of human character.
(c) buy, sell
(d) legal, illegal
(e) animal (superordinate), deer (hyponym)
(f) deep, profound
(g) One cannot use *profound* of physical objects like mineshafts so it is a synonym only of the metaphorical sense of *deep*.
(h) buy, by

Part III

Chapter 7

7.1

an ancient monument, fell down during the bombing, during the bombing.

several young Latvian artists, danced gracefully before the Empress, before the Empress.

7.2

(a) elephants, (b) books, (c) women, (d) material, (e) thick, (f) pleasant, (g) delighted, (h) sitting, (i) bored, (j) delayed, (k) rhythms,
(l) lovely, (m) in, (n) out, (o) above, (p) unimpressed, (q) eating.

7.3

(a) preposition, (b) verb, (c) verb, (d) adverb, (e) adjective, (f) noun,
(g) preposition, (h) adjective, (i) adjective, (j) preposition.

7.4

The head of *some very old cars* is the noun *cars*. It is modified by *some*
and the adjective phrase *very old*, which contains the head adjective *old*
modified by the degree adverb *very*.

The noun phrase *six plants in the shop* has the head *plants*. There are two
modifiers of the head, the numeral *six* and the prepositional phrase *in the
shop*. This phrase has *in* as head and that head is modified by the noun
phrase *the shop*, whose head is *shop*. *Shop* is modified by *the*.

7.5

(a) head, *mare*; modifiers: *the, old, grey, down in the paddock*
(b) head, *uncle*; modifiers: *my, with the fish and chip shop*
(c) head, *bus drivers*; modifiers: *these, three, intelligent, I met
      yesterday*
(d) head, *person*; modifiers: *an, other, I don't know*
(e) head, *goblins*; modifiers: *six, in green*

7.6

Pronouns are in italics:

her: 3rd pers., poss., fem., sing.; *it*: 3rd pers., subj., neut., sing. *I*: 1st
pers., subj., sing.; *them*: 3rd pers., comp., plur. *you*: 2nd pers., subj.,
sing/plur. *them*: 3rd pers., compl., plur. *he*: 3rd pers., subj., masc.,
sing. *she*: 3rd pers., subj., fem., sing.

7.7

other, very hard, big, rather clumsy-looking, big, heavy, long, flat, big,
expressionless, broken-nosed, surprising.

7.8

about, far down the beach, to where the surf was breaking, under a beach
umbrella, towards her, down, on the white sand, with her back *to the
land*, out *to sea*, above her, with white frills and tassels that swayed *in
the breeze*, by the breeze *from the sea*, in proportion *to her long tapering
back and narrow waist*, to Smith, on either side, from where Smith

watched, above her, in green, up the sand, against the white froth and the blue *of the sky*, in the relative quiet *between breakers*, of music, among her things, about the beach towel *on which she sat*.

Discussion
The prepositional phrases are important in relating things, people, events to each other in time and space. Since the central aim of a description in words is giving a picture, such relating is very important.

You may also have noticed that many of the prepositional phrases have still other prepositional phrases embedded within them. Such embedded PPs are in italics above.

7.9

noun phrases

(a)

Figure 7.18

(b)

Figure 7.19

(c)

Figure 7.20

(d)

Figure 7.21

(e)

Figure 7.22

(f)

Figure 7.23

(g)

Figure 7.24

(h)

Figure 7.25

(i)

Figure 7.26

(j)

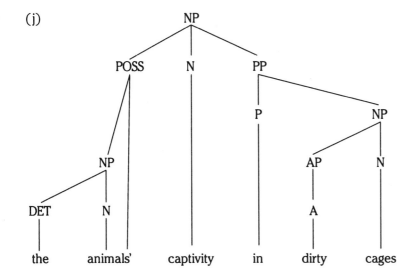

Figure 7.27

Prepositional phrases

(a)

Figure 7.28

(b)

Figure 7.29

(c)

Figure 7.30

(d)

Figure 7.31

(e)

Figure 7.32

(f)

Figure 7.33

(g)

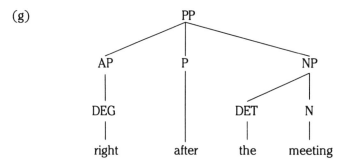

Figure 7.34

Adjective phrases

(a)

Figure 7.35

(b)

Figure 7.36

(c)

Figure 7.37

(d)

Figure 7.38

(e)

Figure 7.39

(f)

Figure 7.40

(g)

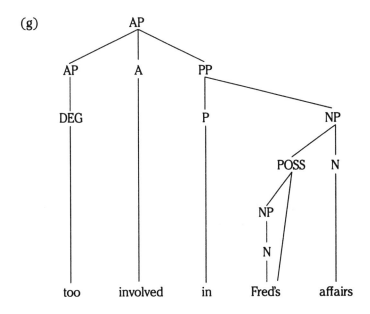

Figure 7.41

7.10

(a) B and C; (b) R, S, and T; (c) B, C, and D; (d) B, C, D, P, Q, R, S, T, and X; (e) C; (f) B, C, and D.

7.11

(a)

Figure 7.42

(b)

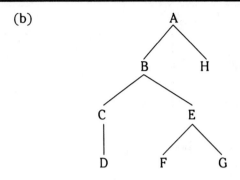

Figure 7.43

(c) [$_A$[$_B$DE][$_C$F]]

(d) [$_A$[$_B$DE][$_C$FGH]I]

7.12

(a) Peter, (b) the greatest magician of all time, (c) three monkeys, (d) they, (e) that Lionel saw the escape.

7.13

(a)

Figure 7.44

(b)

Figure 7.45

(c)

Figure 4.46

(d)

Figure 7.47

(e)

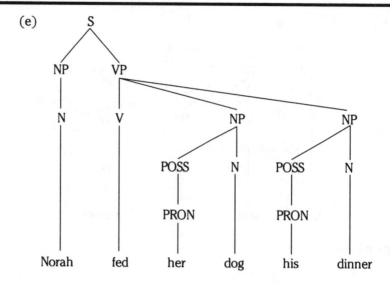

Figure 7.48

7.14

(a) *Freda* is an indirect object and *a bicycle* is a direct object.
(b) *a new camera* is a direct object.
(c) *her breakfast* is a direct object and *hot* is in intensive complement.
(d) *very shy* is an intensive complement.
(e) *Harriet* is a direct object and *the most valuable player* is an intensive complement.

7.15

(a) *Heather* is the subject, *the ferry* is the direct object, and *across to Istanbul* and *yesterday* are adverbials.
(b) *Isabelle* is the subject, *the lamp* is the direct object, and *lightly* is an adverbial.
(c) *Bricks* is the subject, *best* is an intensive complement, and *because they are heavy* is an adverbial.
(d) *Cotton fabrics* is the subject, *everyone* is the direct object, and *this season* is an adverbial.
(e) *Everyone* is the subject, *expensive presents* is the direct object, *to their friends* is the indirect object, and *this season* and *for Christmas* are both adverbials.

7.16

(a)

Figure 7.49

(b)

Figure 7.50

(c)

Figure 7.51

(d)

Figure 7.52

(e)

Figure 7.53

(f)

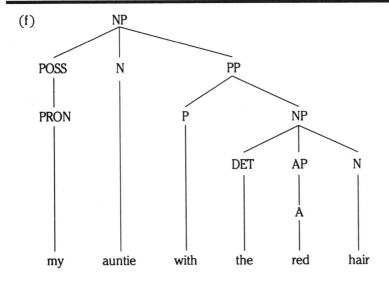

Figure 7.54

7.17

(a) We SUBJECT
    gave him a raise PREDICATE
    him INDIRECT OBJECT
    a raise DIRECT OBJECT

(b) He SUBJECT
    donated his stamp collection to the gallery. PREDICATE
    his stamp collection DIRECT OBJECT
    to the gallery INDIRECT OBJECT

(c) She SUBJECT
    put the wombat in the alligator's cage. PREDICATE
    the wombat DIRECT OBJECT
    in the alligator's cage PLACE ADVERBIAL

(d) Xavier SUBJECT
    cried. PREDICATE

(e) The key SUBJECT
    opened the door. PREDICATE
    the door DIRECT OBJECT

(f) The alligator SUBJECT
    ate its prey. PREDICATE
    its prey DIRECT OBJECT

7.18

Use LEXV: ACTION a preserving jar which *contains* LEXV: STATE about 10 cm of soil to which peat *has* AUXV *been* AUXV *added* LEXV: ACTION in the proportion of two measures of soil to one of peat. *Cover* LEXV: ACTION the top of the jar with muslin.

You *must* AUXV *keep* LEXV: ACTION the atmosphere moist, but *be* LEXV: STATE careful that no mould *is* AUXV *allowed* LEXV: ACTION to *grow* LEXV: ACTION as this quickly *kills* LEXV: ACTION the animals. *Should* AUXV the muslin *feel* LEXV: ACTION dry *sprinkle* LEXV: ACTION it lightly with water. Slugs *will* AUXV *eat* LEXV: ACTION carrot discs, which *may* AUXV *be* AUXV *supplemented* LEXV: ACTION occasionally with pieces of potato and green food. When the food *begins* LEXV: ACTION to *decay* LEXV: ACTION it *must* AUXV *be* AUXV *removed* LEXV: ACTION from the jar.

Chapter 8

8.1

Figure 8.8

(b)

Figure 8.9

(c)

Figure 8.10

8.2

(a)

Figure 8.11

(b)

Figure 8.12

(c)

Figure 8.13

(d)

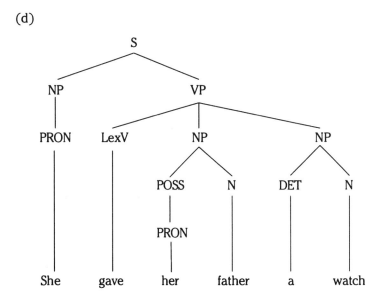

Figure 8.14

8.3

(a) noun phrases
(b) prepositional phrases
(c) verb phrases
(d) whole clauses
(e) noun phrases and verb phrases
(f) noun phrases
(g) verb phrases
(h) verb phrases
(i) noun phrases
(j) verbs

8.4

(a)

Figure 8.15

(b)

Figure 8.16

(c)

Figure 8.17

(d)

Figure 8.18

(e)

Figure 8.19

(f)

Figure 8.20

(g)

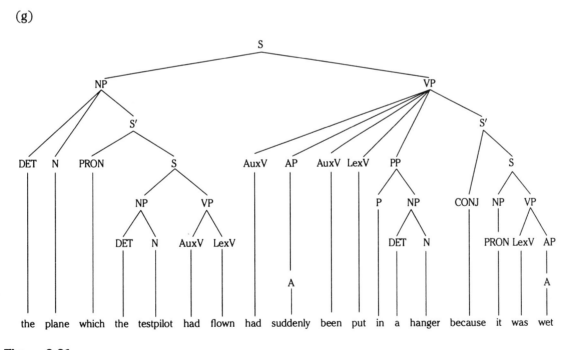

Figure 8.21

8.5

is suited, would be, can be converted, is developed, are shaken, directed, transfers, holding, permits, to be shaken, may be used, are bolted, to remain, is stapled, connects, is formed, permitting, carrying, to be shaken.

The auxiliary verb *be* in one or other of its forms is used a great deal, particularly to form passives. Passives are often found in technical writing such as this.

8.6

(a)

Figure 8.22

(b)

Figure 8.23

(c)

Figure 8.24

(d)

Figure 8.25

(e)

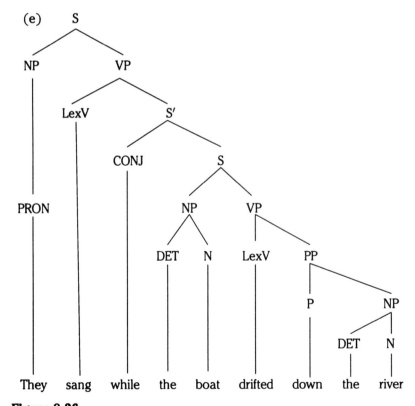

Figure 8.26

8.7

Like can take noun phrases and clauses as objects, e.g. *They liked games, They liked James to come.*

Sob does not typically take complements unless they are redundant, such as *He sobbed great sobs.*

Clean normally takes NPs as direct objects, e.g. *He cleaned the curtains.*

Preserve is a transitive verb which takes a direct object, as in *They preserved the old family customs.*

Declare takes clause complements with *that* as a complementiser, e.g. *They declared that the meeting was very dull.* It can also take an NP direct object followed by an intensive complement, e.g. *The Chair declared the meeting closed.*

Drag is transitive and therefore takes an object, as in *They dragged the chair.*

Place is like *put* in normally requiring both a direct object and a location, e.g. *They placed the chair on the carpet.*

Agree can be intransitive in sentences like *The partners agreed.* It can also take a clausal complement, e.g. *They agreed to come tomorrow, They agreed that Henry should be prosecuted.*

8.8

(a) Philip Swallow had been made and unmade by the system in precisely this way.
(b) He liked examinations and always did well in them.
(c) In the preceding months, he had prepared himself with meticulous care
(d) that *hot distant* June
(e) the *supreme* moment *of his life*
(f} with meticulous *care*
(g) was *taking* the examinations again OR
    filling his mind with distilled knowledge OR
    it was almost *brimming* over
(h) had *been* made and unmade by the system in precisely this way
    OR
    had *been*, in many ways, the supreme moment of his life OR
    had *elected* to answer on every paper that hot distant June OR
    he had *prepared* himself with meticulous care

Index